INDIA–JAPAN RELATIONS IN EMERGING ASIA

India–Japan Relations in Emerging Asia

Edited by

TAKENORI HORIMOTO

LALIMA VARMA

MANOHAR

2013

First published 2013

ISBN 978-93-5098-001-9

Published by
Ajay Kumar Jain *for*
Manohar Publishers & Distributors
4753/23 Ansari Road, Daryaganj
New Delhi 110 002

Typeset by
Umesh Chand Nailwal
Delhi 110 092

Printed at
Salasar Imaging Systems
Delhi 110 035

Contents

Preface 7

1. Strategic Convergence of Japan–India Relations and China's Emergence
Takenori Horimoto 19

2. Enhancing Strategic Ties between Japan and India: Japan–China Relations as a Factor
Lalima Varma 41

3. China's Foreign Policy and Indo–Japan Relations
Srikanth Kondapalli 63

4. Japan–India–US Relations and Rising China
Emi Mifune 93

5. 'China Threat' Theory in Indo–Japan Relations
Toru Ito 113

6. US–Japan–India Trilogue: The China Factor
Swaran Singh 133

7. Explaining the Similarity: Comparative Analysis of Japan and America's India Policy
Kazutoshi Tamari 153

8. India, Japan and Maritime Security Cooperation in the Asia-Pacific
Marie Izuyama 175

9. Prospects and Challenges for Expanding Japan–India Economic Relations
Makoto Kojima 201

10. India–Japan Economic Partnership: Scope and Prospect
Srabani Roy Choudhury 223

11. Present Status of Japanese Studies in India: Prospects and Problems
P.A. George 245

12. Problems of Youth Employment in India and Japan: A Call for a Joint Comparative Study
Mayumi Murayama 265

List of Contributors 287

Index 291

Preface

This volume is an outcome of an international seminar on 'India–Japan Relations: Contemporary Trends' organized by the Centre for East Asian Studies, School of International Studies, Jawaharlal Nehru University, New Delhi, India and Shobi University, Saitama, Japan, on 7 September 2011 in New Delhi. The seminar was supported by Grant-in-Aid for Scientific Research; Japan's Ministry of Education, Culture, Sports, Science and Technology (MEXT); and Japan Society Promotion of Science (JSPS), Tokyo, Japan.

Since the turn of the twenty-first century rapid progress has been witnessed in the development of close relations between India and Japan. Relations between the two countries during the last sixty years have mostly remained cordial. For a decade after Japan regained its sovereignty in 1952 the relations between the two countries were upbeat. India was among the first countries in Asia to conclude a Peace Treaty with Japan in 1952. Japanese Prime Minister Kishi Nobusuke visited India in 1957 and Indian Prime Minister Pandit Jawaharlal Nehru visited Japan in the same year. The following year Indian President Rajendra Prasad visited Japan. Japan's Crown Prince Komatsu Akihito visited India in 1960. In 1958 India was the first country to receive Japanese Official Development Assistance. However, the tempo of promoting good relations could not be maintained in the succeeding decades.

Relations between India and Japan were affected by the Cold War politics which largely determined the foreign policy pursued by a particular country. Japan was closely aligned with the United States of America and India followed a policy of non-alignment and was considered to be closer to the erstwhile Soviet Union. The fact that political relations were not a top priority for both the countries is evident from the fact that after Prime Minister Ikeda Hayato's visit to India in 1961 it was only after 23 years that Japanese Prime

Minister Nakasone Yasuhiro visited India in 1984. During this period economic relations were maintained but it was far from satisfactory. One of the stumbling block was the different path of economic development pursued by both the countries. Japan pursued market economy and India a mixed economy making it difficult for the two countries to expand economic relations.

A major breakthrough in the relation between India and Japan was witnessed after 1991. India initiated the process of liberalizing its economic policy which gave a lot of impetus to the business community to exploit opportunities provided by changed economic environment in India. Economic ties between the two countries since the early 1990s has improved greatly but still not to the level expected. In fact, there was a setback in the relationship in May 1998 when India conducted nuclear tests at Pokharan. Japan's reaction to the tests was sharp and aid to India was suspended.

With the beginning of the twenty-first century, however, relations between the two countries were not only restored to normal but the aim was to establish a 'Strategic and Global Partnership'. This change in perception was instigated by several developments in the region. One was the rapidly growing economies of India and China. Most Western countries were making quick advances in strengthening economic ties with these countries. The other major concern was the security of the sea lanes in the region. Cases of piracy in the seas bordering India and Southeast Asia were on the increase and it was imperative that combined effort be made to tackle this major problem. Japan imports three fourths of its energy requirement from the Middle East countries and the oil tankers pass through the sea lanes in the region.

Thus, during the last one decade effort has been to make the relations more multidimensional. Strategic aspect of the relation in particular has gradually assumed great relevance. In addition to maritime security other developments such as 'rise of China' have now necessitated that the strategic relations between the two countries be expanded and consolidated further. During the last one decade China's rise has not only been rapid but much more faster than was expected. China has also presented itself as power which can be assertive and that it is set to play a dominant role in the region. With a population of 1.3 billion, an annual average economic growth of about 10 per cent for more than ten years and a strong military and navy China has become a matter of concern for the countries not only of the region but for most countries in the world. China's profile has grown phenomenally in recent years. It is not surprising that often the question is asked if this century is 'China century'.

Expanding relations between India and Japan have to be viewed against this background. Both India and Japan have several problems with China, the solution to which seem to be quite remote. However, though the two countries' objective is not to alienate or challenge China but at the same time they are concerned about their interests and security being threatened by China in future. The aim is to maintain a strong relationship which will deter China from acting aggressively and unilaterally.

Economically East Asia is one of the most dynamic regions in the world, hence, it has become the focus of all major powers including the United States. The main interest of most countries is to maintain a balance of power in the region. In achieving this goal, US and Japan feel that India has a role to play. There is also a concerted effort to establish close bilateral relations and have regular dialogue which will contribute to settlement of issues by dialogue and negotiations.

This edited volume consisting of 12 chapters deals with various aspects of India–Japan relations. The relationship between the two countries is discussed in the context of a 'Rising China'; the possible threat which China poses or might pose in the future; the nature of problems between Japan and China; irritants in the relations between India and China and the possibility of trilogue between India–Japan and the US to limit China's growing influence in the region is the subject matter of the first 8 chapters. Economic relations are also an important component of the relations between India and Japan. Two chapters in the volume deal with this aspect of the relationship. Despite the fact that for more than a decade there has been an emphasis on strengthening relations between the two countries and making it one of the most important relationships in the future, still the study of Japan and Japanese language has not really expanded as it should. What is the status of Japanese studies in India and what are the problems and prospects of promoting Japanese studies in India is dealt with in one of the chapters. An interesting chapter on the comparative study of the problems of youth employment in Japan and India is included which throws light on a very different aspect of the problems existing in the two countries and whether there are lessons which we can learn from each other.

The first chapter is by Takenori Horimoto on 'Strategic Convergence of Japan–India Relations and China's Emergence'. He claims that at the moment, Japan–India bilateral relations are at their best in the past six decades. The two nations' overall perceptions, interests, and concerns were dovetailing. Since the 1950s till the 1980s, the two countries have pursued incompatible policy orientations in terms of foreign policy and economic policy lines. Such incompatibility has been reflected in their infrequent interaction. At the prime ministerial level, Japanese Prime Minister Nakasone visited India in 1984, two decades after Ikeda visited in 1961. Similarly, Indian Prime Minister Indira Gandhi visited Japan in 1982, more than a decade after her 1969 visit.

After the end of the Cold War, bilateral relations entered a second phase. Major contributing factors were the dissolution of the Soviet Union and liberalization of India's economic policies. The period up to the end of 1990s could be designated as a first phase. The period from 2000 onward to the present day could be designated as the second phase of bilateral relations. Twenty-seven VIPs undertook mutual visits in the 1990s, increasing to eighty-four VIP visits between 2000 and 2009.

Since 2005, prime ministerial visits have become more common. The two established a Strategic Partnership in 2006; subsequently, a Joint Statement on security cooperation was declared in 2008. In August 2011, the Comprehensive Economic Partnership Agreement was put into effect. Emphasis might be placed on strategic convergence among other matters. A quadrilateral security approach adopted during 2005–6 has been transformed into Indo–US, India–Australia and Japan–India bilateral security frameworks. The backdrop of such a development is attributable to China's metamorphosis into a maritime power with maritime assertiveness and proactivism.

For tiding over the present security milieu, it seems that the two countries must implement hedging-engagement policies jointly to be effective and sustainable. Furthermore, Japan–India relations should be used not only for mutual benefit but for the benefit of the whole Asian region.

Lalima Varma writes on 'Enhancing Strategic Ties between Japan and India: Japan–China Relations as a Factor'. According to the author economic relations between India and Japan are undoubtedly important, however, it is the strategic relations between the two countries which have assumed greater importance during the last one decade. There are several reasons for the enhanced strategic relations such as the security of the sea lanes, but one of the important factors is China. There are several irritants between Japan and China which pose problems in the continuance of cordial relations. Relations dipped to the lowest level in 2010 due to the controversy over the Senkaku/Diaoyu islands issue. Anti-Japan feelings in China have not faded away despite the growing economic relations and attempts by the two countries to cement ties over the years. There is also a perceptible change in Japanese attitude towards China.

It appears that resolution of the problems between the two countries is not likely to be achieved in the near future. Given the sensitive nature of Japan's political relations with China and China's growing stature in the region, Japan's main concern is to build a network of bilateral relations with countries in the region so as to reduce the impact of the threat which China may pose before Japan. Building close bilateral relations is more important for Japan given the fact that constitution prevents Japan from possessing hard power; role of ODA seems to reduce over the years and there are no well established multilateral organizations in the region which can tackle problems. In this strategy, enhanced relations with India is an important component. India also has a share of its problems with China. However, the nature of the relations between India and China is qualitatively different from that of Japan and China.

Srikant Kondapalli in his paper entitled 'China's Foreign Policy and India–Japan Relations' says that as the other two major powers in Asia, India and Japan are important elements in China's minimalist as well as maximalist foreign policy objectives. At a minimum, both India and Japan have territorial disputes with China and this factor overweighs China's considerations on security and stability in its periphery. China spends enormous amounts of diplomatic energy on resolving the territorial disputes with these states, as with others. To build a 'well-off society' – the strategic objective of China till 2020 – it needs to evolve stable and mutually beneficial relations with both India and Japan, the other rising or already risen countries in Asia. Geopolitically as well, China watches carefully the emerging strategic relations between India and Japan, specifically as these have potential implications to the security and rise of China. In order to pursue these objectives, China had followed a number of policies – including engagement, balance of power, joining multilateral groups, market-based economic incentives, or even coercive diplomacy – with mixed results. It is argued that China's rise is triggering security dilemmas for both India and Japan.

Emi Mifune in her paper on 'The Japan–India–US Relation for Rising China' examines how China views the relation between Japan–India–US. She claims that India has already become a prominent and influential actor in eastern Asia. This article is divided into five sections. The first section deals with the changing structure and power shift in Asia. The recent Great Recession she writes has strongly influenced the world economy and politics. Thus, economic changes and shifts that have occurred in East Asia should be understood as a process of changing global implications. The most important among these processes are the relative decline of the US as a unipolar power and Japan as a major economic power. On the other hand, the relative economic importance and political influence of India and China is expanding and the global balance of power is shifting from a structure centred on the United States. In the second section, the role of emerging Indian economy in East Asia is dealt with. India has already been included in the East Asian trade network. In addition to Indian economic growth, the US's changing strategy towards the Pacific region has boosted India's diplomatic importance. The third part deals with Chinese views of the trio under the US policy of 'return to Asia'. The last section points out the difficulties confronting India and China to form a more comprehensive partnership. This chapter also examines the impact of the Japan–India–US relations on China.

Toru Ito in his paper on '"China Threat" theory in Japan–India Relations' analyses as to when and why Japan started to strengthen its political and security relationship with India in spite of their long 'estranged' relationship during the Cold War period. The author draws attention to the expanded sense of vigilance against China following anti-Japanese riots throughout China in the spring of 2005. The 'China threat' theory has been adopted as a central motivation for Japan to approach democratic India since then. However, the author concludes that it might be difficult to understand Japanese intention, considering the disagreement between Japan and India over China. In terms of diplomacy, China is an extremely important partner for India as it faces the global economic order with efforts such as the United Nations Framework Convention on Climate Change (UNFCCC), World Trade Organization, and International Monetary Fund as the largest developing/rising countries. China's cooperation is indispensable if India is to grow further in Asia and the world. In terms of security, Japan and India do not share any specific threat perception against China in spite of common vague images of a 'China threat'. For that reason, each country, especially Japan, must overcome the narrow-minded and nationalistic notion of targeting China if a Japan–India 'Strategic and Global' partnership is to be realized.

Swaran Singh in his paper on 'US–Japan–India Trilogue: The China Factor' seeks to specifically examine the contours of an emerging US–Japan–India trilogue and assess its impact on Asian relations in general. It also examines the logic that India – a peer civilization and rising neighbouring power of a billion-plus people – has an important role to play in this Asian transformation; and how it is partly this increasing recognition of emerging India that explains both US and Japan seriously engaging New Delhi across various forums including this trilogue.

He sums up by stating that the fact that US–Japan–India triangle seems set to address issues like energy security, piracy and environment – which are equally critical to China – their deliberations as well as future formulations are likely to be responded to and influenced by China's initiatives and formulations on these themes. Whether China should be co-opted into this US–Japan–India triangle, and/or will China be interested in joining such a forum remains a subject of interest for future explorations on this theme of Asian triangles and quadrilaterals.

Kazutoshi Tamari in his paper on 'Explaining the Similarity: Comparative Analysis of Japan's India Policy and America's India Policy' states that since 2000 Japan has sought to have closer relations with India. Since 2005 he says the effort is to expand strategic relations with India. The United States has also enhanced its relations with India during the same period. Consequently, this chapter describes that Japan's foreign policy related to India has resembled America's foreign policy towards India since the end of the Cold War. By setting and testing four hypotheses, he attempts to analyse and explain why the policies of the two countries are almost similar. The first hypothesis is that Japan is merely following the US. The second is that Japan's India policy is formed under pressure from the US. The third hypothesis is that Japan and the US have decided to have separate and closer relations with India based on their respective calculations and interests. The fourth hypothesis is that Japan has recognized its interests in relation to India by learning from the policy initiatives of the US and other countries. This chapter concludes that the fourth hypothesis explains best the similarities in the policies of US and Japan towards India. Conclusions show that similarity in policies can be understood considering the common interests of Japan and the US as independent variables and the US policy as an intervening variable.

Marie Izuyama in her paper on 'India, Japan and Maritime Security Cooperation in the Asia–Pacific' elucidates the fundamental impetus and rationale for India–Japan maritime security cooperation. Although maritime history of India and Japan are diverse, there is she states one common feature in the evolution of maritime power: move to outward-looking policy during last two or three decades. Indian Navy and Japan Maritime Self-Defense Force (JMSDF) expanded the area of operations and enhanced their intensity so as to fulfil their 'responsibility' for maritime security and safety. The author argues that either US pressure or US endorsement has been a catalyst for fostering this sense of responsibility.

Evolving cooperative security and maritime multilateralism is largely built on non-traditional security such as HADR and piracy. Indian Navy and JMSDF were quietly endorsing the line by participating in various kinds of multilateral exercises in the Western Pacific region. Both have the will and capability to share responsibility, as was proven during the tsunami relief operation of 2004-5. Although India and Japan are actively engaged in Southeast Asia, their approach is different. Learning from the experience that ReCAAP process and India–Japan Coast Guard cooperation have grown *in tandem*, bilateral navy-to-navy cooperation should be based on India–Japan collaboration on, or at least understanding of, designing regional security architecture.

Makoto Kojima in his paper on 'Prospects and Challenges for Expanding Japan–India Economic Relation' argues that while India has become the largest recipient of Japanese ODA since 2003-4, both bilateral trade in goods and Japan's foreign direct investment (FDI) into India had almost been stagnant until quite recently. The Japan–India CEPA/EPA came into effect in August 2011, which is expected to stimulate the bilateral trade expansion, including India's export of generic medicine to Japan.

Compared to trade, he says there is a conspicuous expansion in the field of investment since 2007. More and more Japanese companies have entered into wider range of manufacturing sector with a view to exploit the huge Indian market. Both the Japanese government and private companies are now more willing to commit themselves to infrastructure development in India. Japanese financial institutes, including commercial banks, insurance and security companies, are also taking a keen interest in the Indian market.

Japan now faces an acute shortage of IT engineers to meet these demands. As for the destination of Japan's IT offshoring, still 80 per cent of Japanese companies have outsourced to China and 25 per cent to India. While there is still some hesitation among Japanese companies to outsource to Indian IT companies, some leading Japanese IT companies are becoming more aggressive in directly tapping Indian IT capability.

The promotion of human exchange is vital for improvement of mutual understanding and thereby consolidating further expansion of India–Japan relations. However, the level of people-to-people exchange between India and Japan is far from satisfactory. Currently, Japanese companies are desperately in need of young qualified people for promoting business in emerging economies.

Prior to full-fledged closer economic relations, both Japan and India have been progressively forming strategic and global partnership amidst growing concern over geopolitical issues. The new perception has been observed in Japan to expand Japan–India relations based on mutual complementarities.

Srabani Roy Choudhury writing on 'India–Japan Economic Partnership: Scope and Prospect' says that cultural relations between India and Japan can be traced back to as far as the sixth century. India–Japan relations have prospered by the advantage of having no ideological differences or historical baggage. Starting with Buddhism, followed by the visit of Rabindranath Tagore to Japan and association of Netaji Subhas Chandra Bose with Japan has resulted in a warm relationship between both the countries. A natural consequence of this should have resulted in stronger economic ties between them. However, in the area of trade and investment India could not reap the benefits that many Southeast Asian countries garnered during Japan's rise in its economic stature. While there have been enough reflections on the reasons for this apathy, especially when overseas development assistance has been forthcoming, the signing of the Comprehensive Economic Partnership Agreement (CEPA) between both the nations augurs a new direction to the relationship. This paper focuses on the development in foreign direct investment (FDI) and trade from the year 2000 onwards and shows how interest by Japanese business houses and a growing Indian domestic economy ensured a move in the direction of a CEPA.

P.A. George in his paper on 'Present Status of Japanese Studies in India: Prospects and Problems' deals with the growth of Japanese language education in India since the beginning of the twenty-first century. With the support of statistical data he gives a detailed account of the status of Japanese language teaching in universities and other institutions. The study shows that there is a substantial increase in the number of students offering to study the language especially after 2009. There is also about 60 per cent increase in the number of institutions teaching Japanese language. The impetus given for studying the Japanese language during the last one decade is due to the realization on the part of both India and Japan the need to build a strong Indo-Japan global partnership and increase the level of strategic cooperation. The paper gives a brief description of Japanese studies, language, and culture in India with special reference to Japanese studies and language programme at the Jawaharlal Nehru University, New Delhi, India.

An attempt is made to highlight some of the major factors which are the root cause for the stagnation of Japanese language education and Japanese area studies in India. Some of the reasons for slow growth of Japanese language is linked to lack of government policy for developing area studies programme especially Japanese studies; lack of job opportunities for Japanese studies scholars; shortage of institutions offering Japanese language and disinterest of students studying the language to pursue higher studies in Japanese studies.

Mayumi Murayama writing on 'Problems of Youth Employment in India and Japan: A Call for a Joint Comparative Study' calls for a joint comparative study on the problem of youth unemployment in India and Japan. Youth unemployment has become a global concern although the nature and extent of the problem she says varies from country to country, and within a country. In post-war Japan, it was not until the early 1990s that the smooth transition from school to stable employment got disrupted. Youth unemployment rate as well as the share of non-regular employment among the young people has increased significantly. Since vertical mobility from non-regular to regular jobs remains limited, many people are trapped among the working poor. In India, although youth unemployment was recognized even in the First Five Year Plan, the problem was not given adequate attention. The core of the problem lies in the unemployment of educated young people.

India and Japan differ considerably in terms of their economic, social and cultural parameters as well as historical trajectories, especially with respect to the development of the economy and modern education. Nevertheless, young people in both countries who are struggling to find good employment and share many common difficulties, irrespective of differences in social and cultural contexts, economic status, educational background, and in many other attributes. Therefore, the experiences of youth in India and Japan can be a good subject for joint research. Through this collaborative work involving young people themselves, it would help in understanding each other's problems, similarities and differences and also find some solutions to the problems.

The year 2012 marks the 60th anniversary of the establishment of diplomatic relations between India and Japan. We do hope this volume helps and contributes to deeper understanding of relations between the two countries. Finally we would like to express our gratitude to Manohar Publishers and Distributors for publishing this book.

March 2012

TAKENORI HORIMOTO
LALIMA VARMA

CHAPTER 1

Strategic Convergence of Japan–India Relations and China's Emergence

TAKENORI HORIMOTO

The present Japan–India relations can be said to be the closest in the last six decades. It has developed gradually since the end of the Cold War. However, real and substantial changes have taken place only since 2000. Japan and India have mutually dovetailing strategic necessities in the fields of economics, trade, investment, security and maritime interests. They have both found each other as filling complementary roles and have almost identical shared perceptions with respect to China. Furthermore, they share a more or less common affinity towards the US.

Among other matters, a basic challenge for Japan–India relations in the coming decades will be coping with China, who has been a major factor nudging the two countries to come closer. As will be discussed later, Japan–India relations started converging around 2005, when China started to show rapid emergence on the Asian stage and implement its assertive diplomacy in the region.

The main thrust of this essay is to examine how Japan–India relations have developed, what are the factors and circumstances prompting the two countries to come closer and what the two countries can achieve through their relations.

DEVELOPMENT OF INDO–JAPAN RELATIONS: 1950s–1980s

Bilateral relations between Japan and India during the 1950s and 1980s have been marked by their mutual incompatibility. Such an incompatibility has been conspicuous in the fields of foreign policy as well as economic policy (Table 1.1).

TABLE 1.1: INCOMPATIBILITY OF JAPAN–INDIA RELATIONS BETWEEN THE 1950s AND 1980s

	Japan	India
Foreign Policy	Japan–US Alliance	Non-Alignment and subsequent Indo–Soviet Alliance
Economic Policy	Free economy	Closed economy

In the field of foreign policy, Japan had aligned itself with the US, by forming Japan–US Alliance. This alliance was antagonistic towards the Soviet-led block, regarding it as an enemy, reflecting the Cold War environment prevailing throughout the world, while India maintained first a non-alignment policy during the 1950s through the 1960s, and later forging an Indo–Soviet Alliance during the 1970s and 1980s. Only a narrow room remained for the two countries India and Japan to come closer.

In the matter of economic policy, Japan has persistently pursued a free economic policy, although India has not fundamentally altered its closed economic policy orientation. Both countries have lacked inducements and requirements to improve their mutual economic relations.

These diametrically opposite policy orientations relegated the bilateral relations to its lowest ebb, reflected by the infrequent interactions of political VIPs between them. A typical example has been prime ministerial visits. The prime ministers of both countries have rarely visited each others' country. In Japan's case, after Prime Minister Ikeda's to visit India in 1961, it took two decades for Prime Minister Nakasone to visit India in 1984. In India's case, Prime Minister Indira Gandhi visited Japan in 1969; and it was more than a decade later that she visited again in 1982.

CLOSE RELATIONS FROM THE 1990s ONWARD

The international situation until the end of the 1980s – particularly the Cold War – affected Japan–India relations. However, the end of the Cold War has brought about a mutually conducive atmosphere to the improvement of bilateral relations. The two countries have gradually developed and shared mutually acceptable international perceptions and strategic objectives, especially common concerns of maritime security in the oceans and coping with a rising China. Brahma Chellaney pointed out that 'India and Japan look like natural allies as China drives them closer together'.[1]

As Table 1.2 illustrates, VIPs including prime ministers have started visiting each other frequently from the 1990s onward.

The list reveals a great deal of difference between the 1990s and 2000 to the present day. The author designates the former as the first phase and the latter as the second phase.

First Phase of the 1990s

In this phase, there emerged mutually conducive circumstances: the collapse of the Soviet Union, acceptability of the US (especially on the Indian side), and India's economic liberalization policy. In the case of Japan, it has evaluated India favourably as a new partner in the fields of a new market, a new political ally, Indian Ocean policy, and China policy.

India's perceptions toward Japan have been almost identical to Japan's. Japan has become India's partner as a new market, a new investing country, and a collaborator of its China policy. However,

TABLE 1.2: VIP VISITS BETWEEN THE TWO COUNTRIES IN THE 1990s ONWARD

	Japan to India	India to Japan	Total
1990-9	13 (2)	14	27
2000-4	12 (1)	11	23
2005-9	31	30	61

Notes: Calculated from the website of the Ministry of Foreign Affairs Website (http://www.mofa.go.jp/mofaj/area/india/data.html) accessed 31 October 2011.

Numbers in brackets are economic missions sent by the Japanese government.

during this phase, Japan has simply represented major foreign policy options for India.

A diametrically opposite divergence has persisted: India's atomic weapons policy, as clearly demonstrated in India's atomic explosion in 1998. Immediately following the explosion, Japan suspended its new ODA to India. Therefore, this phase could be termed as a *kaccha* (imperfect) phase or formative period of new bilateral relations.

Second and Present Phase: 2000 and Thereafter

The second and present phase could be designated as a *pakka* (perfect) phase. This phase began in 2000,[2] when Japanese Prime Minister Mori visited India in the August of 2000 with Indian Prime Minister Vajpayee declaring a Japan–India Global Partnership. His visit was intended to bridge the rift in relations between the two countries created by India's atomic explosion in 1998. Japan's ODA to India was resumed and India became the top recipient of Japan's ODA; it has remained so since 2003.

Now, in almost every aspect, their mutual interests and concerns dovetail mutually, a win-win bilateral relationship has gradually emerged. Even though there remain fundamentally different policies – climate change and India's nuclear weapon policy – they have been somehow been overshadowed by multilateral positive factors.

Such situations have been reflected in Prime Minister Manmohan Singh's annual Independence Day speeches underscoring the importance of relations with the US, China, Japan, and EU – once in 2006 and again in 2009.

One famous India strategist has remarked frankly in relation to India's present weakness and its necessity to cooperate with likeminded countries to cope with an assertive China, in a conference in Tokyo in October 2011, that

> India is acutely conscious of its position as the weakest among the major powers and its vulnerability to the shifting alignments between Washington and Beijing. At the same time, Delhi is deeply aware of an expanding strategic gap with China and the need for partners in its internal and external balancing against China.

Japan has shown perceptions and policy orientations that are more or less similar to those of India, with the result the two countries have cemented their bilateral relations through various interactions, as demonstrated by the chronology of events shown in Table 1.3.

Why 2005?

A look at Tables 1.3 and 1.2 reveals a sudden spate of interactions since 2005. Why did the year of 2005 become such an apparently important turning point? Several factors have brought about such a development.

First, China became Japan's largest trading country in 2004, replacing the US. Second, China has shown its rapid emergence in terms of economic growth and defence capabilities. Third, there occurred fierce anti-Japanese upheavals in China in 2005.

In the light of such developments, Japan began to have second thoughts about closer economic ties with China, and sought to diversify its external relations aside from those with the US. In other words it sought diversification of its foreign relations by introducing

TABLE 1.3: MAJOR EVENTS BETWEEN JAPAN AND INDIA

Year	Major Events
2000	Prime Minister Mori's India visit
2001	Prime Minister Vajpayee's Japan visit
2002	Foreign and Defence Director-General level meeting
2003	India as the top recipient of Japan's ODA
2005	Visits in alternate years by two PMs started
2006	Declaration of Global and Strategic Partnership
2007	Japan has de-hyphenated India and Pakistan: PM Abe's India visit did not accompany Pakistan visit as in the past
2008	Joint Statement on security cooperation: Japan's first such declaration aside from those of the US and Australia
2010	2+2 Meeting of Foreign and Defence Secretary level
2011	Comprehensive Economic Partnership Agreement (CEPA) effective

a policy of bilateral and multilateral approach. Concretely, Japan has chosen India as an important partner, particularly in the Asian region.

India might have had identical motivations to foster closer relations with Japan. Probably from the perspective of India, Japan can be regarded as *a major safe card.* Japan is a formidable economic power and has sufficient defence capabilities, but it is geographically distant from India. Historically very little negative baggage has been shouldered between the two countries.

Another significant factor is apparent: Japan's close relations with the US. Japan has remained an ally of the US, with which India has developed increasingly closer relations since 2000 when President Clinton visited India in March of that year. More or less, Japan has viewed India as India has viewed Japan in terms of relations with the US.

Such mutual perceptions have prompted the two countries to expedite closer cooperation, particularly in the fields of economy and security.

Japan–India Economic Relations

In terms of economic cooperation, the most noticeable achievement has been the Comprehensive Economic Partnership Agreement (CEPA). It became effective in August 2011. CEPA is expected to contribute to significant expansions in trade, investment and other economic activities between the two countries. Particularly, CEPA can facilitate the expansion of Japan's total trade from 10 billion dollars in 2010 to 250 billion US dollars within 3-4 years.

Second, Japan has taken huge strides to increase cooperation on infrastructural development in India, particularly the Dedicated Freight Corridor (DFC), the Delhi–Mumbai Industrial Corridor (DMIC), high-speed rail system, and environmental technologies including renewable energy development.

However, big hurdle remains between the two countries: an atomic cooperation agreement by which it is necessary for the two countries to trade hardware and technology related to India's burgeoning nuclear power sector. Especially after the 11 March

Great East Japan Earthquake in 2011, Japan has been vacillating over nuclear-related exports between pacifism of the past non-nuclear stance and pragmatism of benefits accruing from such trade.[3]

Nevertheless, on 5 November 2011, Mr. Edano, the Economy, Trade and Industry Minister of Japan clarified the basic stance of the nuclear technology exports taken by the Japanese government, saying that no contradiction exists between reducing atomic power generation in Japan and nuclear-related technology exports. Furthermore, the 179th Diet between 20 October and 9 December 2011 ratified nuclear cooperation agreements with Jordan, Vietnam, Korea, and Russia.

Consequently, Japan might proceed with the agreement with India. When Japanese Prime Minister Yoshihiko Noda visited India on 27-8 December 2011, he and Prime Minister Manmohan Singh 'directed their negotiators to exert further efforts towards a conclusion of the Agreement' in their joint statement. The negotiations started in June 2010, but were suspended after the Great East Japan Earthquake.

Strategic and Security Relations

Both countries have conducted annual Foreign Office Consultations at the Foreign Secretary level. A Security Dialogue between the two countries was set up in 2001, and six rounds of dialogue have been conducted since. During Prime Minister Manmohan Singh's visit to Japan in 2008, a Joint Statement on security cooperation between Japan and India was issued. The Japan–India 2 + 2 Dialogue, which is the framework established and based on the agreement by the prime ministers of both countries at the Annual Summit in December 2009, was held in New Delhi in July 2010.

High-level exchange is continuing between the defence authorities.[4] From Japan, in 2005, General Masaki, Chief of Staff, and in 2006 Admiral Saito, Chief of Maritime SDF, General Mori, Chief of Ground SDF, and General Yoshida, Chief of Air SDF visited India.

From India, Admiral Prakash, Chief of Naval Staff, visited Japan in 2005. Defence Minister Antony visited Japan in 2009 and a Joint

Press Statement was issued to promote defence-related exchanges and cooperation. He visited Japan again in November 2011. In 2009, Maritime SDF joined in the 'Malabar 09' which was co-hosted by the US and India.

Not only at the naval level, the coast guards of Japan and India have been conducting combined exercises to serve anti-piracy, and search and rescue missions since 2000. Contingents of the nations' respective coast guards conducted their eighth joint exercises when the Indian coast guard ship *Sagar* sailed to Nagoya in May 2007. Heads of the respective coast guards visit each other almost every year. A Memorandum on Cooperation was also exchanged on the occasion of Commandant Ishikawa's visit to India in November 2006.

JAPAN AND INDIA'S CONVERGENCE OF OCEAN STRATEGY

The most conspicuous bilateral cooperation in the field of security and defence might be that in relation to maritime security. In short, their emphasis has been on coping with China, which is metamorphozing into a land-power-cum-sea-power from being just a land-power in the past two decades.[5] Their principal areas of concern are the Western Pacific and, to a certain degree, the Indian Ocean. Actually, both seas have become the new main stage of naval activities in the world aside from the pirate-infested Arabian Sea. Reflecting their common concerns, the two countries decided to hold their first joint naval exercise in 2012 in the joint declaration of December 2011.

JAPAN'S ORIENTATIONS

In the past two decades, the axis of Japan's maritime policy and Japan–US security alliance have shifted gradually from the *Fight Against Terrorism* to China's oceanic assertiveness and its pro-activism.

Put another way, it is Japan's emphasis on maritime security. It is natural to say that Japan has been facing fierce Chinese claims over the Senkaku Islands (or the Diaoyu Islands) located in the East

China Sea, where East Asian countries have harboured disputes over various islands and territorial waters with China similar to those of Southeast Asian countries in the South China Sea.

The Ministry of Defence of Japan has expressed concern in the annual defence report of 2011 over China's claims and activism in the sea.[6] In fact, when Prime Minister Noda met Prime Minister Singh at New York on the sideline of the UN General Assembly on 23 September 2011, they agreed to strengthen security cooperation through bilateral and multilateral consultations.

Japan, for its part, has been concretizing its maritime policy overall in its operational levels aside from various capacity build-ups in the recent past. For example, it established a Self Defence Force (SDF) *facility* in Djibouti on 7 July 2011 to strengthen its anti-pirate operations. The facility, which is the first ever of its kind for Japan, could be designated as an overseas *base* in reality.

Similarly, the Japanese government has dispatched a Ground SDF engineering unit to the United Nations Mission in the Republic of South Sudan. The first batch of GSDF members will be dispatched as early as January 2012. As the Japanese daily, *The Yomiuri Shimbun* of 3 November 2011 noted 'We hope the South Sudan mission will serve as a turning point that will enable Japan to work positively on international peacekeeping activities again in the future,' certainly such cooperation is a part of international contribution under the strict peaceful Japanese constitution. Nevertheless, it is possible to regard such overseas activities including the Djibouti facility as a covert power projection of a kind by Japan.

In terms of power projection, Japan Maritime SDF has two helicopter destroyers: the *Hyuga* and *Haruna*. The basic mission of such carriers is to function in support of anti-submarine and peacekeeping and relief operations. Nevertheless, comparable to light aircraft carriers,[7] they are the largest combat ships operated by Japan since the old Imperial Navy.

India's Orientations

Similar to China, India is metamorphozing during the past decade into a land-power-cum-sea-power from being just a land-power.

Defence modernization and expansion have represented this metamorphosis. India intends to have its blue water navy with power projection capability through which it tries to achieve twin objectives. Clearly, one objective is to equip itself with a capable navy as a prerequisite of a major power. These efforts have been underscored by India's large-scale defence procurements. A typical case would be its introduction of the Russian carrier, now named *INS Vikramaditya*, estimated to enter service in the Indian Navy after 2012. India has sought to become a regional power across the Indian Ocean basin and has secured agreements from partners in this region that support this goal, while building up expeditionary capabilities in its navy and air force.[8]

According to the Stockholm International Peace Research Institute report released in March 2011, India accounted for 9 per cent of all international arms imports during 2006–10, making it the largest weapons importer in the world, surpassing even China.[9]

Another objective is to unfold its countermeasures against China's encirclement of India. China has been establishing closer ties with countries such as Pakistan and Sri Lanka. Putting it another way, India's Look East Policy introduced since the early 1990s seems to have transformed from an economy-oriented policy into an economy-cum-security oriented policy:[10] with its close relations with Japan, Korea, and the ASEAN countries. India has shown its maritime activities: closer relationship with Maldives, Mauritius and Seychelles, the formation of Bay of Bengal Initiative for Multi-Sectoral Technical and Economic Cooperation (BIMSTEC), Indian Ocean Rim-Association for Regional Cooperation (IOR-ARC) and Indian Ocean Navy Symposium (IONS), in addition to various joint naval exercises.

CHALLENGES BEFORE JAPAN AND INDIA: SHAPING A COMMON STRATEGY

Although Japan and India have continued their close cooperation to form a common cause in terms of their China policy, this cooperation has been developing into a multilateral configuration. Such a configuration has been contemplated in the form of a combination of countries: Japan, India, US, and Australia. The configuration exemplifies a quadrilateral (quad) framework.

Quad Approach

From around 2005 onward, a move was underway to construct a quadrilateral framework among the US, Japan, Australia, and possibly India. At the Sydney APEC Summit in September 2007, the heads of the US, Japan, and Australia held a summit meeting for the first time. An Indian newspaper, the *Economic Times*, reported it by quoting the Japanese press secretary's statement that India had been requested to participate in such a meeting as a country with similar concerns of democracy and freedom.[11]

The quad approach died a natural death, especially after the exit of Prime Minister Shinzo Abe and Australian Prime Minister John Howard, in addition to fierce criticism by China. However, it remains alive in the form of bilateral arrangements as a part of a hedging policy. They are the Indo–US defence agreement (June 2005), India–Australian Defence MOU (March 2006), and the Joint Declaration of Security Cooperation (January 2009).

The Japan–India Joint Declaration on Security Cooperation (October 2008) was also released during Prime Minister Singh's visit to Japan. This was only the third such agreement that Japan has ever made, following those with the US and Australia. Japan's Prime Minister Aso and Dr. Singh emphasized that security cooperation should not target a third country. Dr. Singh clarified that the Indo–Japan economic partnership and security cooperation 'are not at the cost of any third country, least of all China'. Although the quad process was put on the backburner, 'Japan's alliance with the US and its new security ties, no matter how loose, with Australia and India sends the signal of a new security order in the region.[12]

China's Riposte

China has levelled a great deal of criticism against the Japan–India Joint Declaration as a policy of containment of China.[13] Furthermore, China has implemented its countermeasures against the quad approach persistently. China regards various measures adopted by surrounding countries as an encirclement policy. A Chinese magazine *Qiushi* (Seek Truth) article dated 10 December 2010 'How China Deals with the U.S. Strategy to Contain China' claimed that the US encourages neighbouring countries to resist China.[14]

China itself has been relaxing its ASEAN policy. For example, China has been adamantly adhering to ASEAN+3 (Japan, China, and Korea) formula for ASEAN's economic community in the past, thereby excluding India, Australia, and New Zealand. However, Chinese Prime Minister Wen Jiabao has reported that the expansion of ASEAN economic zone could be finalized by ASEAN when he attended the ASEAN summit meeting on 17 November 2011.[15]

A popular proverb in China is that *two tigers are not necessary on one mountain.* China aspires to establish a hierarchical power structure: first in Asia and then in the rest of the world.[16] To concretize its aspirations, China has been implementing various policies: the PLAN's expansion, the String of Pearls operation, the Island Chain strategy in the Pacific, and vast claims of territorial waters and islands in neighbouring seas and land.

Challenge of Japan and India: A Common Bilateral Strategy of Engagement and Hedging

Japan and India do not necessarily see eye-to-eye regarding the pursuit of bilateral relations. Some strategists and rightists in Japan argue for a much closer bilateral relation (i.e. quasi-alliance). Former Japanese Prime Minister Shinzo Abe (September 2006–August 2007), presumably a rightist in Japanese politics, once argued, 'it is no wonder the Japan–India relationship will outdo Japan–US and Japan–China within ten years'.[17]

New Delhi will be entering into economic partnership and strategic dialogues, but not for a balancing role with China.[18] India's foreign policy line at the moment might be best regarded as that of defining a strategic partnership. India has established strategic partnerships with 20 major countries since 1997 (Table 1.4).

TABLE 1.4: INDIA'S STRATEGIC PARTNERSHIPS

Year	Country
1997	South Africa
1998	France
2000	Russia
2001	Germany
2004	US, UK, EU
2005	China, Indonesia, Fiji
2006	Japan, Brazil
2007	Nigeria, Vietnam
2009	Australia
2010	Korea, Canada, Malaysia, Saudi Arabia
2011	Afghanistan

Note: MEA, Annual Reports and other sources.

Strategic partnership cannot, however, jeopardize the solid and fundamental diplomatic orientation of an independent foreign policy. As Shyam Saran, India's former foreign secretary and special envoy of the prime minister, said in March 2011, 'Indian foreign policy strategy must be simple in its conception: engage all great powers, but align with none'.[19] India has been persistent to pursue its strategic autonomy and as Ashley Tellis pointed out, 'Yet the desire to pursue an autonomous course in international politics remains the bedrock of New Delhi's grand strategy....'[20]

For China itself, India is not merely another South Asian country. Fu Xianquiang of the Chinese Institute of Contemporary International Relations has said, China's policy is not to pursue 'strategic equilibrium' between India and Pakistan, with Beijing looking at relations between the two neighbours differently.[21]

Under the present prevailing circumstances, how would Japan and India find a common strategy with respect to China? At the moment, the two countries appear to be applying an engagement policy *vis-à-vis* China. When Prime Minister Singh was asked by Prime Minister Kan during his visit to Japan in November 2010 why India has been so good at dealing with China, he replied: deep studies, engagement, and much patience.[22]

Simultaneously, the two countries are unfolding their hedging policy to China. Japan and India have been expanding their defence capabilities, as described above, with India's defence expansion and Japan's changed defence policy in 2010.[23]

In other words, Japan and India have been commonly deploying the twofold policy of engagement and hedging *vis-à-vis* China. The main objective of each of the two countries would be to constrain and not to contain China, which might be possible only to a slight degree. Such a double-edged policy might be designated as a common and holistic strategy of combination of an engaging and hedging strategy toward China, seeking to achieve a good chemistry of realistic and liberalistic approach. At the moment, the engagement policy would be inclusive, whereas the hedging policy would be exclusive.

The fundamental reason for applying a common and holistic policy of hedging and engagement is to be effective and sustainable. Japan–India Strategic cooperation based on such a policy orientation should be so oriented that it would create an Asian environment where China would find it tough to become a hegemon and instead accept cooperation for a regional framework. After all, as Kondapalli and Mifune point out, 'Asian vicissitudes to a large extent are dependent on how China evolves its relations with its neighbours – in mutually beneficial interdependence or unending and costly conflicts'.[24]

Involvement of US and ASEAN Countries

If the Japan–India cooperation should be oriented to develop a common strategy of engagement and hedging, then the next step would be how to expand this framework to involve the US and the ASEAN member countries.

As clarified earlier, the US has shown keen interest in the Asian region since 2010. For example, Secretary of State Hillary Clinton, has manifestly indicated USA's intention to devote its efforts to closer relations with Asian countries after its withdrawal from the Middle East. She noted in her article in 2011 that in the coming decade, the US would put all its national energies into the Asia-Pacific region.[25]

President Obama has shown such policy orientations during November 2011. Obama announced on 16 November that the United States has planned to deploy 2,500 Marines in Darwin, Australia to shore up alliances in Asia. The following day, in an address to the Australian Parliament, Obama said he had 'made a deliberate and strategic decision – as a Pacific nation, the United States will play a larger and long-term role in shaping this region and its future'. After Australia, he arrived in Bali and became the first American President to participate in the East Asian Summit meeting.

During 2011, the US, Japan, Australia, and India moved to a trilateral meeting. In addition, a US–Japan–India trilateral director-generals meeting on maritime security was held on 19 December 2011.[26] Furthermore, the Heritage Foundation report of November 2011 has advocated the formation of a US–Australia–India cooperative structure in the Indo-Pacific.[27] Trilateral meetings of two kinds might be merged into a quadrilateral meeting. The Heritage Report said,

> This paper provides ideas for establishing a US–Australia–India dialogue and coordination across a host of economic, political, and security issues. In addition to the great value of trilateral cooperation in its own right, the dialogue could lay a policy foundation for the US, Japan, Australia, and India to revive formal quadrilateral security talks if they decide it is in their collective interests at some point.[28, 29]

The quad approach has been advocated clearly by a cable of 5 May 2006 from the US Embassy in New Delhi to its home office.[30] After all, it is only barely possible to maintain an Asian balance of power without the US, as ex-Minister Mentor of Singapore, Lee Kuan Yew reightly pointed out.[31]

For Japan and India, the US could be designated as an indispensable ally to a greater or lesser degree. Japan signed the Japan–US Security Treaty in 1951. Subsequently, bilateral relations turned into an alliance when Prime Minister Suzuki and President Reagan designated them as such in their Joint Statement of 1981. In terms of economy and security, bilateral relations have the most significant implications for Japan.

In the case of India, the US is regarded as an important ally roughly since the turn of the century. Initially the Congress government led by Prime Minster Narasimha Rao had commenced the attachment of great importance to the relation with the US in the first half of the 1990s. When the Bharatiya Janata Party came to power in 1998, it sought a new diplomatic policy by setting up a group of ministers led by L.K. Advani on April 2000. The group emphasized the utmost importance of the US in its foreign relations in its report of February 2001.[32] Since then, BJPs foreign policy line has underscored the importance of the US in India's foreign policy. Such a foreign policy line has been strengthened by the following government led by the Congress under Prime Minister Manmohan Singh.

Therefore, Japan and India must include the US in their calculus of their foreign relations and in the two's bilateral relation. This approach could be especially important in forging bilateral strategic formations related to their Asian policy.

Another issue would be how to involve ASEAN countries. The countries have shown their anxiety over China in terms of security and economy. For them, the US annual defence cut from 600 billion US dollars to 500 billion US dollars in the coming decade has presented the largest headache in the field of security.[33]

Additionally, the ASEAN countries have been anxious about the omnipresence of China's goods and people in their respective countries, with the fear that their economies would be engulfed into the Chinese economy. Such concerns have been a major factor for Singapore and Brunei (both original signatories) and Malaysia and Vietnam (both under negotiations to join) to be member countries of the Trans Pacific Partnership (TPP) framework. These four countries face not only China's large and looming economic might – though economic interactions with China are an inescapable reality – but also territorial disputes in the South China Sea.

In other words, the engagement and hedging policy framework should be pursued in a bilateral (Japan and India) and multilateral way: putting engagement and hedging into a bilateral and multilateral Asian matrix. Engagement alone would yield elusive results, although a hedging only policy would turn out to be antagonistic. By combining these two policies, one might expect an effective and sustainable mechanism in Asia.

BILATERAL RELATIONS AS A NEW PUBLIC GOOD IN ASIA

How should the bilateral relations between Japan and India be oriented? The relation could be formulated preferably as a *public property (or good)* to be shared by all of Asia.

In the past, Japan–US relations have sometimes been compared to a public property of Asia, which have been said to contribute to stabilization of the Asian political environment. In other words, these relations are not meant for beneficial bilateral relations – private property – but for Asia as a whole. However, the Japan–US relationship has tended to be regarded as a relation of junior partner and senior partner. Therefore, the discourse of Japan–US relation as public property has not been readily acceptable in Asia in the past. This has been especially so in India. Satu Limaye pointed out that India had basically written off Japan as an American surrogate in Asia during the Cold War period, and that the view persists today.[34]

Now would be an opportune time for Japan and India to look forward to the future to consider their bilateral relations as public property and not simply to promote bilateral benefits as private property but for public property which would render services. The two countries should apply the present closest relation for institutionalizing a security system, something like an Asian regional security mechanism for Asia's prosperity, peace, and stability.

More concretely, strategic cooperation between Japan and India should be so oriented as to create an Asian environment in which China would find it difficult to become a hegemon and would instead accept cooperation for a regional framework. Furthermore, it must be emphasized that such a framework should be formulated in an inclusive manner to remain effective and sustainable in future decades. Japan–India relations have sufficient potential to emerge as a *public property* benefiting all of Asia, and not merely benefiting the two nations themselves.

For achieving the objectives described above, Japan and India must have more frequent interactions. As one former Indian diplomat has remarked, 'Clearly, the destinies of India and Japan are linked better today. Experts will have to reflect and interact more before crafting a consensus view.'[35]

NOTES

1. Brahma Chellaney, *Asian Juggernaut: The Rise of China, India and Japan*, Harper Collins Publishers, 2009, p. 224.
2. He said 'Indo-Japanese ties have witnessed a paradigm shift since 2000, when Prime Minister Yoshiro Mori called upon both countries to launch a global partnership...', K.V. Kesavan, 'India and Japan Changing Dimensions of Partnership in the Post-Cold War Period' (ORF Occasional Paper #14), Observer Research Foundation, May 2010, p. 37.
3. Takenori Horimoto, 'The Japan–India Nuclear Agreement: Enhancing Bilateral Relations?,' *Asia Pacific Bulletin*, no. 107, 15 April 2011 (http://www.eastwestcenter.org/fileadmin/stored/pdfs/apb107.pdf); 'After the Great Earthquake', *Pragati* (*The Indian National Interest Review*), 5 August 2011 (http://pragati.nationalinterest.in/2011/08/after-the-great-earthquake/).
4. Website of Ministry of Foreign Affairs (http://www.mofa.go.jp/mofaj/area/india/data.html) and press reports.
5. Takenori Horimoto, 'Major Country of South Asia and Japan', in Nishihara and Horimoto, eds., *India as a Rising Military Power*, Askishobo, 2010 (in Japanese), pp. 22-32.
6. Ministry of Defence, *Defense of Japan 2011*, 2011. In the report, reference to individual country is the US 155, China 85, and India 70. These references themselves show Japan's basic stances toward foreign countries.
7. Harold C. Hutchison, *Japan's Secret Aircraft Carriers*, 25 August 2007 (http://www.strategypage.com/htmw/htnavai/articles/20070825.aspx) accessed 1 October 2011.

8. Brian K. Hedrick, *India's Strategic Defense Transformation: Expanding Global Relationship*, Carlisle: Strategic Studies Institute, p. vi.
9. *The Times of India*, 14 March 2011.
10. John Garver shared a similar view: 'India's "Look East" policy, which originated in the 1990s, essentially had an economic logic, but now it has been given a geopolitical logic, in order to counter-encircle the encircler', *The Washington Post*, 27 November 2011.
11. *The Economic Times*, 7 September 2007.
12. Purnendra Jain, 'Tokyo's Nexus with India Deepens', *Asia Times*, 25 October 2008.
13. Hayoun Ryou 'India-Japan Security Cooperation, Chinese Perceptions', *IPCS Issue Brief*, no. 89, January 2009.
14. The English version appeared in *Chinascope* in February 2011.
15. *Asahi Shimbun* (Japanese daily), 19 November 2011.
16. An Indian expert on China interviewed in New Delhi on 6 September 2011.
17. Shinzo Abe, *Utsukusii Kuni He* (Towards a Beautiful Country), Tokyo: Bungekisyunju, 2006, p. 159.
18. Purnendra Jain, 'Global Insider: Japan–South Asia Relations', *Worldpoliticsreview.com*, 22 September 2011 (http://www.scribd.com/doc/65964598/Global-Insider-Japan–South-Asia-Relations).
19. *Business Standard*, 17 March 2011; Shyam Saran has also said that since India's closer bilateral relations with major powers will bring about softened Chinese attitudes toward India, India would have more diplomatic cards, *The Asahi Shimbun*, 14 January 2011.
20. Ashley J. Tellis, 'The Changing Political-Military Environment: South Asia', in Zalmay Khalilzad et al., eds., *The United States and Asia*, Rand, Santa Monica, 2001, p. 209.
21. *Press Trust of India*, 25 December 2010.
22. *The Hindu*, 26 October 2010; *Tribune online* (http://www.thetribuneonline.com/foreign-archives12.html) accessed on 11 December 2011.
23. The latest *National Defence Program Guidelines* decided by the Japanese Cabinet on December 2010 have scrapped the old guidelines of fundamental defence for the modern concept of dynamic defence capability emphasizing mobile and responsive

deployment in the backdrop of PLAN's advance into the Nansei Islands (Southwest Islands) in the East China Sea, North Korea's development of Ballistic missiles, and international terrorism. Japan's 2011 Annual Report has further emphasized China's increasing naval activity near its shores and measures to bolster its coastal defences. Beijing has expressed strong dissatisfaction with Japan's stated concern. *The Japan Times*, 5 August 2011.

24. Srikanth Kondapalli and Emi Mifune, 'Introduction', in Srikanth Kondapalli and Emi Mifune, eds., *China and its Neighbours*, New Delhi: Pentagon Press, 2010, p. xiii.
25. Hillary Clinton, 'America's Pacific Century', *Foreign Policy*, November 2011.
26. Mark C. Toner (Deputy Spokesperson of the US State Department) said on 5 December 2011 at the daily press briefing that, 'this meeting is going to be an opportunity to hold comprehensive discussions on a range of Asia–Pacific regional issues'.
27. The Heritage Foundation, *Shared Goals, Converging Interest: A Plan for US–Australia–India Cooperation in the Indo-Pacific*, November 2011.
28. Ibid., p. 15.
29. Lalima Varma pointed out a similar evaluation on Japan's policy toward South Asia. She said 'Japan almost until recently did not have a well defined policy towards South Asia. It was guided by US policies in South Asia, especially during the Cold War era', Lalima Varma, 'Japan's Policy Towards South Asia: Shifting Paradigms', *International Symposium on India 2009 Changing Perceptions of Japan in South Asia in the New Asian Era: The State of Japanese Studies in India and Other SAARC Countries*, Kyoto: International Research Center for Japanese Studies. Another expert said that 'The imperative for Japan was to view India without "the US prism". Japan's preference for "the hub and spokes approach" (with the US as the hub) needs to be reinforced by the spokes (such as Japan and India "networking" with each other more closely', Rajiv Bhatia, 'Growing Proximity between India and Japan', *The Hindu*, 7 November 2011.
30. The cable pointed out that the stars had aligned for closer trilateral relations among the US, Japan, and India. *The Hindu*, 23 April 2010.

31. *The Asahi Shimbun*, 11 May 2010.
32. *Recommendations of the Group of Ministers Reforming the National Security System*, February 2001. The Recommendations said 'US pre-eminence in the global strategic architectures is unlikely to diminish in the foreseeable future. Meaningful broad-based engagement with the United States spanning political, economic, and technological interests and commonalities will impact beneficially on our external security concerns with a resultant albeit less visible impact on our internal security. Conversely, an adversarial relationship with that State can have significant negative repercussions across the same broad range of issues and concerns.' (p. 7)
33. 'Asian Anxiety', *The New York Times*, 25 October 2011.
34. He said 'Japan was undoubtedly influenced by U.S. policies and consequently reduced its own ties to India. India in turn responded by basically writing off Japan as an American surrogate in Asia. Japan's close relations with the United States, and the latter's troubled relations with India, have strongly shaped the Japan–India encounter – a theme that persists to this day.' Satu Limaye, 'Japan and India after the Cold War', in Yoichiro Sato and Satu Limaye, eds., *Japan in a Dynamic Asia Coping with the New Security Challenges*, Lanham: Lexington Books, 2006, pp. 226-7.
35. Bhatia, op. cit.

CHAPTER 2

Enhancing Strategic Ties between Japan and India: Japan–China Relations as a Factor

LALIMA VARMA

Cordial relations between Japan and the Peoples Republic of China (China) are one of the most important key to the future prosperity and stability of the East Asian region in particular and Asia in general. However, unfortunately political relations between these two major countries of the region are more often than not strained. This paper intends to understand the nature of the problems between the two countries. It also deals with the shifts in the manner in which the Japanese and the Chinese have perceived each other over the last few decades and how Japan endeavours to grapple with the security challenges posed by China's growing stature in the region.

JAPAN–CHINA RELATIONS: UNRESOLVED PROBLEMS

There are several controversial issues which have created barriers in the development of relations between the two countries. China's memories of atrocities committed by Japanese military during the pre-Second World War period; Japan's close relations with Taiwan; territorial issues, i.e. Senkaku islands; problem of rights over the gas fields in East China Sea; contents of the school textbooks which China claims tones down atrocities committed by the Japanese military are few of the major problems between the two countries. These issues have existed between the two countries since the end of Second World War but still have not been resolved and the resolution of these problems in the near future or even distant future seems bleak. Since Japan regained its sovereignty in 1952, its effort has been to achieve 'normal and cordial' relations with China.

Japan was convinced that its strategic and economic interest would be best served by maintaining close ties with China.

For two decades from 1952-72 Japan had no diplomatic ties with China. In September 1972 relations between the two countries were normalized and a Peace Treaty was concluded in 1978. Aware of the fact that Korea, China and some of the Southeast Asian countries had suffered under its rule, Japan apologized for its past behaviour. Majority of the Japanese nurtured a sense of guilt. Thus, Japan tried to compensate these countries by providing reparation or Official Development Assistance (ODA). Since 1978 China has been one of the major recipients of Japanese ODA. Even after the 1989 Tiananmen Square incident when China was criticized for human rights violation and sanctions were imposed against China by most of the developed countries, Japan was one country which worked for the 'non-isolation' of China.[1] The Japanese Emperor visited China in 1992. This was the first time ever that an Emperor of Japan had set foot on Chinese soil. It was an indication of Japan's keenness to maintain friendly relations with China. However, problems existing between the two countries continued to pose obstacles at regular intervals in the development of a more lasting friendship but at the same time were not allowed to be blown out of proportion both by Japan and China. The problems as and when they occurred were managed diplomatically. China's 'somewhat positive' attitude towards Japan at this point of time could be to some extent attributed to its vested interest in Japan's ODA for its developmental projects.

A serious downturn in the relations between the two countries began during former Prime Minister Koizumi Junichiro's premiership (2001-6). Koizumi's visits to Yasukuni Shrine where the Japanese war martyrs are enshrined led to strong protests in China. In April 2005 anti-Japan demonstrations spread over large parts of China against prime minister's visits to Yasukuni shrine, and Japan's aspiration to become a permanent member of the Security Council of the United Nations. The Japanese were taken aback by the enormity of the anti-Japanese mood in China. Japanese attitude till the end of the last century was generally to make efforts to bridge differences.

However, after the April 2005 anti-Japan demonstrations in China, a visible change was evident in Japanese feelings towards China. Response of most Japanese to the anti-Japanese demonstrations at all levels was one of disbelief and anger.

One of the opinions which became widely prevalent in Japan after the April 2005 incident was that ODA to China should be discontinued. It was felt that China despite being a major recipient of Japanese ODA was not appreciative and continued to promote anti-Japanese sentiments. The anger was all the more acute considering that Japan was providing aid despite the fact that since the bubble burst in 1991, Japan's economic growth was slow. At the domestic level there was a growing dissatisfaction that the budget for improvement of social security, education and other areas was reduced by the government. Consequently, increasingly many Japanese questioned the necessity of providing aid when the country itself was facing an economic crisis. In case of China the argument was that China's economy since the late 1990s was growing at a fast pace and that it was itself extending aid to several countries.

However, as it had happened before, the governments of both countries realized the need for preventing the relations from deteriorating beyond repair. Bringing back relations to 'normal' was necessary to protect not only the political, strategic but also economic interests of both the countries. It was clear that economic interdependence of both China and Japan over the years had deepened. By the mid-2000s China had emerged as the largest trading partner of Japan. Japanese investments in China were also considerable. Understandably the Japanese business community was not very supportive of Koizumi's policy towards China.

The opportunity to open a dialogue was provided with the change in the Japanese administration in September 2006. Abe Shinzo became the prime minister of Japan on 26 September 2006. Topmost on his agenda was reviving relations with China and the Republic of Korea. The urgency of restoring damaged relations can be gauged from the fact that Abe visited China within two weeks of assuming office. Abe's official visit to China from 8-9 October was in response to an invitation from Chinese Prime Minister Wen Jiabao. Abe's visit was termed as a 'turning point' in the relations between the two countries. China also responded positively and gave Abe a red-carpet welcome. The process of bringing back relations on track had begun. China's top legislator Wu Bangguo described the relations between the two countries as 'the most difficult' during the Koizumi period.[2]

After Abe's visit the succeeding years witnessed exchange of visits by top leaders of the two countries. Chinese Prime Minister Wen Jiabao visited Japan in April 2007. During his visit Wen also met the Japanese Emperor. Both Abe and Wen agreed to promote mutually beneficial strategic relations. The two leaders agreed to settle their dispute in the South China Sea regarding the development of oil and gas fields in the disputed area. The joint statement issued during the visit avoided reference to any sensitive issues. Prime Minister Fukuda Takeo visited China from 27-30 December 2007. Chinese President Hu Jintao visited Japan from 6-10 May 2008. This was the first visit by a Chinese President after ten years. During this visit an important Joint Statement was signed on 'Comprehensive Promotion of a Mutually Beneficial Relationship Based on Common Strategic Interests'. This joint statement was one of the important documents which set forth a course which Japan and China were to follow in future.[3]

CHINA POLITICAL RELATIONS REACH A NADIR: CHANGING ATTITUDE OF JAPANESE TOWARDS CHINA

The process of restoring 'normal' relations which started with the advent of the Abe Shinzo's administration received a major setback in 2010. On 7 September 2010 Chinese fishing boats collided with Japanese coast guards near Senkaku islands. Both countries stake their claim over the Senkaku/Diaoyu islands. China's captain was arrested by the Japanese coast guard. China vehemently reacted to the arrest of the captain. Japanese government soon after released the captain. This decision to release the captain infuriated a large number of Japanese. They felt that it amounted to bowing down to

China's pressure tactics such as stopping the export to Japan of rare earth minerals, crucial for the electronic industry. This step taken by China was regarded by Japan as an indicator that China was giving out a loud and clear message that it is a power in the region which cannot be challenged easily. Since then China has expressed its determination to protect the fishing grounds around the Diaoyu Islands in East China Sea.[4]

Japanese reaction to the 7 September incident was much more severe when compared to their reaction to the anti-Japan demonstrations in 2005 in China. All sections of the Japanese society – politicians, bureaucrats, business and general public – expressed their anger and displeasure with China's action. Soon after the incident two of Japan's top airlines – Japan Airlines Corp. cancelled about 1,000 and All Nippon Airways Co. about 5,000 flights between Japan–China. Four Diet members including Haraguchi Kazuhiro in October 2010 made an aerial survey of the islands despite the fact that the Foreign Minister Okada Katsuya asked them to cancel the trip so as to avoid further friction with China.[5]

A Japanese Foreign Ministry official stated that, 'We all realize ... China's true nature, Maybe people and politicians realized the Chinese essence, thanks to the incident'.[6] This strong anti-China feeling probably was also linked to China taking over Japan as the number two economy in the world. The disillusionment was more poignant considering that China for decades was one of the topmost recipients of Japanese ODA. It was probably difficult for Japanese to accept the fact that the position which they occupied as the second largest economy for decades had been taken over by China. A feeling of 'anger' 'vulnerable ness' and concern appears to have seeped into the minds of the Japanese. The fear is that China is set out to 'buy up Japan'. Increasingly, department stores are employing Mandarin speaking staff to deal with the growing number of Chinese customers. Japanese are also watching with concern Chinese conglomerates buying up real estate, forests and attempting to establish their control on uninhabited islands around Japan's coast.[7]

There is a growing concern among the Japanese that their country must not appear to be a 'weak' country that cannot take care of its own interests and security. In a recent public opinion poll the percentage of Japanese who are not in favour of China has increased. A Yomiuri Shimbun survey shows that public opinion towards China deteriorated severely as a result of China's actions following the Senkaku incident in September. About 84 per cent said that they don't trust China. Eighty-nine per cent said that China's apparent retaliation was excessive and 94 per cent said that its demand for an apology was unacceptable.[8]

Most of the Japanese are of the opinion that while Japan has moved forward regarding the history issue, Chinese memories of the past continues to persist. One of the reasons for the persistence of the anti-Japanese feelings in China is attributed to the fact that the memories are kept alive in the mind of the Chinese by a constant dose with which they are supplied with by the government which controls the education and media.[9]

DISCONCERTING DEVELOPMENTS IN THE NEIGHBOURHOOD

For Japan in addition to the China 'problem', other developments in the neighbourhood is equally disconcerting. Soon after the Senkaku problem came Russian President Dmitry Medvedev's stopover at Kunashiri island, one of the northern islands, i.e. Kurile islands on 1 November 2010. This incident was referred by the then Japanese Prime Minister Kan Naoto as 'regrettable'. Medevdev's stopover was a cause of great concern for Japan when seen from the viewpoint of the deepening ties between China and Russia. A joint statement was issued by President Hu Jintao and Medevdev on 27 September 2010 which called for 'mutual support for each other's core interests, including national sovereignty, unity, and territorial integrity'.[10]

The Democratic Peoples Republic of Korea's (North Korea) continuous effort to develop its nuclear capability is also viewed as a serious threat by Japan to its security. Japan also watches with concern North Korea's close relations with China. The frequency of former North Korean leader Kim Jong Il's visits to China is evidence of the level to which North Korea is dependent on China. In the last week of May 2011 Kim Jong Il ended his eight-day visit to China. Prior to this visit the leader had made about three visits to China within just one year. Japan is constantly worried about the close military ties between China and North Korea.

NEED TO PREPARE FOR ALTERNATIVES TO PROTECT NATIONAL INTERESTS: CHANGING CONTOURS OF JAPAN–US RELATIONS

Security arrangements with the US have always been and will continue to be one of the main pillars of Japan's foreign policy. Despite this fact Japan's endeavour especially since the end of the Cold War has been to reduce its dependence on the US for its security. Ironically, however, the importance of the Security Treaty has revived since relations with China deteriorated in 2010. As a Foreign Ministry official opined, 'Japan cannot face China alone. We have to step up cooperation with our main ally and with likeminded countries in the region.'[11] US can also play a role as mediator in crisis between Japan and China. For example, Hillary Clinton, US Secretary of State, who attended the East Asia Summit at the Vietnamese capital as a guest said that US would be more than willing to 'host a trilateral meeting with the Japanese and Chinese foreign ministers as part of efforts to diffuse tension over the islands, which Japan administers but China claims'.[12]

Nevertheless the growing opinion is that Japan must evolve a foreign policy which enables it to manage a crisis situation even if US support is not forthcoming. Japan watches with apprehension US interest in enhancing ties with China. The changing contours of China–US relations needs to be also taken into account by Japan while planning its strategy for protecting and promoting its own interests. Japan has not overlooked the fact that US President Bill Clinton ignored Japan during his visit to China in 1998. It was the longest visit ever made by an American President to any country. Japan seemed to have made a serious note of the fact that Clinton did not even stopover in Tokyo.[13] President Barak Obama visited China in November 2009. Since the beginning of the 2011 relations between the US and China have been upbeat. During Chinese Premier Hu Jintao's visit to the US in 2011, the two countries signed a joint communiqué and more than ten agreements, memorandum of understanding in various areas such as trade, investments, technology, cultural exchange, etc. There are a number of areas on which both Japan and the US have differences of opinion, for example, North Korea and Iran, on human rights, economic policies, etc. The possibility of being sidetracked by the US in the future is not ruled out completely by Japan.

It was for the first time since 2000 when the joint Yomiuri Shimbun and Gallup survey began conducting interviews by telephone it revealed that more people had a bad opinion of Japan–US relations. In a public opinion poll conducted in October 2010, 40 per cent respondents considered Japan–US relations to be 'poor' or very poor. Only 33 per cent had a positive impression of the bilateral ties.[14]

IS THE ROLE OF ODA DECLINING

In the absence of hard power extending Official Development Assistance to developing countries has enabled Japan to play an important and visible role in international affairs. By providing bilateral aid Japan also hoped that it would help to strengthen bilateral relations with the recipient country. However, eventually it has become clear to Japan that despite extending ODA to a particular country it did not necessarily lead to good relations. A case in point is China. It was a major recipient of Japanese ODA for several years and Japan hoped to establish close economic and political relations and erase the bitterness of past history. However, though the economic relations improved greatly, political relations continue to be weak.

Gradually, according to some studies it is seen that the role of ODA as a foreign policy tool seems to be shrinking. Countries such as China and India receive ODA but are also aid-giving countries. Moreover, Japan's budget allocation for ODA has reduced after the

1991 'bubble' burst. From being a topmost aid donor it slipped to a third position by the beginning of the twenty-first century. Few months before the Great East Japan Earthquake in March 2011 disasters, Japan according to the Organization for Economic Cooperation and Development (OECD) was the fifth largest aid donor country. Now after the earthquake and tsunami further reduction in the ODA budget is expected. Even before the disaster the Japanese public was critical about the government ODA policies. Now it would be more difficult for the government to justify giving ODA.

The security environment in the Asian region warrants that Japan formulate strategies at various levels to safeguard and expand its economic and strategic interests. In the Asia-Pacific region there is no well established multilateral collective defense security mechanism like the North Atlantic Treaty Organization (NATO) in Europe. In the absence of such an organization in the region and constitutional constraints which prevents Japan from possessing hard power it is aware that regional stability and balance of power has to be maintained by establishing close bilateral security arrangements. Japan is also making an effort to depend on itself to protect its own security interests. The new National Defense Guidelines adopted on 17 December 2010 is an indicator of Japan's intentions.

MOVE TOWARDS 'SELF-RELIANCE': THE NEW NATIONAL DEFENSE PROGRAM GUIDELINES, 17 DECEMBER 2010

Japan's National Defense Program Guidelines (NDPG) which was first drawn up in 1976 analyses the country's basic defense situation and determines the roles and basic composition of Japan's Self-Defense Forces. It was reviewed in 1995 and again in 2004. The 2004 NDPG was to be revised in 2009, however, due to internal problems, the new guidelines were issued in December 2010. The Ministry of Foreign Affairs has stated that the new NDPG was formulated to 'enhance its own defense'. The guidelines aim at building a flexible posture in response to changes in the strategic environment of East Asia.[15]

The December 2010 NDPG introduces a new 'Dynamic Defense Force' concept, which emphasizes on operations and capability to respond to all kinds of threats and contingencies. The earlier 'Basic Defense Force' concept emphasized on deterrence and not to build defense forces to the level maintained by neighbouring countries. Thus, Dynamic Defense Force concept focuses on 'how to operate' the country's defense force whereas the Basic Defense Force focused on 'how to build' the force.[16] Referring to the security environment in East Asia the guidelines notes with alarm China's growing military budget and regional assertiveness and refers to China as a 'matter of concern'. It also mentions the stepped up activities of China's naval and air forces and the lack of its transparency in its military build-up programme. This is the strongest language the NDPG has ever used for China. 'These movements coupled with the lack of transparency on China's military and security issues ... is a concern for the region and the international community' states the Guideline.[17] In contrast, the 2004 version of the Guidelines merely stated that Japan should 'remain attentive' to China's future action. Yomiuri Shimbun in an editorial stated that, 'The security environment around Japan is growing ominous. To secure peace and safety for the nation under such circumstances, it is necessary to eliminate the remnants of Cold War strategies and construct a more flexible and resilient defense system.'[18] The December NDPG which outlines Japan's strategy for the next one decade clearly aims to counter China's growing military prowess by preparing Japan to deal with the China threat on its own to the extent possible. It also calls for a stronger defense around the remote Nansei islands of south-western Japan including a new employment of Self-Defense Forces.

INDIA–JAPAN IN THE 1990s: FOCUS ON ECONOMIC RELATIONS

One of the countries with which Japan since the last one decade in particular is slowly and steadily strengthening relations is India. Both India and Japan are moving towards making this relationship as one of the most important bilateral relations in the region in the future. Since the end of the Cold War in 1990-1, the change in the international relations environment and India's decision to liberalize its economy gave an impetus to Japan to look towards India more seriously. During the 1990s, however, the strategic aspect of the relations was important but the main thrust of Japan's policy towards India was to establish strong economic relations. On the other hand, during this period, especially during the first half of the 1990s, Japan was more focused on strengthening its ties with China. While developing ties with India, the aim was not so much to 'counter' or 'balance' China's growing influence in the region but explore alternative markets and areas for direct investments. Relations between India and Japan during the 1990s improved but the pace was slow. In fact, relations received a setback after May 1998 when India conducted the nuclear tests at Pokharan to which Japan reacted strongly.

However, as the decade of the 1990s closed Japan could not ignore India's rapid economic growth. Think tanks like Goldman Sachs predicted that India would become one of the leading economies by 2050. India had also emerged as one of the foremost country in the information and technology sector. Countries like the US and other Western countries were keen to exploit business opportunities provided by India's improved economic environment. It was time Japan realized that the stalemate in the relations between the two countries be removed. The process of restoring 'normal diplomatic' relations with India began in 1999 with the visit of Yamamoto Ichita, a member of the House of Councillors.

INDIA–JAPAN: EMPHASIS ON STRATEGIC RELATIONS

Promoting economic ties has always been an important item on the agenda of the two countries, however, enhancing strategic relations became equally important or even more important due to worrisome developments in the region since the late 1990s. Initially it was not so much its relations with China which were still not that strained though it was a factor in the development of strategic relations but it was the security of the sea lanes running through the Southeast

Asian waters which became a prime concern for Japan. Japan imports almost 85 per cent of its oil requirements from the West Asian region. Consequently, the safe passage of the sea lanes is indispensable for Japan's economic development. Since the late 1990s a large number of incidents of looting and hijacking of cargo ships by pirates took place in this region, i.e. Malacca and Singapore Straits and waters around Malaysia, Indonesia and Philippines. Several Japanese ships were also attacked by pirates. Close cooperation with India in safeguarding the sea routes was important.[19]

Japanese Prime Minister Mori Yoshiro visited India in August 2000. During his visit the two countries signed an agreement entitled 'Global Partnership with India in the Twenty-First Century'. The most important outcome of this visit was that both the countries were keen to formalize relations between the Ministry of Defense and Foreign Ministry of the two countries for cooperation on security issues such as safeguarding the sea lanes, joint naval exercises to combat piracy and disaster management. India's Defence Minister George Fernandes became the first Defense Minister to visit Japan from 10-14 January in 2000. He had talks with his counterpart in Japan, Tsutomu Kawara. The decision taken to hold annual security talks indicated that strategic relations were assuming great importance.

THE CHINA FACTOR

The China factor in the relations between Japan and India became more important after the April 2005 anti-Japan demonstrations in China. During Koizumi Junichiro's visit to India in April 2005, a major step was taken in the form of an Action Plan called the 'Eight Fold Initiative for Strengthening Japan–India Global Partnership'. The contents of the Action Plan clearly indicated the resolve of the two countries to enhance bilateral security dialogue and cooperation. It was decided to: (1) Strengthen service to service exchanges between defense establishments of the two countries, (2) Working to ensure the safety and security of maritime traffic through joint exercises against piracy and the annual Japan Coast Guard – Indian Coast Guard talks and (3) Building up cooperation between the Maritime

Self-Defense Force and Indian Navy in recognition of the importance of Maritime security.[20] The most important decision taken during Koizumi's visit was to institutionalize annual visits by the top leaders of the two countries.

After Koizumi's visit the pace for promoting and strengthening political and strategic relations was very marked. In 2006 the joint statement issued by Indian Defense Minister and Japan's Minister of State for Defense, reiterated the necessity of close defense cooperation. In August 2007 the prime ministers of the two countries adopted a Joint Roadmap for New Dimensions to the Strategic and Global partnership between the two countries. It was decided to have a dialogue on security cooperation at various levels.

For the first time in September 2007, the Japanese Maritime Self-Defense Force participated in the multilateral maritime exercise 'Malabar 07-2' conducted in the Bay of Bengal. In October 2008 another important agreement between the two countries which further strengthened security cooperation between the two countries was the conclusion of a declaration which called for joint defense exercises; policing of the Indian Ocean and military-to-military exchanges on counter-terrorism. Since 2008 the visits by the Indian Chief of Naval Staff and Chief of Army staff in August 2008 and 2009; the decision in October 2009 to hold regular India–Japan Maritime Security Dialogue are an indication of the speed with which security cooperation between the two countries was moving ahead. Indian Defense Minister Arackaparambil Kurien Antony's visit to Japan in November 2009 saw a further boost in the security relations between the two countries. During this visit it was decided to strengthen cooperation in areas such as joint military exercises; bilateral and regional cooperation in peacekeeping and disaster relief and ASEAN Regional Forum.

Adoption of a Joint Action Plan to Advance Security Cooperation based on the Joint Declaration on Security Cooperation between Japan and India during Japanese Prime Minister Hatoyama Yukio's visit to India in 27-9 December 2009 can be considered as a landmark in the security relations between the two countries.[21] This Action

Plan included a very comprehensive agenda for cooperation and dialogue at various levels – formal and informal. It included annual subcabinet/Senior officials 2+2 dialogue between the Ministry of Foreign Affairs and Ministry of Defense of both Japan and India; regular reciprocal visits between Service Chiefs of both sides; annual bilateral naval exercises and also multilateral naval exercises. This Action Plan also provided for student and research scholar exchanges and seminars between the defense institutions in the two countries.

INDIA'S 'LOOK EAST POLICY'

If for Japan 'strained' relations with China is one of the important factors for strengthening ties with India, India too is guided by its national interests in developing ties with Japan. India's relations with China are 'cordial' but there are several irritants. The border problem is one of the major hurdles to the fast development of close relations between China and India. Continuous dialogues are held between the two countries to resolve the problem but it still persists. In addition to the border issue, concern over China's issuance of stapled visas to Jammu & Kashmir residents, its increasing presence in Pakistan occupied Kashmir; its claim over Arunachal Pradesh are some of the problems which India is not prepared to overlook. China on the other hand is not pleased with India's refusal to recognize the Tibet Autonomous Region as part of Chinese territory. As China's ambassador to India, Zhang Yan during Chinese Premier Wen Jiabao's visit to India in December 2010 said, 'China–India relations are very fragile, easy to damage and difficult to repair. Therefore it needs special care.'[22]

Indian strategy experts and policy makers are also aware of China's growing naval and military capability. India needs to strategize in a manner that it does not feel threatened by China's growing influence in the East and Southeast Asian region. China according to the present trends is likely to become the largest trading partner of most countries in the region by 2020. It enjoys Free Trade agreements with a large number of countries in the region. In the early 1990s India formulated the 'Look East' policy but not much was achieved. In the last two years, however, Indian government has been shown great seriousness in activating its Look East Policy. In November 2010 Indian Prime Minister Manmohan Singh visited Malaysia and also attended the annual summit in Japan. He also attended the 8th ASEAN–India summit in Vietnam. In 2010, a Free Trade Agreement was concluded between India and ASEAN. This agreement will help to boost trade between India and ASEAN. Negotiations are on to include services and investments. Inviting Indonesian President Susilo Bambang Yudhoyono as chief guest for the Republic Day celebrations in January 2011 was also an indication of the importance that India is attaching to the Southeast Asian region. It was after 60 years that an Indonesian leader was invited to the Republic Day celebrations. President Sukarno Achmed was the chief guest at the first Republic Day celebrations in 1950. Indonesia is an important country which has been supportive of India's enhanced role in the Southeast Asian region. It is in India's interest to build strong relations with as many likeminded countries in the region as possible. India on its own is also an important power and has the confidence to take stands on issues which may not be appreciated by China but like Japan it needs the support of other countries.

PREPARING A SOUND BASE FOR BILATERAL RELATIONS: ECONOMIC RELATIONS

Fostering close economic relations is important to build a sound foundation for long lasting relationship. However, even though economic relations between the two countries during the last few years have improved significantly, it is still not 'satisfactory'. At the moment the total trade between Japan and India is very dismal. In 2010 total trade was about US $13 billion, whereas the total trade between Japan and China is more than US $300 billion. Similarly, Japan's investments in India is also very little as compared to its investments in China. There are only a little more than 800 companies operating in India compared to over 6,000 in China. Japanese business community is keen to diversify its economic interests so as to avoid too much dependence on China. For example, since 2009 Japan has increased its import of knitwears and terry towels from Bangladesh. In one year there was 300 per cent increase. This policy is termed as 'China+one'.[23]

Maeda Tadashi, head of corporate planning of the Japan Bank of International Cooperation and special advisor to the Japanese cabinet, also emphasized on this point when he told the *Business Standard* that, 'There have been some tensions with China and we expect that some investment will be shifted from China to other countries, probably India.'[24] Now that India and Japan have concluded the Comprehensive Economic Partnership Agreement which came into effect on 1 August 2011 the possibility of economic relations becoming very strong in future are bright. Expanded economic ties will only contribute to deeper political and strategic relations. Japan's foreign direct investment in India has increased over the years but the pace has been slow. The Japanese manufacturers found the environment in India not very conducive for investment, one of the major barriers being lack of good infrastructure. Thus, presently Japanese investments are directed more towards strengthening infrastructure facilities in India. The two important projects for which Japan is providing aid is the Delhi–Mumbai Industrial Corridor and the Western Dedicated Freight Corridor.

Japan–Republic of Korea

In an effort to build a network of close bilateral relations Japan is not only set to improve relations with India but also with other neighbours like Republic of Korea (ROK). Korea was a colony of Japan from 1910 to 1945. As in China so in ROK, memories of Japan's harsh rule, territorial problems, issue of comfort women often tends to mar relations between the two countries. It is probably in an attempt to pacify ROK that Japanese Prime Minister Kan Naoto apologized once again last year on the occasion of the completion of 100 years since Korea became a colony of Japan. He said that he felt 'deep remorse and heartfelt apology' over the colonial past.[25] His action was not appreciated by many Japanese who felt that another apology after so many decades was uncalled for.

Nevertheless the developments in the region demand that Japan maintain friendly relations with ROK. In another goodwill gesture Japan's Prime Minister Noda Yoshihiko during his visit to ROK on 18 October 2011 handed over five volumes of Korean royal documents that were taken away during Japanese rule.[26]

Continuous efforts are being made by both countries to maintain friendly relations. At the end of 2010 Japanese Prime Minister Maehara Seiji said the two diplomatic priorities for 2011 would be firstly to create an environment conducive to expediting dialogue over security matters between Japan and South Korea and to building a mutual trust between the two countries to contribute to the stability of East Asia.[27] However, the fact that US is the most important ally of both Japan and South Korea, has to some extent helped in cementing ties between the two countries. Now an effort is being made by the US and Japan to involve ROK in their activities in the region. South Korean military officials took part as observers for the first time in the Japan–US joint military exercises taking place around Okinawa and other areas around Japan in 2010. The exercises were the largest ever involving 34,000 SDF members and 10,400 US personnel and a total of 60 vessels and 400 aircrafts. The nuclear powered aircraft carrier *USS George Washington*, also took part. South Korea and the US conducted joint naval exercises in the Yellow Sea.[28]

JAPAN–SOUTHEAST ASIA

Japan is also proactively involved in strengthening its ties with the Southeast Asian countries. Countries like Vietnam, Malaysia, Indonesia, and the Philippines all have territorial issues with China. The disputed islands which control considerable energy reserves are all located in the South China Sea. These countries are increasingly becoming concerned over China's assertive behaviour in pressing its claims over the islands. Anti-China protests were held in Vietnam in May/ June 2011 which is considered to be unusual. These protests erupted after a Chinese surveillance boat on 26 May 2011 severed the cables of a Vietnamese marine resources exploration vessel in the waters near Vietnam. This common interest Japan aims to convert into building a consensus in the region to deal with China.

CHINA AND JAPAN: EFFORTS TOWARDS MAINTAINING 'NORMAL' RELATIONS

Japan and China, despite the contentious issues, would not like to see a total collapse of relations between the two countries. Hence, continuous effort is being made to establish mechanisms to engage with each other. In January 2011 China–Japan–Korea held Ministerial level conference on culture in Nara, Japan. The Nara Declaration under 'China–Japan–Korea Cooperation Outlook 2020' was concluded with the objective of strengthening cultural cooperation. This was the third meeting. The first was held in Nantong, China and the second in Jeju islands, South Korea. Several such statements have been issued by the three countries bilaterally which reflect their interest in promoting mutual interest and maintaining a certain level of communication. On 20 January 2011, China and Japan agreed to strengthen cooperation on security issues. These talks on security issues were started in 1993.

Considering the fact that China is one of the major concerns for Japan which needs to be attended to regularly, an important point which should be seriously noted in passing is that there needs to be political stability in the country. In the last few years there have been frequent changes in the leadership in Japan which does have a negative impact on important issues confronting the country, including its policy towards China. If the developments since 2010 are taken into account, one can see that China's action near the Senkaku Islands occurred at the time when Japan was busy with internal problems. In September 2010 when Chinese vessels collided with Japanese coast guards, the Democratic Party of Japan (DPJ) was busy with the politics of finding a successor to Kan Naito. In September 2011 again when a Chinese trawler collided with Japan Coast Guard vessel the DPJ was engrossed in party presidential election.

Undoubtedly, China has emerged as major player in world affairs and by any analysis it is not possible to exclude the China factor in the development of bilateral relations between any two countries of the region. However, at the same time China must not be regarded as a major threat. China, like the other countries, is also dependent on other countries for its economic development and security. Moreover, other countries of the region also need not be considered as insignificant players in the region and the world. India is an emerging power, both economically and politically. It is set to be one of the largest economies in the world by 2030. Despite the economic problems since the bubble burst in 1991 and the colossal damage caused to the economy by the Great East Japan Earthquake of 11 March 2011 Japan should not be considered as a power which can be ignored. Japan will continue to be a major player in the region given its wealth, advanced technological knowhow, and national cohesion. Japan's wealth should be assessed not only in terms of the foreign exchange reserves but should also include private and corporate investments abroad. Japan has been investing abroad for decades.

Not only US and Japan but even China intends to maintain good relations with India. It is not surprising that China has expressed its support to India becoming a permanent member of the United Nation's Security Council.[29] China has also expressed its opinion that it wants India to play a larger role in the Shanghai Cooperation Organization.[30] Regular dialogues are held to resolve the border issue. It appears that China is more favourably inclined to accommodate India. However, its 'unfriendly' attitude towards Japan is too deep rooted and protracted to change in the near future. Hence, though the aim is not to 'isolate' but to 'engage' China as China is an important factor in the development of strong relations between India and Japan.

NOTES

1. See Lalima Varma, 'Japan–China Relations: Problems and Prospects in the Twenty-first Century,' *China Report,* New Delhi: Sage Publications, vol. 29, no. 4, 1993.

2. NEWSGD.com. 17 October 2006 (accessed on 13 December 2011).
3. 'Chinese President Says 4th Political Document Represents New Consensus in China–Japan Relations', www.chinaview.cn, 7 May 2008 (accessed on 12 January 2012).
4. 'China Pledges Regular Patrols near Senkaku Islands,' *Japan Times* (Tokyo), 25 December 2010.
5. 'Diet Hardliners Charter Plane to View Senkakus', *Japan Times* (Tokyo), 10 October 2010.
6. 'Japan Abandons Bid to Make China a Key Pillar of its Foreign Policy', *The Christian Science Monitor*, online, 18 November 2010 (accessed on 22 November 2010].
7. 'Japan Watches Nervously as China Flexes its Economic Muscles', *Irish Times*, online, 21 December 2010 (accessed on 22 December 2010).
8. 'Public Opinion of China Slumps/After Senkaku Island Incident, Record High 84 per cent don't trust Country', *Daily Yomiuri Online+Associated Press*, 5 October, 2010 (accessed on 23 December 2010).
9. Jeff Kingston, 'Nationalism and its Discontents', *Japan Times*, 27 February 2011.
10. Hirano Ko, 'Rumored China-Russia Tie Up Testing DPJ's Ability', *Japan Times*, 4 November 2010.
11. 'Japan Abandons Bid to Make China a Key Pillar of its Foreign Policy', *The Christian Science Monitor*, CSMonitor.com, 18 November 2010 (accessed on 22 November 2010).
12. 'Kan Airs China Concerns at Meet', *Japan Times*, 31 October 2010.
13. See, Lalima Varma, 'Japan–United States Security Arragements and Northeast Asia: Its Relevance in the Post-Cold War Period', *China Report*, New Delhi: Sage Publications, vol. 35, no. 1, 1999, p. 94.
14. '40 Per Cent Consider Japan–US Ties "Poor"', *Yomiuri Shimbun + Associated Press*, online, 23 December 2010 (accessed on 23 December 2010).
15. *Diplomatic Bluebook 2011*, Ministry of Foreign Affairs, Japan, April 2011, p. 7.

16. *East Asian Strategic Review*, The National Institute for Defense Studies, Japan, Japan Times Ltd., 2011, p. 254.
17. For the text see, Ministry of Defense of Japan, http://www.mofa.go.jp/e/d_act/d_policy/national.html. (accessed on 5 December 2012).
18. 'New Thinking Welcome on Defense Strategy', *Daily Yomiuri-Online*, 20 December 2010 (accessed on 20 December 2010).
19. Lalima Varma, 'Japan's Policy Towards East and Southeast Asia: Trends in Re-Asianization', *International Studies* (New Delhi, London), vol. 43, no. 1, 2006, pp. 33-4.
20. For the text of 'Japan–India Partnership in a New Asian Era: Strategic Orientation of Japan–India Global Partnership', see Ministry of Foreign Affairs of Japan, http://www.mofa.go.jp/region/asia-paci/india/partner0504.html#eight/ (accessed on 9 January 2012).
21. Text see, Ministry of Foreign Affairs of Japan, 'Joint Statement by Prime Minister Dr Yukio Hatoyama and Prime Minister Dr Manmohan Singh – New Stage of Japan–India Strategic and Global Partnership', http://www.mofa.go.jp/u_news/2/20091230_003059.html (accessed on 30 December 2009).
22. Rajesh Mahapatra, 'It's the Trust Deficit, Stupid', *Hindustan Times*, (New Delhi) 15 December 2010.
23. 'Knitwear Recorded 300% Growth in Japan Market in One Year', www.fibre2fashion.com. 22 December, 2010 (accessed on 23 December 2010).
24. Jyoti Mukul, 'JBIC to Provide Equity Funding in India's Private Sector', *Business Standard*, 12 February 2010 (accessed 2 December 2010).
25. 'Kan Offers Govt Apology to South Korea/Looks Past Colonial Rule to Future', *Daily Yomiuri Shimbun*, online, 11 August 2010 (accessed on 18 January 2012).
26. 'New Japanese Prime Minister in South Korea for Key Summit', *Voice of America*, online, 18 October 2011 (accessed on 18 January 2012).
27. Yoshimura Kenji, 'Analysis/ Security Ties Big Step, but no "Alliance"', *Yomiuri Shimbun/Daily Yomiuri*, online, 5 January 2011 (accessed on 18 January 2012).

28. Yoshiro Makino, 'Japan, US, South Korea Deepen Defense Links', Asahi.com, 12 June 2010 (accessed on 12 June 2010).
29. Saibal Dasgupta, 'China to Back India's UNSC Bid without Japan Support', *Times of India*, New Delhi, 18 July 2011.
30. Editorial, 'Welcome Overture: India Must Push for Full SCO Membership', *Times of India*, New Delhi, 27 July 2011.

CHAPTER 3

China's Foreign Policy and Indo–Japan Relations

SRIKANTH KONDAPALLI

INTRODUCTION

Some broad features of China's foreign policy include protection of its sovereignty and territorial integrity, maintenance of peace and stability in the peripheries, policies conducive for the success of modernization, reform and opening up, developing a 'well-off society' by 2020 and a 'three' or 'five' pillars foreign policy strategy (as mentioned at the 16th and 17th Communist Party Congresses in 2002 and 2007 respectively), etc.[1] While implementing these minimalist and maximalist objectives, China had identified a number of countries that are crucial in the success and failure of its foreign policies. Among these, Japan and India and their bilateral relations are an important aspect of the Chinese foreign policy posture. Although diplomatic relations with Japan were not established till 1972, while that with India in 1950, China's interactions with these two countries since then has neither been uniform nor cordial. With both these countries, China has territorial problems which have not yet been resolved. Also, China clashed with both either historically or in the recent times. Thus relations with these two Asian neighbours are a crucial component in the Chinese foreign policy postures. If China has to economically and technologically advance further, cooperation with Japan is necessary as well. Indeed, this issue of economic, trade, investments and technology transfers from Japan to China is a major and positive input into China's rise, which now India is seeking to learn and benefit from. Bilaterally, Indo–Japan relations are carefully watched by Beijing for any security challenges, as both India and Japan are concerned about China's rise and its implications. Hence, China keeps a close watch on the emerging equations between Tokyo and New Delhi in the recent period. Of these, Beijing considers relations with Tokyo crucial and strategic in nature given the economic and technological advances of Japan. It is only since 2005 that China started considering relations with India 'strategic' in nature. Hence, the number of high-level mutual visits between China and these two countries indicate that there are more number of visits between Beijing and Tokyo (about 21 mutual visits at the prime ministerial level, while there were only 12 such visits between Beijing and New Delhi) (see Annexure 3.1).

TERRITORIAL DISPUTES

Of the issues that are crucial for Beijing, given the historical experiences following the two Opium Wars in the nineteenth century, territorial issues have been identified as one of the most important as this has an impact on the legitimacy of the Communist Party rule in China. China has territorial disputes with both Japan and India on the issues of Senkaku/Diaoyutao Islands and Chunxiao Islands and border dispute with India and its policies on Kashmir. China is also uncomfortable with the Japanese and Indian policies on Taiwan and South China Sea Islands dispute. China is aware that with the US–Japan treaty revisions of 1997, the Japanese Self-Defence Forces could act in 'surrounding areas', while growing US–India relations also have implications to the South China Sea.[2]

With Japan, the main territorial problem is related to the Senkaku Islands. These are uninhabited (*wuzhudi*) islands located about 150 km north-east of Taiwan and are claimed by China, Japan and Taiwan.[3] Known for their potential oil reserves according to the 1966 UN committee report, and valuable for its rich fisheries and economic zone, these islands could be a flash point between China and Japan, as the late 2004 Japanese reports indicated. The dispute arose as a result of Japanese occupation of these islands from late nineteenth century and the subsequent events of withdrawal in the mid-1940s. China claims that these islands came under its jurisdiction during the Ming Dynasty period in AD 1373. Subsequently, the AD 1403 documents assert the China linkages, as do the maps published in 1701. In support of its argument, China stated that before its occupation as a result of the Sino-Japanese war in 1895, none of the Japanese maps show that these were ever Japan's territories. Japan imposed its rule over the islands from 17 April 1895. However, during the December 1943 and July 1945 agreements with the US and UK, China was supposed to get these islands from Japan along with Taiwan. However, the Chinese argue, Japan still controlled these islands as witnessed with events related to 1951, June 1971 and May 1972. Though the Chinese foreign minister on 30 December 1971 sought for returning these islands, no progress was made in this regard.[4]

The 1990s saw China incorporating these islands as its territories, thus raising tension in the region. In February 1992, China passed the 'Laws of Territorial Waters and Contiguous Zone' which incorporated Diaoyutao Islands along with Paracels and Spratly's Islands that were disputed territories with neighbouring countries for a long time.[5] Article 8 of this law stated that the Chinese Navy 'can order the eviction of foreign naval vessels' operating in these waters. On 16 November 1994, the United Nations Convention on the Law of Sea came into being. China ratified this convention in 1996.[6] According to this law, the jurisdiction of China over several million square kilometres of sea has been extended.[7] Japanese ratification of the International Convention on the Law of the Sea in 1996, its 1,000 nautical mile limit jurisdiction and so on further complicated claims on the overlapping exclusive economic zones (EEZs) of the three in this region.

Soon the state sovereignty issues spilled over into issues of patriotism and protests from several civil groups in China and Japan. Mid-1990s became a testing time, though manageable, in the security relations of China and Japan. In July 1996, for instance, the Japanese landed in Diaoyutao four times, leading to protests from not only the Chinese government but also the civilian population in Hong

Kong, Taiwan and Macao. While several in Hong Kong and Taiwan protested against the rising Japanese right-wing resolve to occupy the Senkaku Islands, China's efforts in this regard have been either to scale down the nationalistic rhetoric in the mainland or to send its naval ships for training exercises, or for drilling operations in the region. The sovereignty dispute over these islands was soon clubbed with other related issues of energy security and both the parties to the dispute vied for exploring oil reserves in the region. China's oil-drilling vessel *Kantan* no. 3 reportedly carried out trial drills for oil in this area in February 1996.[8]

After anti-China protests broke out in Japan against the Chinese embassy and consulates in the aftermath of the September 2010 Chinese trawler incident closer to Senkaku Islands, the pro-Beijing newspaper in Hong Kong accused the Japanese government of promoting right wing views against China. Ta Kung Pao stated, 'Japan is trying to exert political pressure on the Chinese side over the Diaoyu Islands sovereignty issue by instigating anti-Chinese sentiment at home'.[9]

In September 2010, tensions between China and Japan came to the fore when the crew members of a Chinese vessel approaching Senkaku Islands, were arrested by the Japanese coast guard. The issued was finally resolved when the two premiers met at Asia–Europe Meeting at Brussels in October. In the wake of the Japanese coast guard arresting of Chinese crew members near Senkaku Islands, Ta Kung Pao, citing Russian cutting off of energy supplies to Europe and other countries, argued that China should take revenge on Japan by stopping rare earth metals exports.[10]

Another contentious issue between the two, which has no direct link with the territorial dispute but disadvantageous to China in terms of energy, mineral and fishery resources, is the status of Okinotorishima and the recent Japanese effort to build infrastructure facilities on the island that submerges with the high tide. If autonomy is conferred on this island some Chinese argued then it will acquire its own exclusive economic zone and continental shelf, to the detriment of Chinese claim on resources in the vicinity.[11]

China has similar territorial problems with India, which are also unresolved so far and potentially destabilizes bilateral relations. As modern nation states by the late 1940s, the respective leaderships tried to resolve this issue, but in vain. The 1959 and 1980 Chinese proposals for swapping of territories in the eastern and western sectors of the border were not acceptable to the then Indian leadership. Three discussions took place in 1960 and later after the brief border skirmishes and normalization of diplomatic relations from 1976, several rounds of discussions took place, including eight talks from 1981-7; 15 Joint Working Group Meetings from 1988 to 2005 and then elevated at the Special Representative level of 14 talks from 2003-10. The 15th meeting to be held in November 2011, was postponed with China citing the attendance of the Dalai Lama at the International Buddhist Convention at Delhi. No short- to medium-term solution to this issue is in sight due to the intransigence on both sides. In the meanwhile, rising nationalism in China also resulted in the hardening of Beijing's position. Thus, while the Western sector of the border was suggested as the 'most important' area of dispute by China in the 1950s, from mid-1980s China had shifted towards the eastern sector. Since early 2000s, official documents of China also started treating the eastern sector as 'southern Tibet' – indicting that this dispute is going to be a long-drawn one unless New Delhi conceded to the Chinese demands. There is also the change in the Chinese attitudes towards Kashmir – from considering in favour of India in the 1950s to support to self-determination movement of Kashmir people in the 1960s (coinciding with the 1962 clashes). From the 1980s, Chinese leaders were in favour of resolving the issue through peaceful means bilaterally between New Delhi and Islamabad, maintaining the sanctity of the line of control, etc. However, in the recent period, China had been investing heavily in the Pakistan occupied areas, indicating a change in its position. Further, China also indicated that Indian held areas are disputed rather than the Pakistan held areas of Kashmir, by issuing stapled visas to residents of Kashmir in India. This had resulted in India shutting down high level military exchanges between the two countries from June 2009-10 – only to resume in June 2011 after the Chinese side reportedly conceded to the Indian demand on discontinuing stapled visas.

Similarities between the territorial disputes between China and Japan and China and India are visible in the above narrative. In both cases, China had suggested (specifically by Zhou Enlai and Deng Xiaoping in their discussions with the Japanese and Indian leaderships respectively) that the territorial dispute is complicated and that the Chinese leaders have no time currently in resolving these disputes. They have also suggested that the dispute be put aside now and the respective leaderships improve relations in other fields. Thus, speaking to Prime Minister Ikeda in December 1974, Premier Zhou Enlai suggested that China has no time in resolving this dispute. Further, Deng Xiaoping in 1978 suggested to the Japanese leadership that 'Let us put this issue aside for the time being. May be people of the next generation will be smarter than us and can find a practical solution.' Similarly, with India, while Zhou Enlai argued that the territorial dispute between the two countries was never resolved in history, nevertheless, he sought time to resolve the dispute. Further, while the Indian side wanted to resolve this dispute 'immediately', the Chinese side suggested that this will be resolved 'ultimately' and by the next generation. Thus in both the Indian and Japanese cases, China had been buying time to resolve the disputes.

ON TAIWAN

Another minimalist agenda of China's foreign policy is to consider the status of Taiwan as its internal matter and that no country can evolve relations with Taipei. China ceded Taiwan to Japan after the Japanese military victory in 1895. Till the Japanese surrender in 1945, Taiwan was incorporated into Japanese rule. China has expressed concerns on these two issues, viz., Japanese 'militarism' and links with Taiwan. Today, China's concerns with Japan include fundamentally two issues, viz., Japan's support to Taiwan and Japan's efforts to become a 'normal' state (meaning militarily strong nation).[12] According to Wang Shan, Japan has initiated three measures:

'internal countermeasures' (*guonei duice*); 'international coordination' (*guoji xietiao*) and; 'constitutional interpretation' (*xianfa jieshi*) that are at the root of Japanese revival policies in the recent period that have implications to the Asia Pacific region in general and on China in particular.[13]

Taiwan factor became crucial in the security aspects of China–Japan relations given the latter's proximity to Taiwan from the nineteenth century and specifically after the Japanese occupied the island prior to Second World War. A general contemporary history of Japan's relations with Taiwan indicates to Chinese security sensitivities on the issue. In April 1952, for instance, when Japan signed a 'Peace Treaty' with Taiwan, the Chinese premier and foreign minister Zhou Enlai criticized the Japanese role.[14] When the Japanese Prime Minister Nobusuke Kishi visited Taiwan in June 1957 and supported the nationalist agenda of marching over the mainland, the Chinese government criticized the visit and viewed it as coming together of US-led alliance system in East Asia.[15] The 1960 US–Japan Security Treaty, for instance, was criticized by China for its potential application to the Taiwan areas. Later, the Chinese government criticized the comments of Japanese chief cabinet secretary Seiroku Kajiyama that Taiwan is indeed included in the overall provisions of the 1960 treaty, though in 1978, the Japanese foreign minister Sunao Sonoda reportedly denied to the Chinese of such validity to the Taiwan case.[16]

Some other instances of tensions between China and Japan on the Taiwan issue include the following in brief:

- Japanese government sending a special plane to escort 11 North Korean defectors to Taiwan on 7 February 1987.
- Kokario dormitory incident in 1987 when the Osaka court rejected Chinese ownership claim on the 1950 Nationalist owned dormitory and awarded it to Taiwan.
- Issuing of visa to Hsu Li-The, vice-president of Taiwan's Executive Yuan to visit Japan for the opening ceremony of the Asian Games at Hiroshima on 12 September, 1994.[17]

- Governor Ishihara's pro-Taipei statements and his five Chinas thesis; viz., dividing China into five areas such as Tibet, Xinziang, Mongolia, Manchuria, and rest of China.
- Former president of Taiwan Lee Teng-hui's visa applications to Tokyo. Lee's five China's thesis in preface to Gordon Chang's book.
- Whether Japan would come to the rescue of Taiwan in the event of Chinese use of force by taking recourse to the US–Japan Treaty revisions of 1997.

Further, in May 2009, the pro-Beijing newspaper in Hong Kong *Ta Kung Pao* criticized the head of Japan's Taiwan Affairs office, Ito's comments that the legal status of Taiwan, as reflected in the 1945 San Francisco Treaty, is 'undetermined'.[18]

Unlike the territorial dispute, China's views on India, in contrast to that of Japan, are not harsh on the Taiwan issue. For, in the negotiations before establishing diplomatic relations with India in December 1949-April 1950, China had been able to impose the 'India model' on India on the Taiwan issue. This model had been suggested by China to other countries as well subsequently. This model suggested that India should sever ties with the Kuomintang or Republic of China, support People's Republic of China's bidding in the United Nations and hand over the remnant properties of the KMT or ROC in India. Later, India had evolved economic and trade relations with Taiwan in 1995, but these do not have much diplomatic significance. Further, Beijing extracted from India, in January 2008 during Prime Minister Manmohan Singh's visit, that both sides will 'oppose any activity which is opposed to one China principle'. Nevertheless, in the light of China revising its position on Kashmir and Arunachal Pradesh, several Indians argue that India should also revisit the 'One China' policy.

ISSUES LEFT OVER FROM HISTORY

In addition to the above list of Chinese grievances on Japan, another category – 'issues left over from history' are there to bog down the bilateral relations even today. These are related to the Japanese military actions in coastal and north-east region of China, Nanjing massacre, use of chemical and biological weapons in the 1930s, visits of Japanese public personalities to Yasukuni Shrine, revisions in textbooks of the historical relations between China and Japan, etc. One other issue is of the 'comfort women'. China and other East Asian countries have accused Japan of deliberately creating sex slaves during the Japanese occupation of the region in the early twentieth century. Several countries and personalities have demanded compensation for the victims. However, this was denied by the Japanese leadership. Nevertheless, in August 1993 a former Chief Cabinet Secretary Kono Yohei publicly acknowledged that Japan during the Second World War had established 'comfort institutes' in the Korean peninsula and China. In February 2007, however, Japanese Foreign Minister Taro Aso at a House of Representatives Budget Committee meeting denied the existence of the comfort women issue. Commenting on this, Shih Chun-yu argued:

> There is an unwritten consensus in international society that a country's ability to properly face historical issues is an important symbol indicating its level of political civilization and national reputation. As such, the ability to honestly recognize historical issues is an integral part of a nation's soft power. By failing to properly treat history, the Japanese Government is effectively undermining its own soft power.[19]

The above Chinese discourse indicates that it has concerns on its unfulfilled identities as a nation state and that relations with Japan and India are below normal. Full-fledged normalization of relations with these two hinges on the resolution of the territorial disputes and 'issues left over from history'. This issue also has links with the relative military balance and balance of power equations in the larger Asian region.

BALANCE OF POWER

While China had been a major beneficiary of the economic and technological 'hollowing out' effect from Japan, in addition to the official development assistance of Japan, thus contributing to the rise of China currently, Beijing had been wary of any emerging equations between Tokyo and New Delhi. For, while Japan had fulfilled its strategic economic and technological objectives nearly two decades ago by becoming the second largest economy then, and despite the current economic slowdown pre- and post-Fukushima crises still retains its edge internationally, there is also the rise of India to contend with. Both Japan and India are also democracies, a factor, though downplayed by New Delhi, creates ripples in Beijing in the larger legitimacy game at the domestic and international levels. Any 'democratic' agenda between New Delhi and Tokyo will have negative consequences for the soft power of Beijing. Also, as a result of rising public protests in China, Hong Kong and Taiwan, the Japanese business communities are toying with the idea of shifting its manufacturing base from China to Vietnam and then to India. Beijing considers that this would be detrimental to China's rise. Also, both Tokyo and New Delhi have indicated that they will work together in several areas – joint bidding for United Nations Security Council membership, cooperation in Africa and Asia, coordination in multilateral institutions such as East Asian Summit, etc. To counter any negative fallout on its rise and leverages in Asia and beyond, China had undertaken several measures at the bilateral and multilateral levels, with mixed results.

At the bilateral level, China's military relations with Japan began in 1974 when the two sides established a military attaché's office. Though there was a gradual enhancement in such relations, these were soon subjected to the overall foreign and security considerations. For instance, these military relations were suspended by Japan following the Tiananmen Square incident in 1989 but resumed only in 1995 when Japanese Chairman of Joint Staff Meeting, Tetsuya Nishimoto, visited China. Security consultations between both the sides began in the 1990s by which six such talks were held. Nevertheless, several suspicions still linger in the bilateral relations. In November 2009, the defence ministers of Japan and China, Toshimi Kitazawa and Liang Guanglie met and concluded the 'nine-point consensus'. For the first time, both countries agreed to hold a joint naval search and rescue operation.[20]

With New Delhi, China had expanded military relations in the last six decades, although interrupted by the 1962 clashes. These include mutual high level visits to each other's facilities, joint operations (not exercises) among army and naval forces so far, participation as observers in each other's exercises, periodic local level contacts across the line of actual control, etc. However, after China refused to issue visa to Northern Area Commander-in-charge of Kashmir, Gen. Jaswal, India retaliated by cancelling high level military exchanges. India also refused to explicitly endorse the 'One China' principle in Wen Jiabao-Manmohan Singh joint declaration of December 2010. Nevertheless, the 4th Annual Defence Dialogue was held on 9 December 2011 with emphasis on enhancing medium-level military exchanges.[21]

At the multilateral levels, China had been wary of the emerging strategic relations between Tokyo, New Delhi and Washington. According to an article published in pro-Beijing newspaper in Hong Kong, China needs to carefully evaluate the Japan–India–US relations and evolve countermeasures of not losing ground in Asia. It stated in 2001, in the background of the April 2001 EP-3 incident,

> Both the developed Japan and the rising India want to take up an important position in Asia and the United States is willing to make use of this. The Japan-US Security Treaty has objectively encouraged Japan to revise its Peace Constitution. When US Deputy Secretary of State Richard Armitage visited India not long ago, he mentioned nothing about the US threat of imposing an embargo on India if it develops nuclear weapons. In exchange, he got India's support for the NMD.[22]

Sending troops overseas for the first time in 1992, the Japan–US defence cooperation guidelines revision, issuing of New National Defense Program Outline, passing of Anti-Terrorism Special Measures Law and two other laws after 11 September events and sending warships to Indian Ocean to coordinate with US military operations in Afghanistan, attack on a 'suspicious ship' in 2001 – the first time Japan ever downed a ship after Second World War – and the third visit of the Japanese prime minister to the Yasukuni shrine, are all termed by Han Min as Japanese spread of 'military tentacles' in the region.[23] Inside China, nationalistic rhetoric further complicated relations with Japan. In Xian University, for instance, Japanese students insulting the Chinese led to mass protests as did Japanese tourists indulging in sexual orgies in Zhuhai in September 2003.[24] Further, the Japan Self-Defense Forces deployments to Iraq, the largest overseas deployment, and participation with the US in the missile defence system in East Asia were frowned upon by Beijing.[25] The US troop's presence in Okinawa – its 'cornerstone of the Pacific' and the 'strategic hub of Asia' – is also considered to be a long-term challenge for China. According to the Chinese military newspaper,

> The vast majority of countries in Asia also have manifested widespread dissatisfaction and opposition to the use of forward bases by the US, their war preparations, and their military intimidation methods. However, with the global strategy pushed by the US and their strategic focus centering more on the Asia-Pacific, it is unlikely that the US military will withdraw from Okinawa easily.[26]

Eventually, in the backdrop of North Korean nuclear and ballistic missile threats and Chinese military modernization, on 19 December 2003 the Japanese Security Council decided to upgrade the ballistic missile defence system Patriot PAC-3 low to high-altitude land-based air defence system and the Standard SM-3/Block 1 short- and medium-range ship-based missiles.[27]

Likewise, the mid-2005 defence cooperation for ten years between India and the US is also been keenly watched by Beijing. A few months before this agreement, the then US Secretary of State Condoleeza Rice, speaking at the Sophia University in Tokyo, stated that the US intends to help India to become a major power in the twenty-first century. This US signalling in Tokyo was not lost on Beijing, which tried to placate India with 'strategic and cooperative partnership' arrangement during Premier Wen Jiabao's visit to Delhi in April 2005. The US military supplies to India, although defensive in nature, are viewed with concern by China. Indian endorsement, initially, of the US ballistic missile defence (BMD) system in 2001, has strategic implications for China as well, since this will limit the deterrence ability of Beijing and in addition brings Taiwan into the BMD orbit. Further, the multilateral naval exercise of US, Japan, India, Singapore and Australia in September 2007 were frowned upon by Beijing, which issued demarche to the participants.

In order to overcome these issues and gain initiatives, China conducted strategic dialogues with both India and Japan separately in order to widen understanding and cooperation.[28] Four strategic dialogues were conducted with India starting in 2005 (just before Premier Wen Jiabao's visit to Delhi in April that year) till 2010. However, while China concluded three such talks with Japan in 2005, Prime Minister Koijumi's visit to Yasukuni Shrine was cited by China as leading to the collapse of the third dialogue. China also has a strategic dialogue mechanism at the vice ministerial level. Ten such meetings took place between the foreign ministries of China and Japan till June 2009.[29]

JAPAN–INDIA RELATIONS

China had also been keenly watching the high level meetings and discussions between the India and Japanese leaders in economic, technological, security and strategic fields.[30] Prime Minister Junichiro Koizumi visited India in April 2005, almost coinciding with that of the Chinese Premier Wen Jiabao's visit. While India and China signed for the first time 'strategic and cooperative partnership', India and Japan had more structured and expansive agenda during Koizumi's visit, including cooperation in economic, trade, technology, aid and investments, dialogue mechanism on non-proliferation, energy, defence cooperation and exchange of personnel. These were reiterated and furthered during the Foreign Minister Abe's visit in early 2006.[31] In July 2005, both became part of the joint bidding process for the United Nations Security Council membership in the Group Four format, along with Brazil and Germany. On the eve of Indian Prime Minister Manmohan Singh's visit to Japan in December 2006, the Chinese foreign ministry spokesman commented that India, Japan and China should come together for resolving common problems in the region and for prosperity and stability.[32] Prime Minister Shinzo Abe's visit to Delhi in August 2007 was considered to be crucial in the emerging bilateral strategic partnership. Abe's speech to the Indian parliament stressed the concept of a 'broader Asia' to include cooperation among Japan, India, US and Australia in the format of an 'ark of freedom and prosperity'.[33] The Chinese side noted, with concern, the lack of any mention of China in this broader Asian confluence of the Pacific and Indian Oceans.[34]

During the October 2008 visit by Indian Prime Minister Manmohan Singh, Japan announced its largest yen credit to India (worth $4.5 billion) for the construction of Delhi–Mumbai Freight Corridor, in addition to announcing 2+2 dialogue mechanism, joint military exercises, counter-terrorism, disaster prevention and maritime cooperation.[35] During the Prime Minister Hatoyama's visit to India in December 2009, bilateral relations were depicted by *Xinhua* as 'inchoate' in nature.[36]

The October 2010 agreements between Japan and India, during Indian Prime Minister Manmohan Singh's visit to Tokyo, were viewed as strategic in significance. In the light of the Senkaku Islands incident of a month ago and in the background of the rare earth metal export ban by China to Japan, the conclusion of the Comprehensive Economic Partnership Agreement (CEPA) and discussions on nuclear technology exports from Japan, etc., were depicted by *Xinhua* reporter as 'a perfectly cogent if not somewhat overdue alliance between two of the top three economic powerhouses in Asia'.[37]

China's analysts assume that India and Japan are poised to join a new security grouping in-the-making, viz., Asian NATO.[38] BMD system, a string of US-led alliances in Asia, especially in the East and Southeast Asian region are said to be part of this Asian NATO system and that China should counter it through Russia, multilateralism and active role in Asia.[39] In March 2007, Australia concluded a security and defence pact with Japan, although both said that this is not targeted against China.[40] However, quickly, Australia moved out of the joint strategic dialogue mechanism with US, Japan and India in early 2008 after China expressed concerns about this a year ago.[41]

UNSC REFORM

As mentioned earlier, in July 2005, India and Japan joined Brazil and Germany in the Group Four format in urging the 59th General Assembly of the UN on expansion of the UNSC to include six permanent and four non-permanent members. This had riled the Chinese government, which stated that this is against developing countries, specifically small and medium countries.[42] The Chinese foreign ministry spokesman Liu Jianchao stated that China 'will resolutely oppose the immature UN reform program'.[43] Wang Guangya, the Chinese permanent representative to the UN dubbed this as 'unpopular' and dividing the members of the UN.[44] China was specifically against the candidature of Japan,[45] while implicitly supporting India and Brazil, under the Russian pressure. In May 2011, Cui Tiankai, vice foreign minister of China attended a ministerial conference meeting of 123 participants in Rome, along with the five Uniting for Consensus group of countries (including Pakistan, Italy, Argentina, Canada and Columbia). Cui argued that the UNSC reform should be broad-based and to include the developing countries, specifically from Africa.[46]

On economic issues as well, there is a widening chasm between China on the one hand and India and Japan on the other, although all the three are involved in mutually beneficial trade and economic ties. After the rare earth export ban by China, Tokyo further intended to improve relations with India. India and Japan also quickly concluded CEPA, while Beijing's request for the same had been pending with both Tokyo and New Delhi. A related issue is also the reluctance of both New Delhi and Tokyo to depend on the Chinese currency Yuan (*renminbi*) for Asian/international financial transactions in future. While the Chiang Mai initiative suggested for striving for financial integration in Asia, China, Japan and India differ on the modalities. While China wants its currency to become the dominant currency in Asia, this is not acceptable to Tokyo and New Delhi, although India had supported, at the Sanya meeting of Brazil-Russia-India-China-South Africa grouping in April 2011, the idea of a basket of currencies. According to Cheng Siwei, a former vice-chairman of the Standing Committee of China's National People's Congress suggested that India and Japan will oppose the idea of Yuan becoming the single Asian currency because of differences in economic conditions and degrees of economic development in Asia.[47]

AREAS OF COOPERATION

While a number of differences between China–Japan–India have been outlined, there are also areas of cooperation between the three in a number of areas. Engagement policies have been successful in bringing together these three countries, as with others, in Asia and beyond for mutual benefit. Trade and investment flows from Japan and India, specifically from the former, has been useful in the rise of China. In 2010, trade between China and Japan amounted to more than $300 billion, while trade with India stood at more than $61 billion (see Annexure 3.2). Substantial growth in economic and trade relations had been conducive for the three and this had enhanced mutual interdependence and to some extent reduced tensions. Specifically trade with Japan had been particularly useful to China as hi-tech products led to substantial benefits to China. China has also been a major beneficiary of Japan's FDI flows, which amounted to more than $7 billion as compared to about $2 billion towards India in 2010. (see Annexure 3.3).

Secondly, in June 2002, Asia Cooperation Dialogue mechanism was formed by 22 Asian countries including Bahrain, Bangladesh, Brunei, Cambodia, China, India, Indonesia, Japan, Kazakhstan, the Republic of Korea, Kuwait, Laos, Malaysia, Myanmar, Oman, Pakistan, the Philippines, Qatar, Singapore, Sri Lanka, Thailand and Vietnam. The aim of this organization is to integrate the existing sub-regional cooperation mechanisms in Asia, and promoting dialogue and cooperation among Asian countries. Member states were urged to launch regional cooperative mechanisms and dialogues.[48]

Thirdly, in July 2005, India, Japan and China, along with Australia, South Korea and the US formed the non-binding Asia–Pacific Partnership on Clean Development and Climate to develop, deploy and transfer cleaner, more efficient technologies and to meet national pollution reduction, energy security and climate change concerns, although not much progress was made in such environmental projects.[49]

Fourthly, in the space arena, lunar probe was launched by all the three, viz., *Chandrayaan* by India, *Kaguya* by Japan and *Chang'e* by China in 2008. Although each had its distinct experiment, since there are several similarities, there could be cooperation among all the three to advance scientific knowledge about moon.[50]

Finally, there was also the suggestion made by the then Japanese ambassador to India, Yasukuni Inoki that Japan, China and India should form a strategic triangle to address and resolve a number of strategic issues in Asia. However, no concrete initiatives have been forthcoming for furthering this idea.

CONCLUSION

The above analyses indicates that in the implementation of its minimalist and maximalist foreign policy objectives, Beijing finds relations with both Tokyo and New Delhi as providing opportunities and also challenges. These are related to market-based considerations as well as protection of its perceived sovereignty claims. As a small country geographically, Japan is concerned about the growing capabilities of China. China is also concerned about Japan which is an ally of the United States. Nevertheless, China considers relations with Japan as strategic in nature for a number of reasons, viz., Japan was the first major challenger to the Middle Kingdom status of China in the nineteenth century when Japan defeated China in 1895. Japan also occupied China in the 1930s and 1940s and had helped establish Manchuria by carving territories in northeast China. Also, despite the current slowdown, Japan's military, economic and technological capabilities are more sophisticated in Asia. These factors suggest that China should adopt policies that are not in direct clash with Japan. More significantly, if Japan adopts policies for shifting its manufacture base in China to other countries such as Vietnam or India, and build strategic/military relations with others in Asia, such as with India, South Korea and others, then China's rise will be in jeopardy. This explains partly the vehement response of China towards the Japanese candidature for the UNSC membership or in keeping alive 'historical' issues.

On the other hand, China views relations with India as tactical in nature, at least till 2005. While India had been maintaining higher economic growth rates and its military modernization is picking up, still China considers India as posing no major challenge either to its security or its rise, except posing short- to medium-term pinpricks such as in the Indian Ocean region. However, with relations between Tokyo and New Delhi improving, this poses a major cumulative challenge to Beijing. China had itself followed similar policies in the past such as the military alliance with North Korea and 'all-weather relations' with Pakistan. China had befriended countries which are opposed to Japan and India, viz., North Korea and Pakistan respectively. While Japan continues its mutually beneficial relations with Pakistan, while India with North Korea, albeit at a low key level (especially in technical assistance), China has closer relations with both Pyongyang and Islamabad. Besides, North Korean assistance to Pakistan ballistic missile programme, in lieu of nuclear technology assistance from Islamabad, had provided the glue for both Tokyo and New Delhi to come together in countering these challenges. The current challenge from Tokyo and New Delhi are formidable to Beijing.

To overcome these challenges, China had followed a number of policies – including engagement, balance of power, joining multilateral groups, market-based economic incentives, or even coercive diplomacy – with mixed results as highlighted above. It is significant to note, however, that while Indian role in the East Asian region in general and relations with Japan in particular were affected drastically after the 1962 border clashes between India and China, in the recent period, the rise of China, territorial ambitions, resource competition and military interventions are triggering security dilemmas for both Japan and India.

ANNEXURE 3.1: HIGH-LEVEL VISITS FROM CHINA TO INDIA AND JAPAN, 1954-2011

Period	Visits to and from India	Visits to and from Japan
1954	June: Premier Zhou Enlai's visit.	–
	October: PM Jawaharlal Nehru's visit.	–
1956	Premier Zhou Enlai visited India three times.	–
1960	Premier Zhou Enlai's visit.	–
1972	–	25 September: PM Kakuei Tanaka visited. Joint statement issued.
1978	–	22 October: Chinese Vice-Premier Deng Xiaoping visited and exchanged instruments of ratification of the Treaty of Peace and Friendship.
1979	–	5 December: PM Masayoshi Ohira visited and announced provision of the first batch of Japanese government loans to China.
1980	–	27 May: Premier Hua Guofeng visited Japan, the first visit ever by Chinese Premier.
1982	–	31 May: Premier Zhao Ziyang's visit.
		26 September: PM Zenko Suzuki's visit.
1984	–	23 March: PM Yasuhiro Nakasone visited.
1988	December: PM Rajiv Gandhi's visit.	25 August: PM Noboru Takeshita visited.
1989	–	12 April: Premier Li Peng visited.

1991	December: Premier Li Peng's visit.	10 August: PM Toshiki Kaifu visited.
1992	May: President R. Venkataraman's first ever visit.	23 October: Emperor Akihito and Empress Michito visited China, the first ever by a Japanese Emperor.
1993	September: PM Narasimha Rao's visit. Peace and Tranquillity agreement and cooperation in media communications signed.	–
1994	–	19 March: PM Morihiro Hosokawa visited.
1995	–	2 May: PM Tomiichi Murayama visited.
1996	November: President Jiang Zemin's first ever visit.	–
1997	–	11 November: Premier Li Peng visited. Visit of PM Ryutaro Hashimoto.
1998	–	25 November: President Jiang Zemin visited Japan. Joint Declaration signed.
1999	–	8 July: PM Obuchi visited.
2000	May: President K.R. Narayanan's visit.	12 October: Premier Zhu Rongji visited.
2001	–	8 October: PM Junichiro Koizumi.
2002	January: Premier Zhu Rongji's visit.	Visit of PM Koizumi.
2003	June: PM A.B. Vajpayee's visit.	–
2005	April: Premier Wen Jiabao's visit	–
2006	November: President Hu Jintao's visit.	October: PM Shinzo Abe's 'ice-breaking trip' to China.

2007	–	April: Premier Wen Jiabao's 'ice-thawing visit' to Japan. December: PM Yasuo Fukuda's 'spring greeting trip' to China.
2008	January: PM Manmohan Singh's visit.	May: President Hu Jintao's visit.
2010	May: President Patil visited. December: Premier Wen Jiabao's visit.	–
2011	April: PM Singh's visit to Sanya to attend the BRICS meeting.	December: PM Noda's visit to Beijing.

Source: China's Ministry of Foreign Affairs Yearbooks (several).

ANNEXURE 3.2: CHINA'S OVERALL TRADE WITH INDIA AND JAPAN, 2000-2010

(unit $ billion)

Year	Exports to India	Imports from India	Exports to Japan	Imports from Japan
2000	1.56	1.35	41.65	41.51
2001	1.89	1.70	44.96	42.80
2002	2.67	2.27	48.43	53.46
2003	3.34	4.25	59.42	73.15
2004	5.92	7.67	73.51	94.37
2005	8.93	9.74	83.99	100.45
2006	14.58	10.27	91.63	115.71
2007	24.01	14.63	102.07	133.95
2008	31.48	20.25	116.11	150.62
2009	29.65	13.71	97.89	130.93
2010	40.80	20.80	149.08	152.80

Source: China's Foreign Affairs (yearbooks) and JETRO estimates for 2010 on Japan (figures rounded up).

ANNEXURE 3.3: JAPAN'S OUTWARD FDI BY COUNTRY/REGION

(Balance of Payments basis, net and flow)

Year	China	India
1996	2,317	262
1997	1,862	485
1998	1,301	460
1999	360	261
2000	934	175
2001	2,158	150
2002	2,622	146
2003	3,980	124
2004	2,863	139
2005	6,575	266
2006	6,169	512
2007	6,218	1,506
2008	6,496	5,551
2009	6,899	3,664
2010	7,252	2,864

Source: Accessed on 14 August 2011 from http://www.jetro.go.jp/en/reports/statistics/data/country1_e_cy10.xls

NOTES

1. See *Zhongguo Waijiao* (China's Diplomacy) (various yearbooks) Beijing: Ministry of Foreign Affairs; and Tan Zaiwen, '*Taoguang yanghui, yousuo zuowei*' *de lilun sikao* (Theoretical insights into 'Biding one's time, accomplishing something) *Guoji Guancha* (International Observer) 1, 2005, pp. 68-73.
2. For the Chinese concerns on Japan, see Liu Qiang, '*Lun Riben "zhengchang guojia" hua*' (Japan's endeavour to be a 'normal state'), *Shijie Jingji yu Zhengzhi* (*World Economics & Politics*), 290/10 (2004): 22-6; Wang Xinsheng, '*Riben xianghe quchu*' (The direction of Japan), *Shijie Zhishi*, 16 June 1999: 12-14 and Yuan Yang, 'Japan Further Breaking the Shackles on Military Development', *Liberation Army Daily*, 15 December 2003 in

FBIS-CHI-2003-1215 (Foreign Broadcast Information Service available at <http://wnc.fedworld.gov>, 17 December 2003).

3. According to a draft white paper on maritime policy of Taiwan's Cabinet-level Research, Development and Evaluation Committee in June 1999, Taiwan reiterated its jurisdiction over the Spratly's and Diaoyudao Islands. See for details, 'White Paper Stresses Sovereignty Over Two Sets of Disputed Isles', *Central News Agency* (Taipei), 22 June 1999 in SWB FE/3569 F/2 24 June 1999.
4. These arguments are reflected in Ying Nan, '*Diaoyudao lishi yange ji zhanlue jiazhi*' (History and the evolution of the strategic value of Diaoyu Islands), *Xiandai Junshi* (Contemporary Military), Beijing, vol. 21, no. 3, Issue 242, March 1997, pp. 51-2.
5. See Liao Wen-Chung, 'China's Blue Waters Strategy in the 21st Century: From the First Islands Toward the Second Islands Chain' Occasional Paper Series, Chinese Council of Advanced Policy Studies, Taipei, September 1995, pp. 2 & 10. Two months later, in April 1992, the Commandant of China's Naval Command College, Li Dingwen stated that China's sovereignty extends to about three million square kilometres. Li cited in ibid., p. 10. See also Wang Guangxin and Huang Caihong's report, 'Navy Deploys 3,000 Coastal Navigation Marks', *Xinhua Domestic Service*, 18 April 1995 in FBIS-CHI-95-107, 5 June 1995, p. 37.
6. For a comparison of the 1958 Chinese resolve on 12 nautical mile limits and the recent 1992 law of China and subsequent international responses, see Li Jie, '*Haiyangfa zhishi mantan zhisan: Qiantan linghaiji pilianqu zhidu*' (Free Chat of the Law of the Sea Part III: Brief Talk on Territorial Sea and Contiguous Zone System), *Xiandai Junshi*, vol. 20, no. 8, Issue 235, August 1996, pp. 53-4.
7. See 'Ocean Law Symposium Held', *China Daily* (Beijing), 5 November 1997.
8. See 'PRC; Spokesman Reiterates Diaoyudao Islands Belong to China' *Kyodo* (Tokyo), 15 February 1996 in FBIS-CHI-96-32, 15 February 1996, p. 3.
9. However, this paper was silent on the anti-Japanese protests in China and Hong Kong in the last decade. See 'TKP Slams Right-Wing Groups in Japan for Staging Anti-Chinese Protests', *Ta*

Kung Pao Online, 18 October 2010; NewsEdge Document Number: 201010181477.1_6f5502d90025764f File No. 985, Accession No. 306750673.

10. See for the views of Li Chia-ching and Feng Chih-cheng, researchers at the Research Institute of Hong Kong International Studies, 'TKP Urges China to Deny Japan Rare Earth Resources as Form of Punishment', *Ta Kung Pao Online*, 7 October 2010, NewsEdge Document No. 201010071477.1_d60d02792e19631b File No. 985, Accession No. 306200096.
11. See for a critique, Li Yong, 'Okinotorishima Has No Exclusive Continental Shelf', *Ta Kung Pao*, 30 March 2007, NewsEdge Document No. 200703301477.1_e96007341d1e315c File No. 985, Accession No. 241850852.
12. See for these views, on the eve of Hu Jintao's visit to Japan in May 2008, Qiu Bo, 'China and Japan Break Through Crux and Build Mutual Trust', *Ta Kung Pao*, 8 May 2008, NewsEdge Document No. 200805081477.1_eaa804ac2ae3cdc8 File No. 985, Accession No. 262051283.
13. See Wang Shan, '*ZhongRi guanxi ruhe mianxiang weilai*', in Fu Mengzi, ed., *Yadai zhanlue chang-Shijie zhuyao liliang de fazhan yu juezhu* (Asia-Pacific Strategic Arena: Development and Rivalry of Global Major Powers), Beijing: Shishi Publications, 2002, pp. 229-51 (p. 250).
14. See Tang Jiaxuan, ed., *Zhongguo Waijiao Cidian* (Dictionary of Chinese Foreign Policy), Beijing World Knowledge Publications, 2000, p. 287.
15. See, ibid., p. 287 and *Mao Zedong On Diplomacy*, Beijing: Foreign Languages Press, 1998, p. 319.
16. This is cited by Wang Jianwei & Wu Xinbo, 'Against Us or with Us? The Chinese Perspective of America's Alliances with Japan and Korea', Asia/Pacific Research Center, Institute for International Studies, Stanford University, May 1998 at <http://www.taiwansecurity.org> (accessed on 7 July 2005).
17. This is based on Wang & Wu, ibid.
18. Wang Chi-Wen, 'Ito Picking Up Historical Garbage' *Ta Kung Pao Online*, 14 May 2009, NewsEdge Document No. 200907171477.1_787e049f5ca7f49c File No. 985, Accession No. 283801123.

19. Shih Chun-yu, 'Denying History Will Undermine Japan's Soft Power', *Ta Kung Pao*, 15 March 2007, NewsEdge Document No. 200703151477.1_8d2e02689a766200, File No. 985, Accession No. 241100922.
20. 'Column Hails PRC, Japan's Plan To Hold Joint Search, Rescue Operations', *Ta Kung Pao Online*, 30 November 2009, NewsEdge Document No. 200911301477.1_bc07024e9b1e79f2, File No. 985, Accession No. 290600434.
21. Srikanth Kondapalli, 'Military Ties: India and China Try to "Break the Ice"', 12 December 2011, accessed on 12 December 2011 at <http://www.rediff.com/news/column/military-ties-india-and-china-try-to-break-the-ice/20111212.htm>.
22. Ma Ling, 'What Should China Do?', *Ta Kung Pao*, 18 May 2001. AFS Document No. CPP20105180000041 FBIS-CHI-2001-0518, NewsEdge Document No. 200303191477.1_ f8ae002d70f19342, File No. 985, Accession No. 134701266.
23. Qi Bin, 'Military Expert Points out That Japan's Erroneous Outlook on History Will Lead to Dangerous Consequences', *Zhongguo Xinwen She*, 21 January 2003 in FBIS-CHI-2003-0121, 22 January 2003; and Yan Guoqun and Dong Yinge, 'What is the "Emergency Legislation" About?' *Liberation Army Daily*, 7 June 2003 in FBIS-CHI-2003-0609, 7 July 2003.
24. 'Troublesome Background of China-Japan Relations', *Kanwa News*, 20 November 2003.
25. Yuan Yang, 'Japan Further Breaking the Shackles on Military Development', *Liberation Army Daily*, 15 December 2003 in FBIS-CHI-2003-1215, 17 December 2003.
26. Lu Baosheng and Guo Hongjun, 'Okinawa: "Hub" of the Pacific' *Liberation Army Daily*, 22 June 2003 in FBIS-CHI-2003-0623, 25 June 2003.
27. See for details, Robert Karniol, 'Japan Boosts Missile Defence System', *Jane's Defence Weekly*, 7 January 2004.
28. According to Zhao Qinghai, the three main characteristics of China's strategic dialogue mechanism include non-involvement of third parties, discussion of topics in a wide range of fields, and enhancing mutual trust and cooperation. See 'Strategic Talks: New Mode for China's Diplomacy With Major Countries', *Xinhua*,

21 October 2005, NewsEdge Document No. 200510211477.1_485f007262bdfb02, File No. 985, Accossion No. 215550802.

29. 'PRC Scholar on US-PRC-Japan Triangular Relations' *Ta Kung Pao Online*, 8 July 2009, NewsEdge Document No. 200907081477.1_dd7201be87e63b77, File No. 985, Accession No. 283350772. Wang Ping, research fellow of the Japanese Research Institute of Chinese Academy of Social Sciences argued here that China, Japan and the US are making efforts to build a new strategic relationship.

30. Hou Jinliang, '*Riyin "jingji lian" shengwen de beihou*' (Behind the warming 'economy love' of Japan and India), *Lianhe Zaobao* (United Morning Post), 22 February 2011 accessed at <http://www.chinaelections.org/Newsinfo.asp?NewsID=200524>.

31. 'Japan Seeks Closer Ties With India' *Xinhua*, 7 January 2006, NewsEdge Document No. 200601071477.1_cd0100461929c206, File No. 985, Accession No. 219450101.

32. China's foreign ministry spokesman Qin Gang stated that the three should enhance dialogue, exchanges, and cooperation in order to jointly work for peace and prosperity in the region. See Chang Lu and Ma Wenbo, 'Foreign Ministry Spokesman Says China, India, and Japan Should Jointly Work For Regional Stability and Prosperity', *Xinhua Asia-Pacific Service*, 12 December 2006, NewsEdge Document No. 200612121477.1_9317002ca23a153b, File No. 985, Accession No. 236450677.

33. Zhang Hua, 'Abe Concludes Asia Tour With Tangible Harvest', *Xinhua*, 25 August 2007, NewsEdge Document No. 200708251477.1_59ef0084b2f31829, File No. 985, Accession No. 249250390.

34. 'Japanese PM in India Urges "Broader Asia" Partnership', *Xinhua*, 22 August 2007, NewsEdge Document No. 200708221477.1_d5b10054607293ca, File No. 985, Accession No. 249100514.

35. 'Japan To Help India To Build Key Railway', *Xinhua*, 22 October 2008, NewsEdge Document No. 200810221477.1_a550002a6a48de6f, File No. 985, Accession No. 270401194. On the other hand, with China's GDP surpassing that of Japan, the latter had planned to cut aid to China. Thus, Seiji Maehara, the Japanese foreign minister in March 2011 had announced a

review of such aid policies to China. Overall, Japan began Official Development Assistance to China in 1979 and had disbursed till 2005 about '3.1331 trillion yen in loan aid (yen loans), 145.7 billion yen in grant aid, and 144.6 billion yen in technical cooperation'. See 'Overview of Official Development Assistance (ODA) to China', accessed on 4 July 2011 at <http://www.mofa.go.jp/policy/oda/region/e_asia/china/index.html> On the other hand, Japan's ODA to India started in 1958 and today India has become the largest recipient of such aid amounting to 3.6 trillion yen by June 2011. See 'Overview of Japan's ODA to India' accessed on 14 August 2011 at <http://www.mofa.go.jp/policy/oda/region/sw_asia/india_o.pdf >

36. See 'Japan Warms Relations With India But Future Accord Remains Hazy', *Xinhua*, 30 December 2009, NewsEdge Document No. 200912301477.1_a90f01f506681418, File No. 985, Accession No. 292100541.
37. Jonathan Day, 'Japan and India Head for Broad Economic Alliance, Nuclear Pact', *Xinhua*, 26 October 2010, NewsEdge Document No: 201010261477.1_d6e201efba2803d0, File No. 985, Accession No. 307150178.
38. See the views of Zhao Qinghai on this issue, Yang Qingchuan, 'New Pact Puts Growing U.S.-India Military Ties Under Spotlight', *Xinhua*, 20 July 2009, NewsEdge Document No. 200907201477.1_527f016ce11c8b1c, File No. 985, Accession No. 283951154.
39. Chang Ching-wei, 'China Faces Containment by "Asian NATO"', *Ta Kung Pao*, 16 August 2007, NewsEdge Document No. 200708161477.1_6fce06c38720da48, File No. 985, Accession No. 248800746.
40. Lung Chih, 'Japan-Australia Security Pact Obviously Targeted at China', *Ta Kung Pao*, 30 March 2007, NewsEdge Document No. 200703301477.1_c97e05d75210da6a, File No. 985, Accession No. 241850965.
41. See the comments of the then Australian foreign minister Stephen Smith, after the strategic dialogue meeting with the Chinese foreign minister Yang Jiechi, 'Australia No Longer Takes Part in Strategic Dialogues With the US, Japan And India', *Xinhua*, 5 February 2008, NewsEdge Document No. 200802051477.1_7e900049a6be35ce, File No. 985, Accession No. 257450465.

42. 'Chinese Foreign Ministry Spokesman Says: Japan's Comment That China Will Eventually Not Oppose the G-4's Proposal is Groundless', *Xinhua Domestic Service*, 30 July 2005, NewsEdge Document No. 200507301477.1_b5f9002d954af802, File No. 985, Accession No. 211400353.
43. Xu Song and Ren Ke, 'Foreign Ministry Spokesman Says China Resolutely Opposes the Immature UN Reform Program Proposed by a Small Number of Countries', *Xinhua*, 9 June 2005, NewsEdge Document No. 200506091477.1_db930045db96bf0e, File No. 985, Accession No. 208850539.
44. Yang Zhiwang, 'Wang Guangya: The Group of Four Should Withdraw Its Unpopular Draft Resolution', *Xinhua Domestic Service*, 5 August 2005, NewsEdge Document No. 200508051477.1_ b9d000d996553dbb, File No. 985, Accession No. 211701044.
45. Tadashi Ito, 'UNSC Expansion: PRC Spells Out Basic Position, Makes Clear Desire to "Stop Japan"', *Sankei Shimbun*, 9 June 2005, NewsEdge Document No. 200506091477.1_d5750047109fc10f, File No. 985, Accession No. 208850059.
46. The United for Consensus group was raised to counter the Group Four (India, Japan, Germany and Brazil) bidding for the UNSC expansion. See Silvia Marchetti, 'Consensus Grows on Need to Reach Compromise on UN Security Council Reform', *Xinhua*, 17 May 2011, NewsEdge Document No. 201105171477.1 _3a1300905b907f2e, File Number 985, Accession No. 317300142.
47. Cheng cited by Elizabeth Hsuat, 'Chinese Economist Says Chance of Yuan Being Adopted as Asian Currency Low', *Central News Agency*, 8 June 2009, NewsEdge Document No.: 200906081477.1 _d6490047e62b90c0, File No. 985, Accession No. 281851013.
48. 'Asia Cooperation Dialogue', *Xinhua*, 22 June 2004, FBIS-CHI-2004-0622, NewsEdge Document No. 200406231477.1_ 02fa0007f23af558, File No. 985, Accession No. 191250250.
49. 'Six Asia-Pacific Countries Agree To Form Partnership on Climate', *Xinhua*, 28 July 2005, NewsEdge Document No.

200507281477.1 _0a06006dd857a1ad, File No. 985, Accession No. 211300171.

50. See Oyang Ziyuan, 'The Lunar Exploration Projects of China, Japan, and India All Have Their Own Value, and They Should Strengthen Their Cooperation', *Xinhua Domestic Service*, 26 November 2008, NewsEdge Document No. 200811261477.1 _411300dacad95351, File No. 985, Accession No. 272150298.

CHAPTER 4

Japan–India–US Relations and Rising China

EMI MIFUNE

INTRODUCTION

In June 2010, S.M. Krishna, the Minister of External Affairs of India, delivered a lecture at the Institute of Diplomacy and Security in the Republic of Korea (ROK, Korea). He emphasized that India has already been an East Asian country since India adopted its 'Look East' policy 18 years prior.[1] His speech presented the fact that India is now a prominent and influential player in eastern Asian politics and economic affairs. Indian and Chinese strategic weight, at both the regional and global levels, forms an important element in contemporary changing international politics.

The importance of China reflects two stark realities. One is the sustained growth of the Chinese economy and its implications for rising Chinese power. Another is its increasing military capabilities and its continued transfer for military technology to many parts of the world. Chinese economic development has supported its military expansion (Figures 4.1 and 4.2). China's rise, manifested not only economically but also militarily, has altered international relations in Asia.

Then, how about India? How do the Chinese regard emergent India as a political player in eastern Asia and as part of the triangular relationship of Japan–India–US? Does this trio strongly influence Chinese policy? Although many Japanese politicians, scholars, and journalists have insisted upon strengthening relations among Japan–India–US, is it possible to prevent or balance an expanding and rising China? Does the trio function as a deterrent power against China?

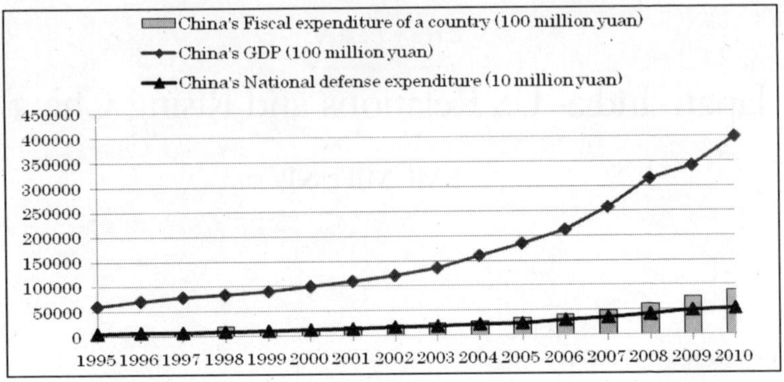

Source: Based on Statistics compiled by *China Statistics Summary 2011*, drawn by the author.

FIGURE 4.1: CHINA'S GDP, FISCAL EXPENDITURES, AND NATIONAL DEFENCE EXPENDITURES.

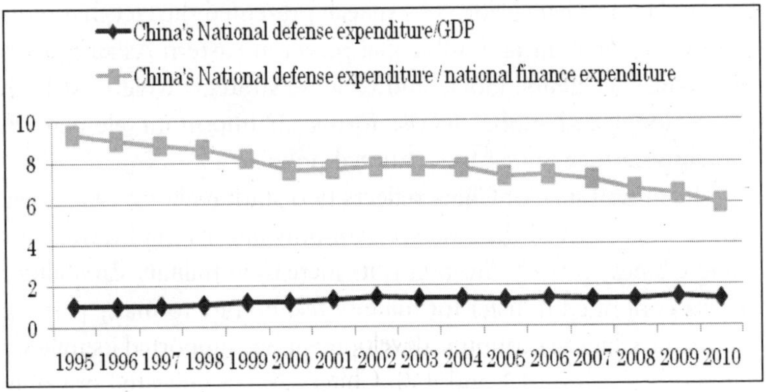

Source: As in Figure 4.1

FIGURE 4.2: RATIO OF CHINA'S DEFENCE BUDGET TO GDP, AND FINANCIAL EXPENDITURES.

In that context, this article presents an examination of how China views the Japan–India–US relation. This article comprises the following five sections. First, the changing structure and power shift in Asia are described. Second, the emerging Indian economy in eastern Asia is presented. Third, Chinese views related to the trio are considered. Fourth, difficulties for India and China in forming a more comprehensive partnership are examined. Subsequently, the influence of Japan–India–US relations towards a rising China is assessed.

CHANGING STRUCTURE AND POWER SHIFT IN ASIA

The recent Great Recession has strongly influenced the world economy and politics. Recently, economic power has shifted gradually to Eastern Asia. China has shown itself to be more resilient to the impact of this crisis and has shown its ability to overcome the effects of the crisis sooner. Economic changes and shifts that have occurred in eastern Asia should be understood as a process of changing global implications. The most important among these processes are the relative decline of the US as a unipolar power and of Japan as a major economic power.

The radar chart presented as Figure 4.3 shows the share of regional trade in the six major world economies (NAFTA, EU, China, Japan, MERCOSUR, and ASEAN) in 1990, 2000, and 2008. The share of trade among economically developed nations and several regions – NAFTA–EU, NAFTA – Japan, and EU–Japan –

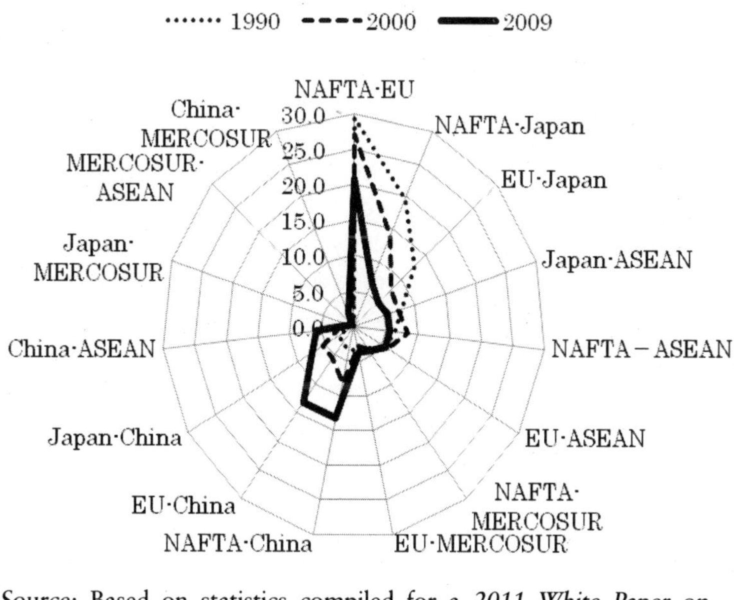

Source: Based on statistics compiled for a *2011 White Paper on International Economy and Trade* drawn by the author.

FIGURE 4.3: TRADE TRANSITION OF SIX MAJOR ECONOMIES (NAFTA, EU, CHINA, JAPAN, MERCOSUR, ASEAN) IN 1990, 2000, AND 2009.

were 61.5 per cent in 1990, 48.9 per cent in 2000 (China entered the WTO in December 2001), and 32.6 per cent in 2008 (it was the year of Lehman Shock). The trade structure in 1990 was pulled by economically developed countries. However, the presence of Japan in trade has decreased markedly. The share of NAFTA–Japan trade was 19.6 per cent in 1990, 14 per cent in 2000, but only 6.8 per cent in 2008 (it was the year of the Lehman Shock). The share of EU–Japan trade was 12.6 per cent in 1990, 7.8 per cent in 2000, but only 5.1 per cent in 2008. In contrast, the share of NAFTA–China trade grew from 3.3 per cent in 1990, to 8.2 per cent in 2000, and 13.2 per cent in 2008. The share of EU–China trade was 3.0 per cent in 1990, 5.5 per cent in 2000, and 13.2 per cent in 2008. The share of Japan–China trade was 2.5 per cent in 1990, 5.5 per cent in 2000, and 7.5 per cent in 2009.[2] The sum of NAFTA–Japan trade in 2009 was 1.1 times that in 1990. In stark contrast, the sum of NAFTA–China trade in 2009 was 16.0 times that in 1990.

Figure 4.3 exhibits the structural change of trade that took place during 1990-2008: Japan's presence in world trade declined but China's presence in terms of world trade rose remarkably.

Although Japan had been recovering gradually from the Lehman Brothers shock of 2008, the Great East Japan Earthquake and Fukushima Daiichi Nuclear Power Station accident of 2011 have affected Japan's society and industry very strongly. Regarding the foreign exchange rate, the Japanese yen is becoming stronger more rapidly than anticipated by exporting firms. Through overseas business expansion, corporations are earning lower revenues in the US and EU countries, but are earning more revenues in markets in Asia. Asian emerging economies, including those of India and China, have risen remarkably since the global economic and financial crises. They have been pulling the world economy. With expansion of their relative economic importance, the political influence of India and China is rising and the global balance of power is shifting from a structure centred on the United States and other industrialized countries to a multi-polar structure that China has insisted upon.[3] The Asian region is becoming increasingly important for Japan both economically and politically.

During the last decade, the US has allocated vast resources to the Middle East and Central Asia. At a time when eastern Asia is building a new security and economic architecture, the presence of the US in Asia has declined gradually.[4] Simultaneously, the status of Japan as the core economy in Asia has been assumed by China instead.

To make matters worse, Japan has had 10 prime ministers since 1996. Japan's frequent changes of top leadership are dizzying and increasingly counterproductive. Perhaps this situation has left Japanese leaders with only barely sufficient time to introduce effective policies. Japan needs experienced and reliable leaders who can offer principled leadership during their terms of office, and who can present and propose and then execute appropriate economic and security policies with a vision for the future of Japan. To make matters worse, the Yukio Hatoyama Administration of the Japanese Democratic Party harmed the Japan–US relationship, thereby degrading the relative status of Japan in Asia.

China's rise has engendered changes in international relations in Asia not only economically but also militarily.[5] China, while expanding its outreach to the world rapidly in terms of its economy, diplomacy, and military affairs, also seeks to increase its influence abroad. Contemporary China is recognized as a great power with global aspirations, which has coloured the relationship between Japan and China.[6] The economic relationship between Japan and China has continued to develop. Is China's rise as a commercial and military power an opportunity, challenge, or threat to Japan? No single answer to this question has ever existed, but the Japan–China relation has never been merely a zero-sum game. The impact of China's rise presents an opportunity, a challenge, and a threat for Japan. The Japan–China relation is moving to a new stage as China raises its international status and consolidates its national power.

EMERGING INDIA AS A PROMINENT PLAYER IN EASTERN ASIA

Another prominent point of changing structure in Asia is that India has already been included in the eastern Asian trade network.

Figure 4.4 portrays the transition of some Japanese companies that have made inroads into the Indian market.

According to a survey by the Ministry of Economy, Trade and Industry (MoETI) of Japan, Japanese companies regard India as an attractive market along with China. In fact, 89 per cent of respondents chose 'development of the Indian market' as the main reason to enter and invest in the Indian market. The respondents cited the following reasons: 44 per cent – low labour costs, 22 per cent – supply bases and assembly plants.[7]

Indian trade with East Asian countries has increased dramatically. Both intermediate goods trade from East Asia to India and final goods trade from India to the US and EU have increased rapidly, which underscores that India has already been included in the eastern Asian trade network. However, many problems now confronting Japanese companies have been pointed out. Some examples are insufficiency of infrastructure and opaque application of laws.

In addition to Indian economic growth, the US's changing strategy towards the Pacific region has greatly enhanced Indian importance.

For US long-term national interests, it must retain its identity as a *Pacific Power.* The Obama administration has articulated a five-

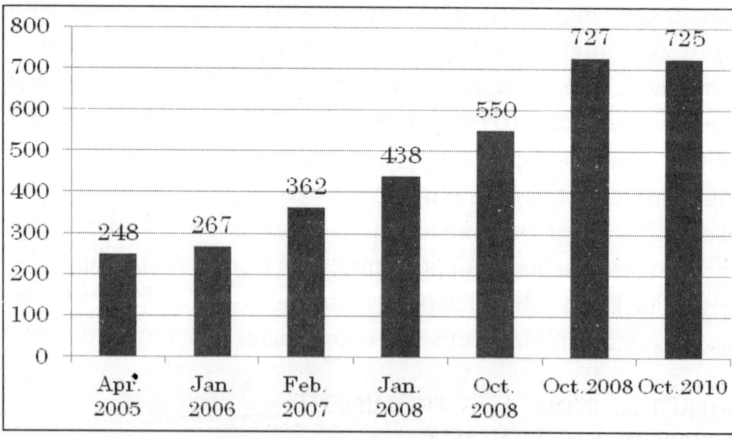

Source: 2011 White Paper International Economy and Trade.

FIGURE 4.4: TRANSITION OF SOME JAPANESE COMPANIES THAT HAVE MADE INROADS INTO INDIAN MARKETS.

part framework for US engagement in the Asia–Pacific region. First, it intends to deepen and modernize the US alliance with Japan, Korea, Australia, Thailand, and the Philippines. Second, it seeks to broaden US engagement with increasingly important partners such as Indonesia, Vietnam, Mongolia, New Zealand, Singapore, Malaysia, and most notably India. Third, it plans to develop a predictable, stable, and comprehensive relation with China. Fourth, it will engage and invest in the region's burgeoning multilateral architecture. Fifth, it intends to pursue a confident and aggressive trade and economic strategy.[8]

HOW CHINA EYES THE JAPAN–INDIA–US RELATIONS

China perceives that US policy related to China has changed from warm to cold during the two years of the Obama administration.

The current changes might be readily apparent. The US directly or indirectly has involved itself in China's relations with neighbouring countries.[9] It took a public stance or indirectly exerted influence related to issues such as Japan's Senkaku Island issue.

Regarding the American policy of a 'return to Asia', Chinese newspapers, magazines, and websites such as *Renmin Ribao* (*People's Daily*) and *Xinhua News Agency* reported analysis by Zhang Jie, Chief of the Office of Security and Diplomacy, Asia Pacific Studies under the Academy of School Science.[10] Zhang said an American return to Asia policy isolates Chinese neighbours from China. It has the weakened mutual confidence between China and its neighbouring countries. Zhang has also said that the US has tried to make a 'Flying Wild Goose Security Model'. This American security model has threatened Chinese security.[11] Zhang has pointed point out inter-dynamic factors of US–India relations has deepened the basic platform of Japan–India relations in view of the US–Japan alliance.[12]

A researcher of the World Economy and Politics Studies under the Academy of School Science, Wang Mingming, presented his analysis in the *People's Daily*[13]: US policy to treat India as a great power is linked to its policy toward a rising China in the following five points.

First, the US strategic focus in Asia is to aim at a balance with China. Wang called attention to this point. Second, the US pursues the US–Japan alliance and the US–Korea alliance to be developed to a trilateral or multilateral military architecture among US–Japan–Korea. Third, the US strengthens security cooperation among the US, Japan, and ASEAN. The US promotes cooperation not only among great powers, but also among small countries. The core of the American 'return to Asia' policy is the policy in relation to ASEAN. Fourth, the US encourages India as a strong and enduring Asia–Pacific partner and promotes India's growing engagement with the region and participation in the regional architecture. The US promotes a trilateral dialogue among the US, India, and Japan. The US encourages India to take a more prominent role in Asia and the world. Fifth, Japan and India agreed to the conclusion of an EPA agreement between the two countries in September 2010. The India and US economic relationships are being reinforced concurrently with deepening relations between India and Japan.

Lu Guangsheng, the Vice Chief of the Institute of Southeast Asian Studies of Yunnan University, has pointed out that leaders have endorsed the Report on APEC's 2010 Economic Progress Towards the Bogor Goals Agreement. Then they agreed to take concrete steps for the realization of a Free Trade Area of the Asia–Pacific (FTAAP), which is a major instrument to advance APEC's regional economic integration agenda. The declaration of APEC 2010 emphasized formulation of the comprehensive and long-term growth strategy for the Asia–Pacific region, which includes India, Australia and New Zealand in addition to '10+3 (ASEAN + China, Japan, and Korea)'.[14]

DIFFICULTIES FOR INDIA AND CHINA TO FORM A MORE COMPREHENSIVE PARTNERSHIP

Certainly, China–India relations have developed in terms of co-operation in the field of commerce. However, it remains doubtful whether these relations can progress further.

Five reasons show the difficulty for China and India to progress to a new stage in their partnership despite progression in their economic relations. An overview of relations between Japan and India is also given in illustration of the rising influence of China.

First, although China advocates a harmonious world, the cornerstone of its strategy for ensuring regional security comprises national development and retention of sovereignty and territory. The overriding mission of Chinese twenty-first-century foreign diplomacy and national defence is to achieve a great reconstruction of Chinese civilization in half a century leading up to the hundredth anniversary of the founding of the People's Republic of China. To achieve this, China is striving to create a peaceful and stable international environment. By being on amicable terms with its neighbouring countries and resolving historical conflicts, China can specifically address economic development. The Chinese 'harmonious world' is a means, not an end. Its neighbourly friendship is a means to advance or rather a step forward for its development. The Chinese ultimate aim is not to construct partnerships but to move ahead with its own development while retaining sovereignty and territory. From the Chinese perspective, for progression of partnership between China and India to the next stage, the partnership must be a means for development and retention of sovereignty and territory. However, in areas other than the economy, many non-negotiable issues remain between China and India for ensuring the security of each country.

Second, in recent years, especially since 2008, the Chinese stance toward foreign diplomacy has become more strident. Traditionally, the Chinese concept of foreign diplomacy was Deng Xiaoping's '24 character strategy', which was to 'observe calmly, forge solid footing, cope with affairs calmly, hide our capacities and our faults, and never claim leadership'. To this, four characters meaning 'do what we can' were added. This 24-character strategy is a stance that avoids friction with other countries and prioritizes domestic economic development. However, since 2008, China has firmly maintained the policy of 'hide our capacities'. This has shifted to a posture of assertive action in foreign diplomacy. In recent years, the presence of China has increased across the Indian Ocean. The United States

Department of Defense Annual Report to Congress: Military Power of the People's Republic of China, points out the possibility of the Chinese military trying to extend the range of its strategic operations to the Western Pacific, which is beyond the Indian Ocean and the second island chain.

The second island chain is a line that runs from the Japanese archipelago to Indonesia, connecting Saipan and Guam. The line that connects Okinawa, Taiwan, and the Philippines is called the first island chain. In the 1980s, Liu Huaqing proposed the following vision for China's Navy: (1) By 2000, have in place a complete offshore defence capacity on China's coastline. This has largely been achieved. (2) Secure maritime control within the first island chain and second island chain by 2000-10 and 2010-20, respectively, and construct an aircraft carrier. (3) By 2020-40, prevent the US Navy from achieving independent control of the Pacific and Indian Ocean. (4) By 2040-50, construct a navy that is equivalent to the US Navy.

What demands attention here is the concept of strategic borders, which differ from national borders. Following Premier Li Peng's pronouncement to the National People's Congress in 1993, to include maritime interests as a target for defence, in 1997, a national defence law was enacted that specified maintaining maritime interests within the scope of national defence. In the same year, when Shi Yunsheng assumed the post of Commander of the Navy, he earnestly set about making the change from a coastal navy to a navy for adjacent waters and asserted the concept of a first island chain and a second island chain in his Strategies for Naval Development. The Chinese consider that the regions where it once conducted tribute trade (from Singapore to the whole of Indochina, Thailand, Nepal, Korean Peninsula, and Japan's Okinawa Islands[15]) were Chinese territories under the Qing dynasty and are therefore territories inherent to China that were taken by force. In China, these are called strategic borders, which differ from original national borders. The Chinese government feels that it should guarantee the security of its strategic borders and conserve its maritime interests. The first island chain is exactly the line that forms this strategic border. China's change in stance to a more active kind of foreign diplomacy signifies a change to a more hard-line foreign diplomacy.

On 3 January 2011, the weekly magazine *Study Times*, published by the Party School of the Central Committee of the Communist Party of China, had an article titled 'A Complete Understanding of the Strategic Thought of Deng Xiaoping for Solving Maritime Disputes'. This article argued that taking Deng Xiaoping's ideas of shelving disputes and joint development as policies for dealing with maritime disputes is a mistake. In addition, this same article pointed out that debating on issues of sovereignty should be of less priority than ensuring the sovereignty and security of the nation. This article in *Study Times* is not just an article: it is a party policy. This article emphasized the enactment of maritime laws, the strengthening of law enforcement at sea, and stepping up of propaganda related to China's sovereignty through domestic and overseas media, as the future policies of China. In addition to peaceful solutions, it pointed to the necessity of increasing military preparations so that China would always win in the event of a war, and emphasized the necessity of making preparations for public opinion on the use of force, and examining the legal aspects of going to war. China specifically has areas such as Japan and the South China Sea in mind. However, for India, a country that harbours border claims with China, this hard-line stance is a cause of concern because when it comes to the problems of sovereignty and territory, the Chinese stance will not be one of compromise but one of recalcitrance and self-assertion.

Third, for China, China–India relations are by no means only a case of relations between two countries, but are influenced considerably by superpowers, such as the US and Russia, as well as Pakistan. China–India relations will come to a halt when India becomes unable to compromise with China regarding China's relations with Pakistan, a country that maintains close ties with China. To date, India has been recognizing the Chinese position that views Taiwan and Tibet as part of China in accordance with the principle of 'one China' in official documents. However, in a joint statement made during Wen Jiabao's visit to India in 2010, no mention was made of this principle of 'one China' that includes Tibet and Taiwan. The issues of Taiwan and Tibet are core interests for China. The fact that these core interests were not featured in this joint statement between India and China can be understood as conveying India's dissatisfaction toward China. During a visit to India last November by the Foreign Minister Yang Jiechi, the Indian government sought to make him aware that the Kashmir problem is, to India, as delicate as the problems of Taiwan and Tibet are to China. In addition, during Premier Wen Jiabao's visit in December, Prime Minister Singh sought confirmation from the premier with respect to Indian policy in which Jammu & Kashmir is regarded as an integral territory of India, just like Tibet is regarded as integral territory of China. However, Wen Jiabao disagreed. In addition, at a summit between China and India in 2010, China did not express its condolences for the 2008 Mumbai terrorist attacks. We infer that the reason for this is China's consideration toward Pakistan.

On the day following the summit between India and China, Wen Jiabao flew to Islamabad, where he was met with a cordial welcome at the airport by Pakistan's top officials, including Prime Minister Gillani, key cabinet ministers, and the Chief of Army Staff of the Pakistan Army, General Kayani. Upon his arrival, Wen Jiabao declared that he would like to strengthen the Chinese strategic partnership with Pakistan, and at a summit, committed to increasing cooperation with Pakistan in fields such as the development of infrastructure and trade. During Wen Jiabao's visit to Pakistan, China established business contracts worth 29 billion dollars between the Pakistani government and private businesses. This greatly surpassed the 16 billion dollars in business contracts formed between China and India.

Wen Jiabao visiting India and Pakistan in December of 2010 was an event that epitomized the relationship between China, India, and Pakistan in recent years. Presently, relations between Pakistan and China have been called 'omnidirectional diplomacy' and 'all-weather relations'. Ever since Pakistan referred to Chinese long-term support for Pakistan as 'an all-weather friendship', relations between China and Pakistan's ruling elite has come to be termed as 'all-weather relations'. When Jiang Zemin visited Pakistan in 1996 and proposed a 'full strategic partnership', the leaders of both countries came to use the term 'all-weather relations'. China and Pakistan affirmed their intention to deepen relations between the two countries in the 2003 'Joint Declaration between the People's Republic of China and the Islamic Republic of Pakistan on Directions of Bilateral Co-operation' and on 5 April 2005, entered into the 'Treaty of Good-Neighbourliness and Friendly Cooperation'. It is said that China had deployed troops in the Pakistan-controlled area of Kashmir.

The US and Russia are also involved intricately with Pakistan. On his visit to India in 2010, Russian President Dmitry Medvedev held talks with the Indian Prime Minister Singh and reached an agreement to implement the joint development of next-generation fighter jets. China views this agreement as India holding China in check. These fighter jets that are being jointly developed with the aim of being operational from 2017 are the T50 models of the Russian Sukhoi Company that were tested this January. China is also developing its own next-generation fighter jets. By partnering with Russia, India has moved against China to restrain Pakistan, which is modernizing its air force equipment with the cooperation of China. The Pakistan factor that exists between China and India is making confidence-building between these two nations difficult.

Fourth, friction between China and India surrounding the issue of resources is one that is difficult to resolve. Friction between the two countries is increasing in relation to diminishing or limited natural resources such as oil, natural gas, and water. India and China are major consumers of resources. Both countries are competing to provide active support for developing infrastructure and military cooperation to obtain resources not only from neighbouring countries in Asia but also from oil-rich and gas-rich countries such as Iraq, Sudan, Nigeria, Angola, and Myanmar.

Moreover, India is deeply concerned with China with respect to water resources. According to the *Global Times*, an international newspaper owned by *People's Daily*, India's Institute of Peace and Conflict Studies has pointed out how the problem of water resources under the influence of global warming will become a major point of contention among various countries in South Asia, China and India being among them. Many of the rivers that flow through countries in South Asia have their source in the Tibetan plateau. If temperatures rise by 2–5 °C by 2060, glaciers in the Tibetan plateau will melt because of the effects of global warming. This will cause floods in the short term, but in the long term it will result in a shortage of water with the largest impact predicted to be felt by 11 countries downstream.

Amid Indian concern over this situation, in November 2010, China commenced construction of the Zangmu hydropower station on the Yarlung Tsangpo River, the largest river in Tibet, having invested 7.9 billion yuan in its construction. It is expected to begin operation in 2014. The Chinese government has commented that the plant will prove useful in resolving Tibet's shortage of electricity, but the Yarlung Tsangpo River, after crossing Tibet from west to east, flows south into the north-east area of India, where it merges with the Brahmaputra River and provides an important source of water for agriculture in this area. Because the plant will undoubtedly affect water volumes in the Brahmaputra River, India is wary of Chinese activities.

The water problem is a severe political problem for China as well. Central Document No. 1, which indicates policy issues for 2011 and which was published on 29 January 2011 by the Communist Party of China, assigned top priority to the reform of water supplies. The document outlined a policy by which the average yearly amount invested in the construction of water supply facilities would be double that of 2010 by 2020 and that 4 trillion yuan would be earmarked for investment in the construction of these facilities over the next ten years. Additionally, it included the policy of allotting 10 per cent of income gained through the sale of land-use rights for the securing of water for agricultural use. In China, a series of droughts has increased prices of agricultural products. Major investments targeting the securing of water resources also aim to weaken inflationary pressure through increased food production. It is predicted that the problem of water will become an even greater source of friction in future China–India relations.

Fifth, although trade relations between the two countries have deepened, India is greatly dissatisfied with China because of the unilateral growth of India's trade deficit. The population of India's middle class, which for China forms their seventh largest export partner, corresponds to approximately the population of the US and twice the population of Japan. In addition, India's economic growth is domestic-demand-led economic growth, rather than growth achieved through the introduction of foreign capital. For China, India is therefore highly desirable as an export market.

Considering that the total amount of trade, between India and China has increased to 1.5 times that of India and the US, and there are areas that remain closed to the export market from India to China, such as branded generic drugs, and the fact that the Indian trade deficit with China, which stood at over 20 billion dollars in 2009, further increased in 2010 has become a source of friction between China and India. Furthermore, there are some fields that are perceived as 'posing a security threat'. An example of this is the possibility that communication equipment made in China contains surveillance devices, which has led the Indian government to place limitations on imports of communication equipment from China. In addition, concern persists within the Indian business community that there will be a huge impact on Indian small and medium-sized businesses if the Indian domestic-demand-led market becomes overwhelmed with inexpensive Chinese products. Posing yet another source of friction between the two countries is the increasing concern in India that an increase in Chinese labourers is taking jobs away from Indians. In September 2009, the Indian government, in principle, placed limitations on the authorization of work visas on 'Chinese labourers that do not possess any special skills' and effectively demanded that over 20,000 Chinese labourers return home. In future, it is expected that Chinese businesses will increase local production in India, which will lead to the creation of jobs for Indian people.

Although China–India relations are developing in a range of fields, confidence-building between the two countries still has a long way to go. This paper has demonstrated that although China and India are increasingly developing relations in the economic field, many problems hinder their attempts at building confidence and constructing a comprehensive partnership.

CONCLUSION

From the examination presented here, the following points can be made.

First, economic power has been shifting gradually to eastern Asia. The most important among these related processes are the relative decline of the US and Japan. With expansion of their relative economic importance, the political influence of both India and China is rising and the global balance of power is shifting from a structure that has heretofore remained centred on the United States. The US is expected to shift diplomatic, political, economic and security policy to retain its identity as a Pacific Power.

Japan, India and the USA have grappled with a rising and expanding China while being hindered by an economic-security duality. Chinese expansion as a military power is a territorial threat to Japan and India, although Chinese eminence as a commercial partner is an opportunity for each nation. Japan and India have been annoyed and at times confounded by that duality. Both Japan and India consequently have few political instruments with which to restrain or contain China. Japan and India play a role as balancing China under the US' pivot strategy. However, neither Japan nor India has concretely effective means or mechanisms to restrain or contain China because of their economic and military duality.

Second, China regards development of the Japan–India–US relations as a US measure related to China. An American policy shift can be expected to influence Chinese policy. A weekly magazine in Hong

Kong presented a special issue assessing American commitment to the South China Sea issue. It pointed out that the mutual commitment of the US, Japan, and India has compelled China to change its foreign policy. Chinese new foreign policy after commitments of the US, Japan and India into the South China Sea issue is 'omnidirectional diplomacy of interest community'.[16]

In this context, strengthening several levels and fields in the relationship with India is extremely important for Japan to form several multinational frameworks. India is a member of the East Asia Summit (EAS), ASEAN Regional Forum (ARF), ASEAN Post Ministerial Conference (ASEAN PMC), but not of Asia–Pacific Economic Cooperation (APEC). Although Japan, the US, and Australia agreed with India's request for APEC membership at the APEC meeting in Yokohama in 2010, this was shelved because of objections from China. This eventuality has led to caution related to the formation of Chinese encirclement within APEC. It is necessary for Japan to encourage India to join APEC and to play a greater role in a diplomatic strategy to confine Chinese hard-line policies in multilayered frameworks. Because cooperation between Japan and South Korea cannot be expected, frameworks among Japan, India, the United States, and Australia must be strengthened.

Third, the Japanese government's improvment of economic ties with India is considered under the US policy toward China. Japan has rapidly developed warm diplomatic relations with India, but their $15 billion level of bilateral trade in 2010 was less than 5 per cent of the trade flowing between Japan and China. Although that amount of trade and investment is important, dispersing superfluous dependence to China is fatal to Japan.

In this context, India is an effective strategic partner for Japan. About 90 per cent of rare earth mineral imports to Japan derived from China until 2009. However, Japan undertook efforts to disperse rare earth imports after 2010. During the first half of 2012, the ratio of Japanese imports of rare earth minerals from China was 49.3 per cent. Japan will continue to expand its rare earth imports from India, Australia, Kazakhstan, and Vietnam in 2013. The expected share of imported rare earth minerals from those four countries will account for about 60–80 per cent of Japanese domestic demand.

Fourth, China does not see the trio as a monolith. Although China is an unpleasant part of the American pivot policy 'return to Asia', China simultaneously and calmly analyses Japan–India–US relations. China sees the relation among US–Japan–India as '*tong chuang yi meng* (sleeping in the same bed but dreaming different dreams)'.

In this context, both governments of Japan and India must explain concrete common profits of mutually shared interests and mutual respect. Although Japanese Prime Minister Noda has announced 'value oriented diplomacy' involving emphasis on 'universal values' such as democreacy, freedom, human rights, the rule of law, and the market economy, when he visited India in December 2011, the visit probably represented a copy of Taro Aso's vision of 'value oriented diplomacy' and an 'Arc of Freedom and Prosperity' or the American idea of a 'Greater Middle East Plan'. Although the United States and Saudi Arabia have never had the same democratic political system and have never shared the same sense of values, they have continually shared good relations. Although the US and Japan share similar ideas related to democracy, soldiers of the US in Okinawa have frequently violated Japanese human rights and criminal law there. Sharing values is important as a political issue, but it does not function as a diplomatic issue. Mutually shared interests and mutual respect are crucial.

Fifth, both India and Japan have developed economic relations with China dramatically despite their mutually controversial issues, including territorial issues. Japan and India have not cooperated on territorial issues. Regarding territorial issues, intergovernmental cooperation stimulates China too much. Japan and India should launch strategic cooperation at the private sector level. For example, the non-governmental sectors of Japan and India must mutually cooperate to diffuse their own justifications of sovereignty and to contest unjustified Chinese claims in front of the US and the world.

NOTES

1. Chen Qinghong, 'Yindu zhanlue tumou de yinying (Shadow of Indian Strategic Plot)', *Liaowang Xinwen Zhoukan* (*Outlook Weekly*), vol. 39, September 2011, p. 59.
2. Ministry of Economy, Trade and Industry, *2011 White Paper on International Economy and Trade*, MoETI, 2011.
3. Emi Mifune, 'US Policy Towards Rising China and China's Policy in the Korean Peninsula', Session 3: Power Shift in Eastern Asia and the Korean Peninsula, *2011 Annual Convention of the Japan Association of International Relations*, 11 November 2011; Emi Mifune, 'China's Policy Towards India', Impact of Rising India: New Deployment of the International Relations in Asia, *2011 East Japan Convention*, 21 May 2011.
4. Hillary Clinton, 'America's Pacific Century', *Foreign Policy*, November 2011. [http://www.foreignpolicy.com/articles/2011/10/11/Americas_Pacific_century].
5. Emi Mifune, 'Richer and Stronger China and the US–China Relation', Satoshi Amako and Emi Mifune (eds.), *Expanding China's Foreign Relations* (*Bohchosuru Chugokuno Taigai kankei*), Tokyo: Keisoshobo, 2010, pp. 237-80.
6. Emi Mifune, 'Japan's Perspectives Toward Rising China', Herbert S. Yee (ed.), *China's Rise: Threat or Opportunity*? New York: Routledge, 2011, pp. 124-33.
7. MoETI, 'Report on Oversea Activities of Japanese companies 2010'.
8. Hearing before Sub-Committee on Asia and the Pacific of the Committee on Foreign Affairs, House of Representative, One-hundred Twelfth Congress, First Session, 31 March 2011, Serial No. 112-15.
9. Zhang Diyu, 'Nanhai: Zhongguo Jueqi Yali de Zuoyongdian (South China Sea: Pressure Point of Chinese Rising)', *Shijie Zhishi* (*World Affairs*), vol. 24, December 2011, pp. 14-23.
10. Zhang Jie, et al., 'Zhoubian Anquan Xingshi Sida Bianhua yu Zhongguo Duice (Four Major Changes of Neighbour Security Situation and Chinese Countermeasures)', *Shijie Zhishi* (*World Affairs*), vol. 2, January 2011, pp. 14-24.
11. Zhong Feiteng and Zhang Jie pointed out that 'Flying Wild Goose Security Model' is the third stage of the US strategy

toward the Pacific region since the Cold War Era (Zhong Feiteng and Zhang Jie, 'Yan Xing Anquan Moshi Yu Zhongguo Zhoubian Waijiao De Zhanlue Xuanze (Flying Wild Goose Security Model and Strategic Choice of Chinese Neighbour Diplomacy)', *Shijie Jingji Yu Zhengzhi* (*World Economy and Politics*), August 2011, pp. 47-64).

12. Zhang Jie, et al., 'Zhoubian Anquan Xingshi Sida Bianhua yu Zhongguo Duice (Four Major Changes of Neighbour Security Situation and Chinese Countermeasures)', *Shijie Zhishi* (*World Affairs*), vol. 2, January 2011, pp. 14-24.
13. *People's Daily*, 27 January 2011.
14. Lu Guangsheng, 'APEC 2011: TPP Chengwei Jiaodian (TPP became focal point)', *Shijie Zhishi* (*World Affairs*), vol. 23, December 2011, p. 25.
15. Ryukyu Islands are called Okinawa today.
16. Mei Ri Yin Jieru Nanhai Wenti Zhongguo Jizhuanbian Yingbian (Commitment of the US, Japan, India into the South China Sea Issue made China Suddenly Change its Policy), *Yazhou Zhoukan* (*Asia Weekly*), 4 December 2011, pp. 68-72.

CHAPTER 5

'China Threat' Theory in Indo–Japan Relations

TORU ITO

India has attracted the interest of quite a few Japanese, mainly because of its abundance of historical, religious and cultural basis for a long time. Today, however, such a traditional image of India has changed completely. Increasingly, young Japanese students as well as policy-makers, business people, and journalists are studying the Indian economy, domestic politics, diplomacy, and security issues. India has become an increasingly important country not only in terms of the humanities but also in terms of its importance for the social sciences.

Actually, Japanese policy toward India has changed completely. The growing amount of trade and investment, frequent high-level government official visits, and expanding defence exchanges between Japan and India are no longer rare.

This paper specifically examines how and why Japan has become so keen to strengthen the political and security relationship that it shares with India. The importance of China in this process is emphasized. Put most succinctly, an expanded sense of vigilance has arisen against China throughout Japan, which has motivated Japan, particularly since 2005, to approach India as a partner and ally. Nevertheless, it might be difficult to realize such a Japanese intention, considering the disagreement between Japan and India over China's intents and affairs. Each country, but especially Japan, must overcome a narrow-minded and nationalistic notion of targeting China if a Japan–India 'Strategic and Global' Partnership is to be realized in a literal sense.

STRUCTURAL FACTORS RELATED TO THE JAPANESE APPROACH TO INDIA

We have experienced substantial change in the international system since the end of the last century. First, the Cold War, which has truly become a fixture of the past, long deterred Japan from building close ties with India. Japan and India might not have been adversaries, but they were very 'estranged' countries by any measure (Figure 5.1).

For several reasons, Japan had hesitated to forge a close relationship with India in spite of holding generally good image of each other.[1] First, independent India, led by Prime Minister Jawaharlal Nehru, chose a policy of non-alignment. In contrast, Japan was closely aligned with the United States. Moreover, it had joined and often supported the Western bloc. Second, with the advent of the 1970s, India chose a quasi-alignment path with the USSR, the most prominent of potential enemies of the Western allies, including Japan. Nehru's daughter, Prime Minister Indira Gandhi, concluded an Indo–Soviet Treaty of Friendship and Cooperation in 1971 to prevent China and other external powers from interfering in Southern Asia immediately before the third war with Pakistan. Third, Indo–Soviet cooperation was ranged against the strengthened US–China–Pakistan relationship after the Soviet invasion of Afghanistan at the end of 1979. In such a situation, India was not a direct enemy, but became a diplomatically

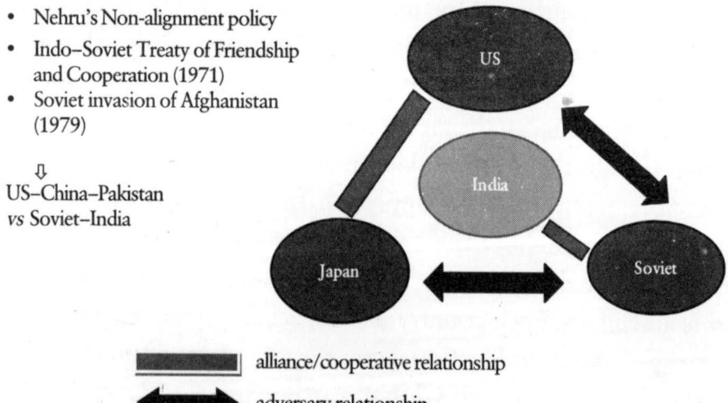

FIGURE 5.1: 'ESTRANGED' JAPAN–INDIA RELATIONSHIP DURING THE COLD WAR.

distant country for Japan. India remained off the Japanese diplomatic radar screen since then.

The collapse of the Cold War order was therefore good news for the Japan–India relationship: it has enabled Japan to approach India. Actually, the United States, an alliance partner of Japan, undertook strategic dialogue with India immediately after India's nuclear tests in May 1998. President Clinton paid a historical visit to New Delhi in March 2000.[2] Even the United States had begun to regard India as an important future partner. Japanese Prime Minister Yoshiro Mori's visit to New Delhi in August of the same year took place under these circumstances.[3]

If we can regard the collapse of the Cold War order as a 'necessary condition' for Japanese approach toward India, its 'factor of sufficiency' was the shift of power relations in Asia and the world. First China and then India had remained on a plateau for so long, harbouring their great potential and enhancing their hard powers. Their rapidly rising importance in the post-Cold War world necessitated major changes in power relations. In contrast, the national power of Japan has been waning.[4]

When Prime Minister Mori visited New Delhi in 2000, however, it seems that this reality was not recognized widely in Japan. It was not until 2005 that conditions had ripened sufficiently. Mori's successor, Prime Minister Junichiro Koizumi, postponed his scheduled visit to New Delhi, so long heavily occupied with the other foreign policy tasks in Afghanistan, Iraq, and North Korea, as well as demanding domestic issues. Security dialogues and Military-to-Military (MM) talks were not held annually but were instead held ad hoc, and only a few times. In that environment of stagnant political and security relations, the development of trade and investment relations also continued to lag.

THE RISE OF THE 'CHINA THREAT' THEORY IN JAPAN

The stagnant situation after Prime Minister Mori's visit in 2000 changed completely in the spring of 2005, when 'China threat' theory became popular in Japan.

As a very populist leader, Koizumi took a hard stand as prime minister, and the Japan–China relationship soured over the history textbook issue, visits to the Yasukuni Shrine, and the Senkaku Islands issue. No official bilateral summit meetings had been held between the countries, with the exception that Prime Minister Koizumi had visited Beijing only once in the early days of his administration. Chinese government and media did not mask their incredulity toward Koizumi. However, it was not until the spring of 2005 that more massive anti-Japanese riots occurred throughout China. Many young Chinese demonstrators who shouted anti-Japanese slogans attacked and damaged Japanese business enterprises, the embassy, and consulates. Moreover, China blocked Japanese ambitions to become a permanent member of United Nations Security Council (UNSC) along with India, Germany, and Brazil. These anti-Japanese movements in China undoubtedly stimulated anti-Chinese sentiment and 'China threat' theory in Japan.

As a result of the rising 'China threat' theory, not a few Japanese politicians, media and opinion leaders, especially nationalists, suddenly began to insist that Japan should forge a strong partnership or even alliance with India to address the looming discomfort with neighbouring China.[5] Japanese people recognized the 'strategic' significance of India in politics and security as well as in business at this time. Nevertheless, one must keep in mind that most Japanese people did not seem to have evaluated India itself but evaluated it in terms of its value as a 'card' to be played against China. An eminent researcher, Hiroshi Sato, properly describes the Japanese perception of India as 'derivative'.[6] In other words, Japan would not have realized the diplomatic importance of India without a China factor.

Japan has become keen on involvement with India in political and security terms since then. Cooperation in political and security matters between the countries, which had remained a mere symbol for boosting slowly developing economic relations, has become substantial now. At last, an Indo-boom has blossomed in every field in Japan.

It is not so difficult to present that evidence in light of subsequent developments. In April 2005, Prime Minister Koizumi visited New

Delhi to hold a bilateral summit meeting with his counterpart, Prime Minister Manmohan Singh, immediately after Chinese Prime Minister Wen Jiabao's visit to New Delhi. Three important points must be mentioned in relation to the joint statement of Singh–Koizumi meeting. First, the new phrase, 'strategic' was added officially to the established global partnership, as a result of which both leaders declared the 'Strategic orientation of Japan–India Global Partnership'. Second is the more emphasized shared value in the document, i.e. not only democracy, but human rights and pluralism, and also an open society and the rule of law, none of which China shares with Japan and India. Third, the Japanese side clearly supported India's membership in the East Asia Summit, whose framework had been under discussion at that time.[7] Japan was believed to be keen on involving India in the East Asia Summit and the future East Asian Community to check the growing Chinese influence. Since then, annual prime-minister-level meetings have been held alternately in the two capitals (Table 5.1).

TABLE 5.1: BILATERAL SUMMIT MEETINGS BETWEEN JAPAN AND INDIA AFTER 1990

April 1990	Kaifu's visit to New Delhi.
June 1992	Rao's visit to Tokyo.
August 2000	Mori's visit to New Delhi: 'Global Partnership'
December 2001	Vajpayee's visit to Tokyo.
April 2005	Koizumi's visit to New Delhi: 'Strategic Orientation of Global Partnership'.
December 2006	Singh's visit to Tokyo: 'Strategic and Global Partnership'.
August 2007	Abe's visit to New Delhi
October 2008	Singh's visit to Tokyo: 'Joint Declaration on Security Co-operation'.
December 2009	Hatoyama's visit to New Delhi: 'Action Plan to Advance Security Co-operation'.
October 2010	Singh's visit to Tokyo.
December 2011	Noda's visit to New Delhi.

After the Koizumi cabinet, the more nationalistic team of Prime Minister Shinzo Abe and Foreign Minister Taro Aso regarded India more clearly as a counterweight to growing Chinese influence.[8] India has become an indispensable partner in their espoused new concepts of 'value-oriented diplomacy' and 'Arc of Freedom and Prosperity'.[9] Prime Minister Abe did not hesitate to emphasize the shared values which Japan did not share with China when he made a speech at the Joint Session of the Indian Parliament in August 2007.[10]

To make an 'Arc of Freedom and Prosperity', he also proposed the so-called 'four-nation alliance' or 'four-way framework' for strategic cooperation among the democratic powers in the Asia–Pacific region, which involved Japan, the United States, Australia, and India. His quadrilateral initiative crystallized as the first official-level security consultation on the sidelines of the ASEAN Regional Forum (ARF) security policy meeting in Manila in May 2007 and the massive joint naval exercise, 'Malabar 07-2' by the four nations listed above plus Singapore, in the Bay of Bengal.

The quadrilateral framework attracted strong protests from China. The Government of China issued démarches to each of the participants seeking their respective statements of purposes behind their meetings in the days leading up to the Manila meeting.[11] Most of the media in Japan, and in the world described the move as a strategy to warn against China in spite of each official side's denial of such an intention. Indeed, the Chinese side doubted the United States and Japan, and feared that they were fashioning a 'China containment' strategy involving India.[12] Later, US Secretary of State Condoleezza Rice urged Japan to exercise caution about Abe's framework over concerns of irritating China.[13]

The political and security relationship forged during Koizumi and Abe's tenure has been maintained and strengthened since. In October 2008, when Prime Minister Singh visited Tokyo, he announced the third 'Joint Declaration on Security Cooperation', this time for Japan, following declarations made in relation to the United States and Australia. Since that year, Security Dialogues and Military-to-Military talks have been held annually (Table 5.2).

TABLE 5.2: MEETINGS OF THE JAPAN-INDIA SECURITY DIALOGUE AND THE MILITARY-MILITARY TALKS

Security Dialogue	Military–Military talk
July 2001 First: Tokyo	July 2001 First: Tokyo
January 2004 Second: New Delhi	March 2005 Second: Tokyo
March 2005 Third: Tokyo	February 2006 Third: New Delhi
February 2006 Fourth: New Delhi	February 2008 Fourth: Tokyo
February 2008 Fifth: Tokyo	February 2009 Fifth: New Delhi
February 2009 Sixth: New Delhi	April 2010 Sixth: Tokyo
April 2010 Seventh: Tokyo	May 2011 Seventh: New Delhi
May 2011 Eighth: New Delhi	

Even after the change of government in Japan to the Democratic Party of Japan (DPJ), no change occurred in the policy of assigning importance to India. Yukio Hatoyama, the first prime minister of DPJ rule, visited New Delhi immediately before the end of 2009 in spite of his hectic schedule to maintain the pattern of annual summit meetings with India established by Liberal Democratic Party (LDP) governments.[14] Prime Minister Singh and Prime Minister Hatoyama agreed with the framework of Subcabinet/Senior Official level annual meeting 2 plus 2 to advance security cooperation. The first 2 plus 2 meeting was held in New Delhi in July 2010.

Hatoyama's successor, Prime Minister Naoto Kan, maintained and strengthened the policy of approaching India. He ultimately decided to enter into negotiations with India to conclude a civil nuclear cooperation agreement despite expanded hesitation to make a nuclear deal with non-NPT and nuclear armed India as the only country that had experienced a nuclear attack.[15] When Prime Minister Singh visited Japan in October 2010, the China issue had become the hidden main topic in the summit meeting. Actually, at just around that time, diplomatic ties between Japan and China worsened sharply again because of the Senkaku Islands issue. Prime Minister Kan sought joint ventures in rare earth minerals with India because China had restricted their exports to Japan after the Japanese Coast Guard detained a Chinese fishing boat captain who had violated 'Japanese' territorial waters. Both leaders were reported to have discussed how to address China at the meeting.[16] Prime Minister Kan recognized India's significance clearly in the face of the diplomatic impasse over China.

It was natural to regard India as an important strategic partner to address China for Prime Minister Yoshihiko Noda, known as more conservative, right-wing, and hawkish than his two predecessors. His government made a decision to resume negotiations on civil nuclear cooperation with India in spite of mounting concern against nuclear power following the Japanese nuclear disaster in 2011. He also fulfilled a promise to pay a visit to New Delhi at the end of that year in spite of his busy schedule.

DISAGREEMENT BETWEEN JAPAN AND INDIA OVER CHINA

As described above, in Japan, a growing trend of using India as a strategic card against the 'China threat' has become apparent.[17] Such Japanese thinking, however, might not serve its interests well because of the existence of several important differences between Japan and India with respect to China.

Since spring 2005, most Japanese politicians, media, and opinion leaders have not hesitated to describe China as a threat. The 'China threat' theory has been emphasized even though the term of 'threat' has been carefully avoided in official parlance in Japanese annual white papers on defence as well as its blue book on diplomacy.[18] In December 2005, the president of DPJ, which was in opposition at that time, Seiji Maehara described China as a 'realistic threat' or 'realistic concern' when he made a speech at the United States' think tank, the Center for Strategic and International Studies, whereas his colleague Katsuya Okada said that China should be regarded as a 'potential threat'. [19] Asked for a comment on Maehara's statement, the LDP Foreign Minister Taro Aso told reporters that China was becoming a 'considerable threat' referring to Chinese increased military expenditure and nuclear weapons.[20] 'China threat' theory has dominated Japanese discourse since then.

In contrast, most Indian strategists have tended to describe China not as a 'threat' or 'enemy' but as a 'rival' or 'competitor'. Some divisions of opinion remain in relation to India–China–Japan relations among Indian strategists.[21] However, as Rajaram Panda writes, India does not see China as a 'threat'.[22] Some 'hawks' such as former Defence Minister George Fernandes, who openly branded China as 'potential enemy no. 1', and Professor Brahma Chellaney, a leading strategist who appreciated Abe's quadrilateral initiative, might use the word 'enemy' or 'threat'.[23] Nevertheless, it seems that their number and influence are much more limited than in Japan. Stephen P. Cohen and Sunil Dasgupta allege that '[t]he hardliners in India's strategic community, alarmed by the China threat, have been largely marginalized'.[24]

Actually, India has been reluctant to become involved in Abe's quadrilateral initiative. Prime Minister Singh explained to Chinese premier Hu Jintao at the G8 outreach summit in Germany in June 2007 that 'there's no question of ganging up against China' and assured that the group was not a military alliance responding to China's articulated fears.[25] India has been cautious about making China uncomfortable by overemphasizing a 'China threat'.[26] India's reluctant stance has led to the disappearance of a quadrilateral meeting and exercises with the fall from power of the conservative trio of US President George W. Bush, Australian Prime Minister John Howard, and Japanese Prime Minister Shinzo Abe, with the exception of bilateral efforts. Later, Abe's initiative seemed to have been reactivated by the launch of the first-ever Japan–US–India trilateral strategic dialogue held in December 2011, but the new framework floated by the United States was more low-keyed and played down by each participant.

Some disagreement between Japan and India over China factors can be analysed in terms of diplomacy and security. In the area of diplomacy, we should not miss the fact that India and China are 'the two biggest developing countries in the world', as emphasized in the Joint Declaration at the time of Hu Jintao's visit to New Delhi in November 2006.[27] In fact, India's interests often coincide with those of China as new rising states with a huge area and population, even though it does not share domestic political values with Communist China. Therefore, India will naturally shy away from showing overt hostility to China if it behaves pragmatically, and not ideologically, as it does.

India has cooperated so closely with China over some key issues in the global economic order, such as the United Nations Framework Convention on Climate Change (UNFCCC), WTO, and IMF. Indo–Chinese cooperation on UNFCCC is widely known. India and China have fought against accepting their legally binding emissions reduction targets, which might curb their growth, attaching historical responsibilities to developed countries. Having thwarted target setting of their gas reduction in the COP13 Bali conference in December 2007 hand in hand, both countries signed a Memorandum of Agreement on climate change and even formed a new group, BASIC, with Brazil and South Africa before the COP15 Copenhagen meeting in December 2009. In agricultural negotiations at Doha Development Round of WTO, India and China, heading G20 developing countries, insisted that developed countries such as the United States reduce their farm subsidies while their own weak domestic sectors remain protected. On the stage of the IMF too, India and China struggled jointly for reforms to the fund's voting power. Cooperation with China on these issues seems indispensable to India's further growth in Asia and the world, while preventing its isolation in the international community.

In contrast, in Japan, China's cooperation in these global issues has not been regarded as necessary in spite of the great amount of bilateral trade and investment. The relationship between Japan and China remains as a 'Mutually Beneficial Relationship on Common Strategic Interests' at best, which suggests that both 'are partners who cooperate together and are not mutual threats'[28] although the Indo–Chinese relationship has already developed to a 'Strategic and Cooperative Partnership for Peace and Prosperity'.

Next, in the area of security, it remains doubtful whether Japan and India really share any specific threat perception against China in spite of the common vague image of a 'China threat' (Table 5.3). Japan and India have had to face their assertive neighbour China and have apparently been confronted by growing pressure over respective border issues.[29] Nevertheless, India has had to face China directly over a 3500 km land border, whereas Japan has the Sea of Japan and the East China Sea with no land border with China. India must be regarded not only as a maritime nation but also as a continental state if Japan is a maritime state.[30]

Related to the Chinese assertive activities around respective countries, China has been expanding its influence in the Indian Ocean, which India had assumed as its own domain through the ages in spite of the United States' overwhelming presence thereafter Second World War. It is often said that the strategy of 'String of Pearls' by which China has embarked on constructing huge port facilities in Gwadar (Pakistan), Hambantota (Sri Lanka), Chittagong (Bangladesh), and Sittwe (Myanmar) as well as deepening diplomatic and military cooperation is a Chinese enterprise designed to encircle India. India has become overtly sensitive about such Chinese proactive activities in the Indian Ocean, surrounding itself in terms of national sentiment and security.[31] The Indian Ocean is apparently the main and almost only region where India has a vital maritime interest.[32] From the perspective of Japan, however, the more irritant activities of China are apparent in the East China Sea, where India has few stakes.[33] The recent Indian approach toward Vietnam might engender extension of its traditional security perimeter, stretching from Aden to Malacca, to include the South China Sea and the Western Pacific.[34] Some

TABLE 5.3: DIFFERENCE IN CHINESE THREAT PERCEPTION

	Japan	India
Border	Sea	Land
Indian Ocean (String of Pearls)	Secondary	Vital
East China Sea	Vital	Secondary
China–Pakistan	Secondary	Vital
China–North Korea	Vital	Secondary

Indian strategists might have had some hand in suggesting a new geopolitical term – Indo–Pacific – that US Secretary of State Hillary Clinton used.[35] Nevertheless, no sign of India's interest in the East China Sea is apparent yet.

Regarding land security with respect to China, India has long viewed the China–Pakistan economic, diplomatic, and military nexus as an important concern. Indian leadership has believed that Pakistan could not have developed its nuclear weapons and missiles without Chinese assistance. It is often said that China has been hesitant to put international pressure upon Pakistan not to export terrorism to the Indian domain.[36] India has remained irritated about Chinese 'all-weather' support to Pakistan. Some Indians argue that China has also supported anti-Indian governments and extreme elements in other Indian neighbours, to a lesser degree.[37] However, again, for the Japanese side, the Chinese connection with North Korea is more worrisome than the China–Pakistan connection. In Japan, China is believed to have played a role mainly as a guardian of North Korea in the United Nations Security Council and Six-party talks on nuclear issues.

Considering the difference in concrete security threats from China, it also remains doubtful whether Japan and India can remove or reduce respective threats from China through their bilateral cooperation. Japan has neither the intent nor the capability to address India's threat perception, the threat from a long land border with China, Chinese 'encirclement', hegemonic activities in the Indian Ocean, or Chinese 'all-weather' support to Pakistan. Its declining national power and inward-looking popular sentiment as well as pacifist constitution prevent it from playing a proactive role in the area far from its soil and will continue to prevent such a role. India will attach more weight to relations with the United States on this score.[38] Related to Japan's threat perception, Chinese offensive action over the Senkaku Islands issue, Chinese hegemonic activities in the East China Sea, and Chinese role as a guardian of North Korea, India might have greater capability, as seen in its recent naval build-up. India has an aircraft carrier (Japan does not) and will have more in the coming decade. Nevertheless, the intent of India is not directed eastward but rather southward, as described above. Regarded in this light, the United States, with which Japan has maintained a firm alliance for almost 70 years, is expected from a Japanese standpoint to be a more reliable partner to address the 'China threat'.[39]

CONCLUSION

As Harsh V. Pant has analysed, a sub-current mindset, not only in Japan but also in India, is to consolidate against China – an entity that must be faced and countered in the near future. He writes that '[t]he rise of China is a major factor in the evolution of Indo–Japanese ties'.[40] Actually, the 'China threat' theory might have triggered substantial political and security cooperation between Japan and India in spring 2005. However, it is readily apparent that overemphasizing the 'China threat' has not helped to deepen bilateral cooperation because of different diplomatic and security situations. In this environment, the United States must be regarded as a more important and crucial partner for both countries to address China in terms of intent and capability.

The Japan–India relationship has been elevated to status as a 'Strategic and Global Partnership' since Prime Minister Singh's visit to Tokyo in December 2006.[41] However, if both countries were to cooperate strategically in the global stage, it would be inevitable for both, especially for Japan, to overcome the facile slogan of 'China threat' theory. How to address their common neighbour, whose influence is growing on the global stage now will become a touchstone of 'Strategic and Global Partnership'. In spite of some different diplomatic and security situations over China, both countries will be able work in concert to encourage arising China to be a responsible stakeholder. In this process, it will also be beneficial to make a concerted effort to build a political and security architecture in Asia that includes Japan, India, and China to relieve concern about China issues.

In addition to the China issue, Japan and India will be able to cooperate to eradicate poverty, terrorism, and piracy on the global stage. Cooperation that focuses upon these fields is not only possible; it will also deepen the 'Strategic and Global Partnership' between both countries and contribute to the stable environment supporting growth and survival for each nation.

NOTES

1. The Japanese army did not invade India during Second World War, with the exception of an abortive enterprise to capture Imphal, a north-eastern city of India. After the end of the war, the Indian people expressed compassion toward atomic-bomb ravaged Japan, and Justice Radhabinod Pal spoke for Japanese 'war criminals' in the Tokyo Tribunal, which was well known to Japanese.
2. Although the Clinton administration imposed economic sanctions on nuclear-testing India and Pakistan, US Deputy State Secretary Strobe Talbott was engaged in as many as 14 meetings with his Indian counterpart, External Minister Jaswant Singh, during the two and half years from June 1998 to September 2000. See Strobe Talbott, *Engaging India*, The Brookings Institution, 2004.
3. Prime Minister Yoshiro Mori himself and Japanese Ambassador to India Hiroshi Hirabayashi, expressed appreciation for his leadership related to this visit despite the bureaucrats' hesitation. See the dialogue record between Mori and Hirabayashi published in the organ of Liberal Democratic Party: *Gekkan Jiyuuminshu*, December 2007. However, some doubt remains about whether Prime Minister Mori, suddenly elevated to his position as Prime Minister in April 2000, really was able to play a leading role in his visit to New Delhi in August of the same year. Pant stresses not only Mori's personal factor but also the structural factor. 'The US has also encouraged Japan to forge close political and strategic ties with neighbouring states such as India and Australia.' See Harsh V. Pant, 'India–Japan Relations: A Slow, but Steady, Transformation' in Sumit Ganguly, ed., *India's Foreign Policy: Retrospect and Prospect*, Oxford University Press, 2010, p. 211. Actually, Ambassador Hirabayashi admits that he really felt the necessity for mending relations with India and asked Prime Minister

Keizo Obuchi, Mori's predecessor, to visit New Delhi when he saw US President Clinton's visit to New Delhi in his article published later. See Hiroshi Hirabayashi, 'Kokko 60 Syunen: Nichiin Kankei wo Kaiko shi Tenbou suru', *Contemporary India Forum*, vol. 12, Winter 2012, pp. 11-12. http://www.japan-india.com/pdf/forum/48-1.pdf.

4. According to the well-known Goldman Sachs report, the Chinese GDP, which surpassed the Japanese figure in 2010 will become the world's largest economy, leaving the United States behind by 2041. The Indian GDP, which is less than one-third of Japanese GDP in 2010, will also surpass the latter by 2032. See Dominic Wilson and Roopa Purushothaman, *Dreaming with BRICs: The Path to 2050*, Goldman Sachs, 2003, p. 10. The economic growth also supports increased military expenditures. China, with military expenditures that are by no means transparent, spends at least twice as much of its budget on its military as Japan. Indian military expenditures, which amount to three-fourths of the Japanese figure in 2009, will surpass Japanese expenditures in the very near future. See Takenori Horimoto, 'Indo wo Meguru Nihon no Ugoki: Juncyou na Nichiin Anzenhosyoukankei to Kongo', in Masashi Nishihara and Takenori Horimoto, eds., *Gunjitaikokuka suru Indo*, Akishobou, 2010, p. 95.
5. *Sankei*, a prominent Japanese conservative and nationalistic newspaper wrote in an editorial that it was necessary to enhance the Japan–India partnership in wide-ranging fields in order to counter Chinese hegemonic movements. See *Sankei Shimbun*, 13 December 2006.
6. See Hiroshi Sato, 'Taiingaikou Higashiajiakyoudoutai ni Indo wo Makikonda Nihon: Haigo ni Bei no Kage', *Ekonomisuto*, 10 April 2006.
7. See http://meaindia.nic.in/mystart.php?id=53059479.
8. Brahma Chellaney, a leading Indian strategist who looked critically at China, gave high praise to Prime Minister Abe as follows: 'Japan has never had a head of government so interested in forging close ties with India as Abe'. Brahma Chellaney, 'Japan, India: Natural Allies', *The Japan Times*, 16 August 2007.
9. Shinzo Abe, *Utsukushii Kuni he*, Bungeishunjuu, 2006; Taro Aso, *Totetsumonai Nippon*, Shinchosha, 2007 and *Jiyuu to Hanei no Ko*, Gentousya, 2008.

10. For the speech titled 'Confluence of the Two Seas' by Prime Minister Abe in the Indian Parliament, see http://www.mofa.go.jp/region/asia-paci/pmv0708/speech-2.html.
11. *The Hindu*, 14 June 2007.
12. Commentary of *People's Daily*, 21 April 2007.
13. *Mainichi Shimbun*, 10 August 2007.
14. At that time Prime Minister Hatoyama was tied up with mountains of internal problems as well as diplomatic issues related to the United States and China. In the middle of December 2009, his Chief Cabinet Secretary suggested the possibility of shelving his visiting plan to New Delhi within that year. See *Yomiuri Shimbun* 15 December 2009. Finally, he was compelled to resign as a result of his failure to resolve the dispute over the Futenma US base in Okinawa in June 2010.
15. Until the Fukushima nuclear accident three rounds of talks on nuclear pact had been held since the first meeting in Tokyo in June 2010 in the early days of Kan's government.
16. *Asahi Shimbun*, 26 October 2010; *The Hindu*, 26 October 2010.
17. On the recent downright point of this view, for instance, see the symposium report titled 'Stand Against China by Japan–Indo Alliance'. Yoshiko Sakurai, Shinzo Abe, Tadae Takubo and Yoichi Shimada, 'Nichiindoumei de Chuugoku ni Tachimukae', *Will*, no. 76, April 2011, pp. 196-209.
18. In the wake of the Senkaku crisis in 2010, the term 'assertive' was used officially to refer to China's response to the territorial issues for the first time in the white paper on defense published in 2011. Nevertheless, no descriptions of 'threat' or 'concern' were included. *Defense of Japan 2011*, pp. 72-92.
19. President Maehara chose the more modest word 'concern' when he made a speech in English, although the term 'threat (*kyoui*)' was written in his original Japanese manuscript. *Asahi Shimbun*, 21 December 2005.
20. *Mainichi Shimbun*, 23 December 2005.
21. Shamshad Ahmad Khan, 'Indo–Japan Strategic Cooperation: Issues, Expectations and Challenges', *Comparative Studies on Regional Powers*, no. 6, 2011, p. 25. http://src-h.slav.hokudai.ac.jp/rp/publications/no06/02_Khan.pdf.
22. Rajaram Panda, 'Changing Dynamics of India–Japan Relations: Future Trends', *Comparative Studies on Regional Powers*, no. 6,

2011, p. 8. http://src-h.slav.hokudai.ac.jp/rp/publications/no06/01_Panda.pdf.

23. Brahma Chellaney, '"Quad Initiative": An Inharmonious Concert of Democracies', *The Japan Times*, 19 July 2007. Chellaney has maintained a stern attitude toward Communist China consistently.
24. Stephen P. Cohen and Sunil Dasgupta, *Arming without Aiming: India's Military Modernization*, The Brookings Institution, 2010, p. 13.
25. *The Times of India*, 29 June 2007.
26. Rajaram Panda, op. cit., p. 15.
27. http://meaindia.nic.in/mystart.php?id=530511988.
28. On the difference between Strategic Partnership and Mutually Beneficial Relationship Based on Common Strategic Interests from a Chinese point of view, see Emi Mifune, 'Senryakuteki Gokeikankeito ha Nanika: Kanseiken no Rikaibusoku de Roteishita Niccyukankei', *JANET* (http://janet.jw.jiji.com), Jiji Press, 8 December 2010.
29. Just one year before Japanese government became embroiled with difficulties with China over the Senkaku Islands issue, border tensions rose between India and China in the wake of the report on Chinese People's Liberation Army's intrusions into Arunachal Pradesh in Summer 2009. China claims sovereignty over both the Senkaku Islands and Arunachal Pradesh, but does not control them effectively. A leading young Indian analyst pointed out that the conciliatory stance toward China by the US Obama government led to the Chinese 'distinctly aggressive stance *vis-a-vis* India'. Harsh V. Pant, 'China's Challenge Moves India to Expect the Worst', *The Japan Times*, 28 September 2009.
30. India itself is clearly cognizant of this situation. 'India Enjoys a Strategic Location with Reference to Continental Asia and the Indian Ocean Region', *The Annual Report 2010–11 of Ministry of Defence*, p. 2.
31. For instance, see Brahma Chellaney, *Asian Juggernaut: The Rise of China, India and Japan*, HarperCollins Publishers, 2006, pp. 197–200.
32. The former Indian Ambassador, Rajiv Bhartia argues that the Indian Ocean has been kept in mind in India's policy-making. 'A Vision for the Indian Ocean', *The Hindu*, 15 October 2011.

33. The Indian Defence Annual Report includes no reference to the East China Sea, but a detailed description of the Chinese activities there is included in the Japanese Defense White Paper, which has no reference to the Indian Ocean regarding China. See *The Annual Report 2010–11 of Ministry of Defence* and *Defense of Japan 2011*.
34. C. Raja Mohan, 'Looking beyond Malacca', *The Indian Express*, 11 October 2011. The Oil and Natural Gas Corporation (ONGC) Videsh, a state-owned Indian company, agreed to explore oil in the disputed marine area between China and Vietnam in co-operation with its Vietnamese counterpart in October 2011, which provoked a Chinese reaction. The relationship between India and Vietnam has been expanding and deepening.
35. Shyam Saran, 'Mapping the Indo-Pacific', *The Indian Express*, 29 October 2011. Saran is a former foreign secretary.
36. According to the United States' cable disclosed by the WikiLeaks, China 'at the behest of Pakistan', has blocked the United Nations Security Council from listing Jamaat-ud-Dawa, a front for the militant group Lashkar-e-Taiba under the UNSC Resolution 1267, until the Mumbai terror attacks in November 2008. *The Hindu*, 7 December 2010.
37. Brahma Chellaney, 'Dealing with China's Increasing Assertiveness', *The Economic Times*, 17 September 2010.
38. As a leading strategist in India writes, 'long-term defence co-operation with the United States could significantly ameliorate India's relative weakness' against China. C. Raja Mohan and Alyssa Ayres, 'Situating the Realignment', in Alyssa Ayres and C. Raja Mohan, eds., *Power Realignment in Asia: China, India and the United States*, Sage, 2009, p. 317. Moreover, a study conducted by a New Delhi-based think tank which assessed India's strategic partnership with the United States, Russia, France, the United Kingdom, Germany, and Japan, sees greater potential for development of defence cooperation with the United States than Japan. *India's Strategic Partners: A Comparative Assessment*, Foundation for National Security Research, November 2011. http://www.fnsr.org/indias-strategic-partners-a-comparative-assessment.pdf.
39. Prime Minister Koizumi and President George W. Bush clearly affirmed that 'robust US–Japan cooperation embraces the dynamism

of China and helps to maintain peace and tranquillity in north-east Asia' at their summit meeting in June 2006, but no official document or statement on Japan–India relations has referred to the China issue. See http://www.mofa.go.jp/region/n-america/us/summit0606.html.

40. Harsh V. Pant, 'India–Japan Relations: A Slow, but Steady, Transformation' in Sumit Ganguly, ed., *India's Foreign Policy: Retrospect and Prospect*, Oxford University Press, 2010, p. 212.
41. Japan–India Strategic and Global Partnership, http://www.mofa.go.jp/region/asia-paci/india/pdfs/joint0612.pdf.

CHAPTER 6

US–Japan–India Trilogue: The China Factor

SWARAN SINGH

Rise of China has been the trigger for US officials and experts revisiting their interest and initiatives across the Asia–Pacific region. This is equally true of most other major Asian powers who have also been reviewing their China policies; and by extension their foreign policies in general. Beginning of the end of Cold War, accompanied by withdrawal of Soviet forces from Vietnam and Afghanistan and withdrawal of US forces from Subic Bay in the Philippines had created this so-called 'power-vacuum' that was to make China's rise especially noticeable. China's immediate neighbours have been particularly preoccupied with this rapid transformation trying to grapple with new formulations around a 'China-model' and 'Beijing-consensus'.

China too has made efforts to reinvent itself as also to reorganize its foreign relations. It has been seriously trying to engage afresh all major players across Asia working hard to appreciate their sensitivities. Nevertheless, there remains widespread concern regarding China becoming increasingly assertive, ensuring that its foreign policy remains geared to serve its core national interests and objectives. This has resulted in a rising China-consciousness amongst major powers leading even to occasional hyperactivity – like the US–Japan–India trilogue – with critical implications for the emerging Asian security and development architecture.

It is in this backdrop that this chapter seeks to examine the triggers, visions and emerging contours of the US–Japan–India trilateral dialogue and to crystal gaze its emerging trajectory and implications for the Asia–Pacific region. The central running thread of this examination remains China that has since come to be the *primus-*

inter-pares amongst Asian powers, and its rise is seen pregnant with systemic implications.

ENGAGING A RISING CHINA

At the end of the Cold War, South Korea was one of the first country to make a major turnaround and evolve closer cooperation with Beijing since the early 1990s. Popularly described as 'China-fever' of the South Korea's elite, this U-turn was expected to not only marginalize the historic China–North Korea axis but also introduce a thaw in North Korea-South Korea rivalry, making Korean peninsula less dangerous.[1] Measured in statistics, this change was to result in China–South Korea bilateral trade rising up from mere $3.2 billion in 1991 to $207 billion for 2010 and the two have set a target of taking it to $300 billion by 2015.[2]

Association of Southeast Asian Nations (ASEAN) likewise also turned around its China policy from early 1990s. Especially after Beijing's proactive engagement of ASEAN during the East Asian financial crisis of 1997, China–ASEAN trade witnessed a rapid rise from a mere $8 billion in 1991 to $230 billion for 2008, making China the largest trading partner of ASEAN.[3] Their bilateral ties has especially picked up momentum since the start of their Free Trade Agreement from 1 January 2010 and it was expected to reach $350 billion at the end of 2011 and to $500 billion by 2015.[4] China, as a result, has come to be a major influence across all ASEAN-led forums, initiatives and deliberations to the peril of other major stakeholders in the Asia–Pacific.

Other major powers like Australia, Japan, India and Vietnam, however, have had mixed results. Japan and India are especially seen as major economies of Asia and both continue to see the rise of China as their major concern. But their efforts at engaging Beijing have been full of complications, including occasional political eruptions and diplomatic showdowns. No doubt this has partly triggered Japan–India *rapprochement* that has witnessed their strategic engagement witnessing an upswing while their bilateral trade with China has also been rising at a rapid pace. Beijing indeed has come to increasingly attach certain scepticism to Japan–India parlays with Chinese media often over-reacting to Japan–India summits calling them aimed at containing China.[5]

Australia and Vietnam have also been occasionally seriously courting China. At least during the years of Kevin Rudd premiership, Australia was known for having witnessed rise in the 'Asia-literate Australia' and their trade was to show a rise from about $3 billion in 1991 to reaching nearly $100 billion for 2010.[6] Vietnam has made inroads in building a 'strategic cooperative partnership' with China based on the 'four good' spirit including good neighbours, good friends, good comrades and good partners.[7] But, it is these four countries – namely India, Australia, South Korea and Japan that are listed as 'US friends and allies' – that continue to face scepticism of Beijing. All four also have had mixed results in engaging rising China. Beijing remains especially sceptical of US motives in Asia–Pacific and sees it behind regional power initiatives, especially those where US also seeks active participation.

US RE-ENGAGEMENT ACROSS ASIA–PACIFIC

As regards the US, its conventional hub-and-spokes strategy of military alliances and defence cooperation arrangements with major regional powers continue to underwrite its strategy across Asia–Pacific.[8] More recently, however, the Bush presidency (2000-8) was to witness visible increase in its military prowess and penchant to use force to resolve international issues. As a result, this behaviour of the sole surviving superpower engenders a subdued caution amongst all major powers of the Asia–Pacific. But the fact that expensive US military interventions did not result in resolving issues and creating sustainable peace has re-enforced this sentiment and lent credence to anti-American formulations especially amongst the media and civil society activists. Recent economic slowdown since 2008 has only made the situation favourable to Beijing's indulgent benevolence in engaging the region. All this has made the US rethink and seek alternative strategies of re-engaging regional powers and forums privileging soft power and diplomacy.[9]

Inside China – which is often viewed as the second pillar in a potential cold war replay of adversarial relations or even in situation of G2 type partnership mode – both these possibilities of US engagement are seen as aimed at circumventing, if not countervailing China's rise. Beijing accordingly has tried it best to remain cautious yet cooperative in its diplomatic interface with US which has been variously described by experts as hedging or bandwagoning strategy.[10] US, on the other hand, have been trying to co-opt and privilege China at least in Asian affairs. But its opposite is also equally true as most of US parleys with other Asian powers remain aimed at ensuring restrain in China's increasingly assertive behaviour across the Asia–Pacific. This is commonplace therefore that Beijing views any mechanism, like the recent US–Japan–India trilateral parleys, as motivated and anti-China in its origins and orientation. It is also equally true that while all these Asian powers, including US, remain determined to ensure restraint on China's rising assertiveness, none of these are ready to confront China upfront, especially not at individual one-to-one level.

It is in view of this inherent limitation of US engagement of Asia–Pacific, generating both cohesive and divisive sentiments at the same time, and a rising China being at the centre of this unfolding Asian reality that this paper seeks to now specifically examine the contours of this emerging US–Japan–India trilogue and assess its impact on Asian relations in general. The following paragraphs also examine the logic that India – a peer civilization and rising neighbouring power of a billion plus people – has an important role to play in this Asian transformation; and how, it is partly this increasing recognition of emerging India that explains both US and Japan seriously engaging New Delhi across various forums including this trilogue which once again makes Asian politico-strategic triangles such a focus of strategic discourses.

ANATOMY OF ASIAN TRIANGLES

Triangles and quadrilaterals, strategic or otherwise, have been the way of life for post-Cold War Asian relations. From time to time, experts and officials have conceived of and launched various triangles that have witnessed evolving pace and shifting focus with fluctuating, activism and efficacy generating various actors and models for Asian relations for the twenty-first century. However, only few of these have been persistent enough, especially when we restrict our choices to only politico-strategic forums amongst major Asian powers. To confine ourselves to these politico-strategic 'triangles' alone, the most visible of these in Asia include US–Japan–Australia trilogue, US–Japan-South Korea, and the Russia–China–India strategic triangle though experts have also written and talked of US–China–India, China–India–Pakistan, US–India–Australia triangles and so on.[11]

Most of these Asian triangles have a few common features. All of these Asian triangles, for example, share following uniformities: three legs of all of these triangles share a strongly asymmetric relationship; all of these feel compelled to re-iterate how these are not aimed at any third country; and, how partners in all of these triangles also have their own share of mutual suspicions; and finally, how these triangular formats are so often meant to resolve their internal trust deficit while projecting a cohesive picture to those who do not fit into their scheme of things. Then of course each partner in each of these triangles is circumvented with multiple domestic constituencies and stakeholders that also influence their foreign policies.[12] In practice, therefore, most of these only facilitate three sets of bilateral relations which also remain the basis for most of their trilateral deliberations.

Amongst these Asian triangles, the US–Japan–India has been the most recent addition which seems to gain credence based on the recent upsurge in their bilateral *rapprochement* which has earned it certain solemnness. The curiosity can also be partly explained from perspective of this being viewed as a mechanism for putting restraint on rising China's adventurism – a common sentiment that binds together most of China's neighbours, including these three powers. This US–Japan-India triangle was formally announced in an US–Japan Strategic dialogue in Tokyo in April 2011, heralding their annual trilateral dialogue amongst their foreign ministries and their first trilateral meeting took place in Washington DC on 19 December 2011. No doubt, most of their official discussions on this had occurred in bilateral format. Also, this had occurred in the backdrop of deepening of their bilateral relations resulting in regular 'feel-good' exchange of visits at the highest levels of their leaderships. But frequency and rootedness of their trilogue has now been robust enough to call for serious scrutiny of its future direction and implications.

Prima facie, this US–Japan–India trilogue was never expected to have any fixed agenda; aiming to deliberate on various open-ended topical regional and global questions. But all three partners are seen as torchbearers of democracy and share a rapidly expanding economic relationship with a rising China whose 'democratic deficit' has been part of their foreign policy narratives. Besides, their trilateral interactions are expected to play a major role in expanding nuclear energy use and safety as also to evolve international cooperation in climate change discourses. This trilogue has also gained increased significance in wake of the 'Indo–Pacific' region becoming the new buzzword in Asian relations. Besides, this tri-lateralization of their interactions was announced after years of bilateral brainstorming of this idea amongst practitioners and experts from these three countries followed by regular trilateral academic and Track-II deliberations since 2006.[13]

US–Japan–India had also a tested trilateral strategic chemistry, and international response to it, by holding trilateral naval exercises from 2007. Besides, their navies already had experienced working together in multilateral collaborations in committing of their naval assets in managing the immediate aftermath of the tsunami disaster of December 2004. They have also had substantial work experience of working together in other forums like the ASEAN Region Forum, the quadrilateral dialogue of democracies, ASEAN Regional Forum, the International Thermonuclear Experimental Reactor (ITER), which is a fusion-energy reactor project, as well as the Asia–Pacific Clean Development Partnership and currently in the UN Security Council and so on. They have increasingly professed having common stakes in dealing with themes like piracy, terrorism, energy security and climate change. On various occasions these three states have had opportunities to coordinate their negotiation strategies which are now expected to move to its next stage of active cooperation.

FROM TRACK II TO TRACK I

The earliest sinews of this US–Japan–India trilateral *rapprochement* can be traced to the early 1990s. At the end of the rigid bipolar system of Cold War years, US–Japan–India interactions had begun grappling with the new uncertainties and undergo gradual transformations in their foreign relations. Academics and experts in all three countries were also trying to make sense of this unfolding reality and to examine new formulations about international relations and foreign policy. It is in this backdrop of intellectual explorations by their think-tanks that Washington-based Centre for Strategic and International Studies (CSIS) was to take the lead in this. CSIS, in collaboration with the Aspen Institute India and Confederation of Indian Industries (CII) and with Tokyo's Japan Institute of International Affairs (JIIA), was to begin holding their trilateral 'Strategic Dialogue' from June 2006 and has since continued to do so, on a regular basis. This amongst others was to stimulate interactions amongst the policy makers from these three countries who have also been working together in several other multilateral forums. And finally, continued rise of China has also been pushing these three powers (US–Japan–India) to calibrate their joint strategies, especially for the Asia–Pacific which has been the region majorly impacted by rise of China.

Given that all these three countries share a difficult relationship with a 'rising' China and that in the face of their expanding interdependence with China none of these three wish to ignore Beijing's sensitivities about such trilateral initiatives, this trilateral of US–Japan–India has remained a cautious enterprise. This has made them (especially India) preoccupied with ensuring that their joint parleys must not be perceived to have any negative influence or implications for any specific third country (read China). Addressing the Japan Society in New York in February 2008, the then Indian

Ambassador to US, Ronen Sen, for instance, had sought to underline how this trilateral dialogue was not aimed at creating any new grouping but only for enhancing cooperation in

> issues ranging from countering international terrorism, responding to global pandemics and natural disasters, protecting the environment, addressing illegal trafficking in narcotics, arms and people, promoting stability and prosperity, are among the many avenues of enhanced cooperation between India, Japan and the United States.[14]

Their caution about a rising China comes primarily from the fact that each of the US–Japan–India has its own shades of differences on their foreign policy trajectories in general and on their China policy in particular. *Prima facie*, while the US and Japan may individually find it difficult yet together, and especially in association with India, they hope to better engage a rising China which is seen as a common stimulus for their trilateral initiatives. India is seen by both the US and Japan as a model of democracy-before-development which provides a counterfactual to China's argument in favour of development-before-democracy. Second, credentials of India's commitment to multilateralism that bring it closer to China's foreign policy formulations is also viewed as potentially useful in achieving socialization of China's power elite and in ensuring peace and stability of this larger Asia–pacific region. But it is intriguing to US and Japan why India remains an active partner in the Russia–China–India strategic triangle which is often perceived as a forum aimed at restraining the unilateral instincts of the US. While this portends a cautious pace of US–Japan–India formulations there are deeper trends that promise to bring strength and promise to their trilateral initiatives.

IDENTICAL TRAJECTORIES OF *RAPPROCHEMENT*

Strength to this US–Japan–India trilogue also comes from their shared values and political cultures. It is also important to note that the three powers also do not share any bilateral territorial disputes which have been the primacy preoccupations of most Asian relationships. In 1991 in view of India's balance of payment crisis,

Japan was one of the first countries to announce 150 million yen emergency assistance to India heralding a new chapter in the deepening of Indo–Japan relations. This soon was to result in forging closer cooperation that was to be briefly disrupted by India's nuclear tests of 1998 and some of that bad taste continues to linger on in certain components of their expanding interactions.

The year 2005 was to mark a breakthrough in India's relations both with Japan and US: India was to sign an 'Eightfold Initiative' with Prime Minister Koizumi as India had signed 'Next Steps in the Strategic Partnership' with George Bush Jr. launching a 'strategic orientation' to India–Japan and Indo–US global partnership creating fertile grounds for trilateral relations.[15] As the fable of Indo–US relations took off from these initiatives, India and Japan were to sign 'Global Partnership for the 21st Century' and work together as co-members of the tsunami core group, as also as partners in the 'G4' group of 2009 seeking together permanent seats on the UN Security Council. Japan was also responsible for pushing ASEAN to include India as an original member of the East Asia Summit from 2007 where India and Japan later worked together facilitating US being invited as a member from 2011. This second half of the first decade of the twenty-first century saw India surpassing China to become the largest recipient of Japan's Official Development Assistance (ODA) and their bilateral trade rose from $6.5 billion to over $10 billion.[16]

It is also interesting to note that while popular imaginations link Japan's foreign policy to be identical to that of the US, in this case the unprecedented tenor and pace of Indo–US agreement for civilian nuclear cooperation was not to show its impact on Japan's continued caution on opening nuclear commerce with India. This perhaps presents a special case and is understandable in view of Japan's unique experience of two nuclear tragedies in 1945 and 2011. But increasing intensity and frequency of their India–Japan military to military cooperation and exchange of visits of military leaders and prime ministers lends hope to closer cooperation in all sectors including nuclear sector where Japan presents Asia's most advanced model of power generation. With such strong and identical trajectories in their bilateral relations in all three legs of their triangle, US–Japan–India trilogue has since resulted in facilitating greater trilateral understanding on several issues. This has re-enforced notional trilateral relations that were around for some time in various academic, media and Track II dialogues taking place in Washington, Tokyo and New Delhi. This is what has facilitated ground-breaking initiatives such as the India–US agreement at the Defence Policy Group meeting of November 2007 to invite Japan to the Malabar 2007 naval exercises off Guam.

Several new ideas have since come under their trilateral deliberations. These include possibilities of a trilateral peacekeeping training under the Global Peacekeeping Operations Initiative (GPOI) to be conducted at India's United Services Institute's Centre for UN Peacekeeping (USI-CUNPK) which has already been training troops for UN Peacekeeping from various countries.[17] Possible programmes of CUNPK include joint seminars training designated personnel in civil-military relations, bridging gaps between peacekeeping and peacebuilding, working in a multinational environment, as also coordinate joint funding of police and medical units training for peacekeepers/trainers from other countries. Other items on their trilateral agenda include synergizing US–Japan Strategic Assistance Dialogue in building Japan's freight corridor project, building maritime infrastructure for India in Indian Ocean, conduct joint maritime security exercises to deal with menace of piracy and terrorism, explore collaborations in trilateral missile defence research, to establish informal yet committed disaster relief response capability to handle situations in the Indian Ocean.

FIRST US–JAPAN–INDIA TRILOGUE

Though this idea had been in vogue for over five years, at the official level, it was Japan that had floated the idea in mid-2010 and both India and US had been cautious and took some time. The other view is that it is the US that has been encouraging Japan for working out this triangle and to maximize benefits from their rapidly improving ties with New Delhi. There were also media reports that this idea had been formally finalized in principle during Indian Foreign Secretary, Nirupama Rao's visit to Tokyo during April 2011. Their first trilateral meeting was reportedly planned for 7-8 October 2011 which could not materialize for lack of preparedness.[18] But this trilateral dialogue remained increasingly part of their regular bilateral meetings. For instance, Indian Foreign Minister, S.M. Krishna at the end of his 29-30 October 2011 visit to Tokyo to participate in India–Japan fifth round of bilateral Strategic Dialogue was to put on record: 'We also discussed the India–Japan–United States trilateral dialogue. We agreed that it will be held very soon. It will cover regional and international issues of concern to all three countries.'[19]

Finally their first trilateral meeting did take place in Washington DC on 19 December 2011 and this was able to bring certain definitiveness on their slow-moving trilateral parleys from early 2000s. A brief note put up by the US State Department at the end of this meeting underlined their shared 'values and interests' and announced that this was not one isolated event and that their next meeting was scheduled to be held in Tokyo in 2012.[20] In terms of hierarchies of bureaucracy, this meeting was co-chaired by Assistant Secretary of State for South and Central Asia Robert Blake and Assistant Secretary for East Asia and Pacific Affairs Kurt Campbell. The Japanese side was represented by Deputy Vice Minister for Foreign Policy, Koji Tsuruoka (who was accompanying Foreign Minister Koichiro Gemba on an official visit to the US) and the Indian side by two Joint Secretaries respectively for Americas and East Asia, namely, Jawed Ashraf and Gautam Bambawale. Briefing the press later they underlined that this meeting provided them with opportunity to 'begin a process of operationalizing Indo-Pacific cooperation as a seamless construct in areas such as maritime security cooperation, counter-terrorism, counter-piracy, counter-proliferation, disaster relief and humanitarian assistance'.[21]

As regards China as a factor triggering this trialogue, while officials were unusually defensive and described it as 'preposterous', most experts believe that this trilateral dialogue was triggered by China's rising influence and US need to recast its relations with

Asian powers.[22] China is also remembered for its sharp criticism of the last quadrilateral dialogue of four democracies (Australia, India, Japan, and US) that had started in May 2007.[23] This had become dysfunctional after Shinzo Abe demitted office and Kevin Rudd took over the Australian premiership. This time round, however, China was to respond with much caution. This was so even while this trilogue was taking place in the backdrop of China's enhanced assertive postures in South China Sea where India's continued joint oil and gas explorations with Vietnam had already triggered sharp responses from Beijing. And in the more immediate backdrop, the death of King Jong-Il had also generated concerns about succession in Pyongyang as also about China's traditional close ties with North Korea. Chinese foreign ministry spokesperson, Liu Weimin was to tell media that, 'US, Japan and India are countries with great influence in the Asia-pacific region. We hope that the trilateral meeting will be conducive to regional peace and stability.'[24]

THE PERENNIAL CHINA FACTOR

Without doubt, China's rising influence (especially in the face of declining US influence) remains the key factor in driving this US–Japan–India trilateral *rapprochement*. Pertinent question remains as to what extent has China's rise overcast this trilogue and is this likely to colour their vision entirely? To the least, experts and officials in Beijing definitely perceive it in this manner; and it feels 'boxed in' by this US–Japan–India trilogue, whatever colour and shape one may give to these deliberations. China has often been vocal about its suspicions and discomfort about these trilateral formulations especially when these are convened in the name of sensitive subjects like democracy and human rights. Individually, these three states have also been vocal about how China's own relentless pursuit of its own interests through several regional multilateral organizations like the Shanghai Cooperation Organisation – which had told US in 2007 to vacate all military facilities from Central Asian Republics – or the way China has organized its 'string of pearls' from Gwadar to Hambantota, to Chittagong to

Coco Islands that does not reflect that Beijing defers to either US or Japanese or Indian sensitivities.

China's forays into the Indian Ocean – from its anti-piracy naval operations in the Gulf of Aden to launching for sea-trials of its ex-Soviet *Varyag* aircraft carrier in August 2011 – can be read both as cause or consequence of cementing US–Japan–India naval cooperation.[25] China has also been the leading country focused on exploiting resources across continents and oceans and it is now the third country with advanced capabilities in exploring deep seas up to 5,000 m deep. China has had UN permission to explore about 75,000 sq km of the Pacific Ocean and it was granted similar permission to explore 10,000 sq km of southwestern Indian Ocean in July 2011.[26] As far as exploitation of resources is concerned, China today is seen as a country in a hurry. China's engagement of Central and Southeast Asia has clearly impacted on the relative influence of other major powers including the US, Japan and India and China's reluctance had been the main factor in delaying entry of US into East Asian summit. China was also reluctant (and remains) to have India in EAS dialogue.[27] This clearly has been a major stimulus for US–Japan–India coordinating their joint strategies for Asian affairs and beyond though it has had limited success as yet in socializing China into norm-based multilateralism.

Amongst US–Japan–India, New Delhi has been perhaps most considerate to Beijing's sensitivities or vulnerable to pressure tactics whichever way one likes to put it. India is also known for its soft-approach to consensus-based decision-making and some of it can be seen even in New Delhi's engagement of neighbours like Myanmar, Pakistan, Sri Lanka where India clearly has the wherewithal to be far more assertive. In 2007, a massive Malabar series exercise was held in the Bay of Bengal with the participation of the five navies of India, the US, Singapore, Australia and Japan. But in 2007, India stopped involving more countries in the Indo–US naval exercise after China issued strong demarches to all the participants of this five-nation naval exercise.[28] Only, over the years, India has gradually become a bit more comfortable with allowing the Japanese

Self-Defense Force to participate in Indo–US naval exercises. So while the US–Japan leg has been the oldest and strongest leg of this triangle, it is the India–US and India–Japan partnership which has been recent and it has had its own share of hiccups even when these two bilateral ties are seen expanding rapidly. This raises the question as to whether the future of US–Japan–India triangle puts greater premium on India's engagement and commitment to it or does it depend far more on the US–Japan indulgence with rising India?

DOES INDIA MATTER?

Questions are often asked if India has earned its place at the big table of great powers, even in Asian affairs? Why should the US and Japan be interested in engaging India that continues to be such a cautious (read reluctant) partner and one which has been equally serious in engaging China and Russia in another strategic triangle? Other than being the world's largest liberal democracy and a booming market of 1.2 billion people with increasing purchasing power, India also remains home for the world's second largest Muslim population, a nuclear power, an educational dynamo, a strategically located regional naval power and an oasis of stability in a dysfunctional neighbourhood.[29] Their common concern about a 'rising' China becomes relevant to their trilateral dialogue only with these qualifications that India has earned since the early 1990s. With our earth becoming flat, India's private business (especially sectors like information technology, pharmaceutical, steel, communications, automobiles and so on) have opened a new chapter in India's foreign relations.[30]

It is in this new India with its advantages of dynamic private business, thriving and yet largely ancient culture, grassroot politics and civil society activism and a promising huge middle class and young population that countries like the US and Japan see for themselves an attractive partner who can help them fulfil their destiny and make a value addition to Asia's regional politics and international relations. Both the US and Japan are also cognizant of the independent streak of India's foreign policy as also of the vagaries of coalition politics in the largest democracy on earth and have evolved their nuanced methodologies of engaging India. Indeed, India being a functioning democracy in a largely dysfunctional region brings a certain aura to Indian participation in democratization of world affairs. India is part of various forums seeking to promote democracy both in internal politics as also in international deliberations and decision-making processes. This is how US–Japan–India have been successfully investing attention and efforts in building their trilateral working relationship to ensure peace and stability in Asia as also to engage and socialize a rising China so as to ensure its positive contributions in Asia's future evolution.

This combination of India's free-market and liberal democracy makes it a textbook case of growth model that, being based on conventional wisdom, engenders trust and determination for partnering of India by major powers. Therefore, it is not unusual that India today, for the first time, has good relations with all major powers. Conversely, it is the nature of China's free-market and democracy which keeps Beijing on the defensive all the time. Therefore, any combination of power across Asia, even when of generic nature being to appear directed against China, especially if it co-opts India; at least this is how scholars in China popularly view this to be. The same is true of the US–Japan–India triangle which is located in such time and space that even if it was not conscious of China being their common concern, the China Factor seems ordained to be a major trigger for evolution of its trajectories, or at least this is how its trajectories are likely to be interpreted by experts the world over, especially Chinese officials and experts. So, the China Factor of US–Japan–India may at best be exaggerated yet, there is no denying that it does remain an important trigger in formulation and potential flourish of US–Japan–India triangle.

CONCLUSION

There are experts who underline the fact that China is physically located at the very centre of the Asian continent. This may have been partly the reason why ancient Chinese sages saw China (*Zhong guo*) as the centre of the human universe. The same has been further re-enforced by the more recent economic resurgence of Asia with China at its core. China has been both the benefactor as also beneficiary of similar growth trajectories amongst its immediate neighbours. So, no doubt expanding economic relations of China with US–Japan–India make them increasingly interdependent but it is intriguing how little dent this economic interdependence has made on the nature of their mutual politico-strategic equations.

Second, China seems omnipresent, if not central, in most Asian multilateral forums. Any Asian multilateral forum that does not include China – while it involves other major Asian power and especially when these are located on China's contentious borders – is bound to have China consciousness writ large in its formulations and deliberations. Thus even when it is not a participant, China still casts a long shadow in any multilateral mechanism, especially so in its immediate periphery. In the Asia-Pacific region this was especially triggered by China's proactive policies in response to East Asian Financial crisis of 1997 and then in providing post-tsunami relief and rehabilitation since 2004. The global economic slowdown since 2008 has only made China confident of repeating its performance now at a global level. China's fast changing equations with the European Union present a good example of this shift. So if the 1997 East Asian Financial crisis gave China lead over Japanese Official Development Assistance and investments the 2008 global economic slowdown has been casting a Chinese shadow on the US global leadership.

Finally, the reality is that unlike South Korea that has managed to relatively resolve issues with China, Japan and India have continued to have rather difficult equations with Beijing. And now with increasing contestation of China's rising influence with that of the US, the latter is seen coming under pressures to revive and recast its equations with other Asian powers. This promises to make US–Japan–India trilogue, not only conscious of but also focused on how to best manage China's rise for ensuring peace and prosperity in Asia. To sum up, the fact that US–Japan–India triangle seems set to address issues like energy security, piracy and environment – which are equally critical to China – their deliberations as well future formulations are likely to be responded to and influenced by China's initiatives and formulations on these themes. Whether China should be co-opted into this US–Japan–India triangle, and/or will China be interested in joining such a forum remains a subject of interest for future explorations on this theme of Asian triangles and quadrilaterals.

NOTES

1. Jae Ho Chung, *Between Ally and Partner: Korea-China Relations and the United States*, New York: Columbia University Press, 2007, p. 1.
2. Robert G. Sutter, *Chinese Foreign Relations: Power and Policy since the Cold War*, Lanham: Rowman & Littlefield, 2010, pp. 193-201; Ye Zicheng, *Inside China's Grand Strategy: The Perspectives from the People's Republic* (ed. and tr. Steven I. Levine and Guoli Liu), Lexington: The University Press of Kentucky, 2010, pp. 219-21; Michael Wines and Choe Sang-Hun, 'Despite Industry Skepticism, South Korea and China Are Said to Plan Trade Talks', *New York Times*, 6 August 2010, p. B3.
3. Yang Mu and Heng Sian-Heng, 'China-ASEAN Relations after CAFTA', in Mingjina Li and Chong Guan Kwa, eds., *China-ASEAN Sub-Regional Cooperation: Progress, Problems and Prospect*, Singapore: World Scientific Publishing, 2011, p. 130.
4. 'Sino-ASEAN Trade Grows 36 Times in 20 Yrs', *China Daily* (Beijing), 17 December 2011.
5. Ananth Krishnan, 'Chinese Media see 'Containment Strategy', *The Hindu*, New Delhi, 29 December 2011, p. 8.
6. Kevin Rudd, 'East Asian Perceptions of Australia', in *Double Vision*, Canberra: The ANU E Press, 2011, p. 13; Zhiqun Zhu, 'China's Warming Relations with South Korea and Australia', in Mingjiang Li, ed., *Soft Power*, Lanham: Lexington Books, 2009, p. 197.

7. Phung Thi Hui, 'China's 21st Century Status and Challenges', in Sudhir T. Devare, Swaran Singh and Reena Marwah, eds., *Emerging China: Prospects for Partnership in Asia*, New Delhi: Routledge, 2012, p. 175.
8. Kai He, *Institutional Balancing in the Asia Pacific: Economic Interdependence and China's Rise*, New York: Routledge, 2009, p. 72.
9. Dominic J. Caraccilo, *Beyond Guns and Steel: War Termination Strategy*, Santa Barbara, Ca: Praeger, 2011, p. 5; Susan B. Epstein, *Foreign Aid Reform, National Strategy, and the Quadrennial Review*, Washington DC: Congressional Research Service, 12 April 2010, p. 4.
10. Rosemary Foot, 'Chinese Strategies in a US-hegemonic Global Order: Accommodating and Hedging', *International Affairs*, vol. 82, no. 1, 2006, p. 77.
11. Michael D. Swaine, *America's Challenge: Engaging a Rising China in the Twenty-First Century*, Washington DC: Carnegie Endowment for International Peace, 2011, p. 142.
12. Michel Oksenberg, 'U.S. Politics and Asian Policy', in Ezra F. Vogel, Yuan Ming and Tanaka Akihiko, eds., *The Golden Age of the U.S.-China-Japan Triangle, 1972-1989*, Boston: Harvard East Asian Monographs, 2002, pp. 32-3.
13. For Details on their Track II deliberations see 'US–Japan–India Strategic Dialogue' (JIIA Report, 22-4 September 2010) at http://www2.jiia.or.jp/pdf/report/101022e-US-J-I_Joint_Statement.pdf
14. 'India, US, Japan Share Values and Aspirations: Ronen Sen', *Rediff News*, 16 February 2008 at http://www.rediff.com/news/2008/feb/16ronen.htm
15. '88132: Time for India–US–Japan Tri-lateral Relationship', *The Hindu*, New Delhi, 23 April 2011.
16. K.V. Kesavan, 'India and Japan: Changing Dimensions of Partnership in the Post-Cold War Period', *ORF Occasional Paper No. 14*, May 2010, p. 10.
17. Please see United Services Institute, Centre for United National Peace Keeping (New Delhi) at http://www.usiofindia.org/CUNPK/
18. Rajaram Panda and Victoria Tuke, 'India–Japan–US Trilateral Dialogue: A Promising Initiative', *IDSA Issue Brief*, 22 November

2011, accessed on 2 January 2012 at http://www.idsa.in/system/files/IB_India-Japan-US.pdf, pp. 2, 4.

19. 'India, Japan Discuss Nuclear Pact', *The Hindu*, New Delhi, 30 October 2011.
20. 'U.S.-Japan-India Trilateral' (Media Note, Office of the Spokesperson, Washington DC), 19 December 2011 accessed on 2 January 2012 at http://www.state.gov/r/pa/prs/ps/2011/12/179172.htm
21. 'First US-Japan-India Trilateral, Say not Aimed at China', *The Economic Times*, New Delhi, 20 December 2011.
22. Rohit Viswanath, 'It's Win-Win for India and Japan', in *Daily News & Analysis*, 27 December 2011 (accessed on 4 February 2012) at http://www.dnaindia.com/analysis/comment_its-win-win-for-india-and-japan_1630451; 'ASIA: US, India, Japan to Meet After Obama's Asia "Pivot"', *AfroAsian Business Chronicle*, 23 December 2011 (accessed on 4 January 2012), at http://www.aabc.co.in/component/content/article/60-focus/3703-asia-us-india-japan-to-meet-after-obamas-asia-qpivotq.html
23. Suisheng Zhao, 'China and East Asian Regional Cooperation: Institution Building Efforts, Strategic Calculations, and Preference for Informal Approach', in Mingjiang Li and Dongmin Lee, eds., *China and East Asian Strategic Dynamics: The Shaping of a New Regional Order*, Lanham: Lexington Books, 2011, p. 184; Amitav Acharya, *Asia Rising: Who is Leading?*, Singapore: World Scientific Publishing, 2008, p. 160.
24. K.J.M. Varma, 'China Reacts Cautiously to 1st India–US–Japan Meeting', *Outlook Magazine*, New Delhi, 20 December 2011 at http://news.outlookindia.com/items.aspx?artid=744973
25. For details see Swaran Singh, 'China's Forays into the Indian Ocean: Strategic Implications for India', *Journal of Indian Ocean Region*, vol. 7, no. 2, December 2011, p. 215.
26. Ibid., p. 221.
27. 'Sino-Japanese Competitive Regionalism', in Michael Heazle and Nick Knight, eds., *China-Japan Relations in the Twenty-first Century: Creating a Future Past?*, Cheltenham: Edward Elgar Publishing, 2007, p. 217.
28. Cdr Gurpreet S. Khurana, 'China-India Maritime Rivalry', *Indian Defence Review*, New Delhi, vol. 23, no. 4 (October-December 2009), p. 91.

29. Sarah Hiddleston, 'How the "Stars Aligned" for Closer Trilateral Relations', *The Hindu*, New Delhi, 23 April 2011, p. 11.
30. Suma Athreye and Sandeep Kapur, 'Introduction: The Internationalization of Chinese and Indian Firms – Trends, Motivations and Strategy', in *Industrial and Corporate Change*, vol. 18, no. 2, April 2009, p. 212.

CHAPTER 7

Explaining the Similarity: Comparative Analysis of Japan and America's India Policy

KAZUTOSHI TAMARI

INTRODUCTION

On 15 December 2006, Prime Minister of Japan Shinzo Abe and India's Prime Minister Manmohan Singh declared in a joint statement that Japan and India had decided to establish a 'Strategic and Global Partnership'. The following is a part of the statement.

> The two Prime Ministers recall that Japan and India share ancient bonds and a proud civilisational heritage. The current context of Japan–India relations is rooted in their similar perceptions of the evolving environment in the region and the world at large. It is driven by converging long-term political, economic and strategic interests, aspirations and concerns and underpinned by a common commitment to democracy, open society, human rights, rule of law and free market economy....
>
> ... Given their shared determination to raise bilateral relations to a higher level, the two leaders decide to establish a Strategic and Global Partnership between Japan and India. This will impart stronger political, economic and strategic dimensions to bilateral relations, serve long-term interests of both countries, enhance all-round cooperation and contribute to greater regional peace and stability.[1]

Since 2000, especially since 2005, one year before the statement of strategic partnership, Tokyo and New Delhi attempted to enhance their cooperation in various issue areas. Among the multiple issues associated with Japan–India relations, the strategic realm came to be regarded as important, as the text of the statement clarifies. Whereas 'strategic' cooperation was emphasized in the joint statement of 2006, the 'Japan–India Joint Declaration' of 2001 by Prime Minister

Junichiro Koizumi and Prime Minister Atal Behari Vajpayee had not included the word 'strategic'.[2] Indeed, both countries have broadened their strategic cooperation through activities such as conduct of joint naval exercises, only recently.

For explaining the emerging closer cooperation between Japan and India, it is common for researchers and journalists to examine the reasons underlying the initiatives. For instance, Rajaram Panda, a Senior Fellow at the Institute for Defence Studies and Analyses (IDSA), lists the following factors as reasons for India's importance for Japan: rapid economic growth of India, Japan's threat perception from China, the uncertain future of Japan's alliance with the USA, and maritime security in and around the Indian Ocean.[3] These are examples illustrating the orthodox mode of explaining the recent Japan–India cooperative relationship in the strategic realm.

However, such an orthodox mode of explanation of Japan–India relations seems strange from the perspective of usual understandings of Japanese foreign policy because the orthodox explanations of the Japan–India engagement subsume that Japan made a decision to pursue closer strategic relations with India based on its own calculations of its national interests. Against this assumption, Japan's external policies are regarded as reactive, not proactive, while some argue that Japan's foreign policy has become autonomous and realistic since the end of the Cold War.[4] Moreover, it is sometimes said that Japan's foreign policies have been subordinate to those of the US.[5] At the very least, one cannot dismiss the argument that the US has influenced Japan's external relations. Accordingly, the orthodox mode of explanations of contemporary Japan–India relations might be problematic in the sense that Japan's decision is assumed to be autonomous.

Indeed, Purnendra Jain, a Professor at the Centre for Asian Studies, University of Adelaide, Australia, argues that 'rather than through independent assessment of India's importance in its own right, Tokyo has viewed relations with India through the prism of Japan's close relationship with its primary strategic partner, the United States' and '[i]n other words, Tokyo's approach towards

New Delhi can be described as reactive rather than proactive'.[6] This mode of understanding Japan's India policy as 'reactive' is well suited to general discussions of Japan's foreign policy.

Therefore, this essay complements the limitations of the orthodox prior literature associated with Japan–India relations with an exploration of the impact of the US factor on relations following the end of the Cold War. For that purpose, it focuses attention on the similarity between recent developments of Japan's India policy and those of America's India policy, and explores the reasons underlying their similarity. This chapter contributes to a more sophisticated understanding of Japan–India relations by exploring the autonomy of Japan's India policy under the US influence.

The first section of this essay overviews Japan's foreign policy related to India in the post-Cold War era. The second section presents a comparison of Japan's India policy with America's India policy after the end of the Cold War. Each of the following four sections sets a hypothesis for explaining the similarity and tests them respectively. The four hypotheses examined in this chapter are as follows:

Hypothesis One: Japan, as a junior partner of the Japan–US alliance, has chosen its foreign policy relative to India merely by following the policy of the US towards India.

Hypothesis Two: Because the US had urged Japan to have closer relations with India, Japan decided to engage India.

Hypothesis Three: Because Japan and the US share common interests in their relations with India, their foreign policies towards India have come to be similar as a result of the rational decisions of each country.

Hypothesis Four: Japan has acknowledged its own national interests in having closer relations with India from learning the behaviours of other countries, especially the US.

The concluding section of this essay sums up the examinations of the hypotheses presented above and presents implications for the study of Japan–India relations.

OVERVIEW OF JAPAN'S FOREIGN POLICY TOWARD INDIA IN THE POST-COLD WAR ERA

Tables 7.1 and 7.2 gives a brief overview of the development of Japan's India policy between 1990 and 2011.[7]

The major developments in Indo–Japan relations between 1990 and 2011, is deputed in Table 7.1, while Table 7.2 lists the number of visits of prime ministers of the two countries.

TABLE 7.1: MAJOR DEVELOPMENTS IN JAPAN–INDIA RELATIONS, 1990-2011

Time	Events
August 1990	Prime Minister Kaifu visits New Delhi
1991	Economic crisis in India; Japan provides emergency assistance
May 1998	India's nuclear tests with subsequent Japanese economic sanctions (through October 2001)
August 2000	'Japan–India Global Partnership in the 21st Century' by Prime Minister Mori and Prime Minister Vajpayee
July 2001	First security dialogue and military–military talks between India and Japan
April 2005	'Japan–India Partnership in a New Asian Era: Strategic Orientation of Japan–India Global Partnership' by Prime Minister Koizumi and Prime Minister Manmohan Singh
December 2006	'Joint Statement towards Japan–India Strategic and Global Partnership' and 'Joint Statement on the Enhancement of Cooperation on Environmental Protection and Energy Security' by Prime Minister Abe and Prime Minister Manmohan Singh
August 2007	'Joint Statement on the Roadmap for New Dimensions to the Strategic and Global Partnership between Japan and India' by Prime Minister Abe and Prime Minister Manmohan Singh
September 2007	Joint Naval Exercise 'Malabar 07' by Japan, India, the US, Australia, and Singapore
October 2008	'Joint Statement on the Advancement of the Strategic and Global Partnership between Japan and India'

	and 'Joint Declaration on Security Cooperation between Japan and India' by Prime Minister Aso and Prime Minister Manmohan Singh
April 2009	Joint Naval Exercise 'Malabar 09' by Japan, India, and the US
December 2009	'New Stage of Japan–India Strategic and Global Partnership' by Prime Minister Hatoyama and Prime Minister Manmohan Singh
June 2010	Negotiation for Civil Nuclear Cooperation started
July 2010	First 2+2 (Defense and Foreign secretaries) Dialogue
February 2011	Signing of the Comprehensive Economic Partnership Agreement (CEPA)

Source: Website of Ministry of Foreign Affairs of Japan, 'Japan–India Relations', February 2011 (http://www.mofa.go.jp/region/asia-paci/india/index.html, accessed on 13 December 2011).

TABLE 7.2: JAPAN–INDIA PRIME MINISTERS' VISITS DURING 1990–2011

From Japan to India		From India to Japan	
April 1990	Kaifu	June 1992	Rao
August 2000	Mori	December 2001	Vajpayee
April 2005	Koizumi	December 2006	Manmohan Singh
August 2007	Abe	October 2008	Manmohan Singh
December 2009	Hatoyama	October 2010	Manmohan Singh
December 2011	Noda		

Source: Website of Ministry of Foreign Affairs of Japan, 'Japan–India Relations', February 2011.

Although the Ministry of Foreign Affairs of Japan says that 'the two countries have enjoyed cordial relations' since the establishment of diplomatic relations between Japan and India on 28 April 1952,[8] Japan–India relations remained limited during the Cold War era. When the Cold War ended at the beginning of the 1990s, signs of improvement in their relations appeared. Prime Minister Toshiki Kaifu visited New Delhi and delivered a speech in the Indian parliament in April 1990. Then the Japanese government provided emergency economic assistance to India when India's economy was faced with a severe crisis in 1991.[9] However, such initiatives for Japan–India relations were not sustained and Pokhran II India's nuclear tests in 1998, worsened the relationship.[10] It would be safe to say the Japan–India relations were at a low ebb during the 1990s.

The estranged Japan–India relations began to change in 2000. Prime Minister Yoshiro Mori visited India and agreed to a 'Global Partnership' between both countries with Prime Minister Vajpayee in August 2000. They also agreed to set-up official-level security dialogues and military–military talks.[11] The visit was said to provide 'the momentum to strengthen the Japan–India relationship'.[12] In October 2001, Japan ended its economic sanctions on India, which had been imposed because of the Pokhran II nuclear tests.[13] Behind these initiatives for closer Japan–India relations at the beginning years of the 2000s, it is said that both countries regarded their national interests economically and strategically.[14]

Since 2005, Japan–India engagement has accelerated. Prime Minister Koizumi and Prime Minister M. Singh declared a 'Japan–India Partnership in a New Asian Era: Strategic Orientation of Japan–India Global Partnership' in April 2005 on Prime Minister Koizumi's visit to New Delhi. They also agreed on an 'Eightfold Initiative for Strengthening Japan–India Global Partnership' to support additional cooperation, with

1. enhanced and upgraded dialogue architecture, including strengthening of the momentum of high-level exchanges, launching of a High Level Strategic Dialogue, and full utilization of the existing dialogue mechanisms;
2. comprehensive economic engagement through expansion of trade in goods and services, investment flows and other areas of economic cooperation, and exploration of a Japan–India economic partnership agreement;
3. enhanced security dialogue and cooperation;
4. the Science and Technology Initiative;
5. cultural and academic initiatives and strengthening of people-to-people contacts to raise the visibility and profile of one country in the other;
6. cooperation for ushering in a new Asian era;

7. cooperation in the United Nations and other international organizations, including cooperation for the early realization of UN reforms, particularly Security Council reforms; and
8. cooperation in responding to global challenges and opportunities.[15]

In the next year, 2006, both countries officially agreed to the strategic partnership in the statement cited at the beginning of this chapter. As these agreements show, Japan–India cooperation has been enhanced at various levels and issues, especially in the strategic field.[16] Regarding a nuclear issue, which is sensitive for the Japanese side, Japan started to negotiate with India for cooperation in 2010. Furthermore, Japan–India trade has expanded rapidly since 2005. (Figure 7.1).

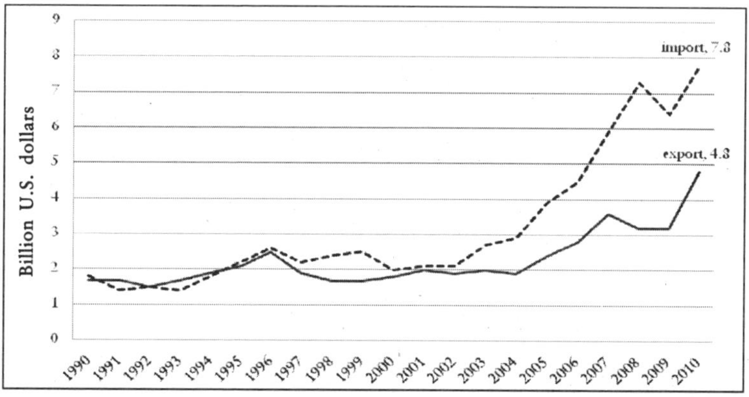

Note: Data refer to India's trade data with other countries in the following sources. Consequently, 'export' denotes the amount of India's export to Japan, and 'import' denotes the amount of India's imports from Japan.

Source: (For 1990–6) International Monetary Fund, *Direction of Trade Statistics Yearbook 1997*, Washington, D.C.: International Monetary Fund, 1997; (for 1997-2003) International Monetary Fund, *Direction of Trade Statistics Yearbook 2004,* Washington, D.C.: International Monetary Fund, 2004; (for 2004-10) International Monetary Fund, *Direction of Trade Statistics Yearbook 2011,* Washington, D.C.: International Monetary Fund, 2011.

FIGURE 7.1: INDIA'S TRADE WITH JAPAN.

COMPARISON WITH THE USA's INDIA POLICY

On comparing the recent developments of Japan's India policy with those of America's India policy, one can easily find similarities: indeed, Japan's India policy seems to mimic America's India policy.

A few examples are likely to be illustrative. President Bill Clinton visited New Delhi in March 2000 and Prime Minister Mori visited India in August 2000. These visits are regarded as important in their relations with India.[17] The US lifted its economic sanctions on India (and Pakistan) in September 2001, soon after the 9/11 terrorist attacks, and Japan followed in October 2001. The US and India declared their 'strategic partnership' in January 2004,[18] and the Japan–India 'Strategic and Global Partnership' statement followed in December 2006.[19] The US concluded a nuclear cooperation agreement with India in October 2008, and Japan started nuclear cooperation negotiations with India in June 2010.

TABLE 7.3: VISITS OF THE US PRESIDENTS AND INDIAN PRIME MINISTERS (1990-2011)

From the US to India		From India to the US	
		May 1994	Rao
		September 1998	Vajpayee
March 2000	Clinton	September 2000	Vajpayee
		November 2001	Vajpayee
March 2006	Bush	July 2005	Manmohan Singh
		November 2008	Manmohan Singh
		November 2009	Manmohan Singh
October 2010	Obama	April 2010	Manmohan Singh
		November 2010	Manmohan Singh

Source: Website of Ministry of External Affairs of India (http://www.mea.gov.in/, accessed on 14 December 2011); a website of Embassy of India in Washington, D.C. (http://www.indianembassy.org/, accessed on 14 December 2011); various newspaper articles (especially, *The Hindu* and *The Washington Post*).

Table 7.4 gives a list of the countries which signed strategic partnership with India.

These specific developments and general trends of Indo–Japan relations and the Indo–US relations have been similar. Both represent estranged relations in the Cold War era. While signs of approaching India were apparent in the early 1990s in both countries,[20] both relations remained low-key during the 1990s. Since 2000, both Japan and the US have strengthened their efforts to enhance co-operation with India. Especially since 2005, strategic cooperation in both Japan–India and India–US relations has been accelerated. As described earlier, these 'peaks and troughs'[21] have been almost mutually coincidental.

There have been differences, of course. For example, whereas Japan concluded the Comprehensive Economic Partnership Agreement (CEPA) with India in February 2011, such an agreement does not

TABLE 7.4: COUNTRIES CONCLUDING STRATEGIC PARTNERSHIPS WITH INDIA

Year	Countries
1997	South Africa
1998	France
2000	Russia
2001	Germany
2004	The United States of America, The United Kingdom, European Union
2005	China, Indonesia, Fiji
2006	Japan, Brazil
2007	Nigeria, Vietnam
2009	Australia
2010	South Korea, Canada, Malaysia, Saudi Arabia
2011	Afghanistan

Note: For the year of conclusion of the India–US strategic partnership, see n. 18 of this chapter.

Source: Takenori Horimoto, 'India's Partnership Diplomacy for Major Power (Taikoku-kawo Mezasu Indo no 'Renkei Gaikou')', *Contemporary India Forum, Quarterly Review* (*Gendai Indo Forum*), no. 10 (Summer 2011), p. 4 (Japanese).

exist in India–US relations. Japan has hesitated to conclude a civil nuclear cooperation deal with India, as of the end of year 2011. These two are the major differences, and many other minor differences must exist too. Considering these differences, however, it seems safe to say that Japan's India policy has closely resembled the US foreign policy relative to India in the post-Cold War era.

The following sections are intended to explain why the policies have been so similar by setting and testing four hypotheses.

HYPOTHESIS ONE: MERELY FOLLOWING THE US

The previous section described that Japan's India policy seems merely to have followed the US foreign policy related to India. This is the first hypothesis that this paper presents for examination. If Japan's India policy is defined by America's India policy, then the similarity can be readily understood.

It is true that some major developments in Japan's India policy occurred soon after similar developments had happened in India–US relations, such as the halt of economic sanctions on India. We might say that these successions occurred because Japan has followed the US. Nevertheless, there exist many cases of discrepancy. For example, Prime Minister Kaifu's visit to India in 1990 cannot be regarded as following the US initiative because no American president had visited India for quite a while before that time. In addition, the Japanese government has hesitated to make a nuclear deal with India, although the US concluded an agreement three years ago and Tokyo is regarded as being under pressure from Washington and Paris to follow suit.[22]

Although it can explain some actions and policies, this hypothesis is not persuasive. Above all, it is far from realistic. Just as it is difficult to assume that Japan's foreign policy is perfectly autonomous, it is

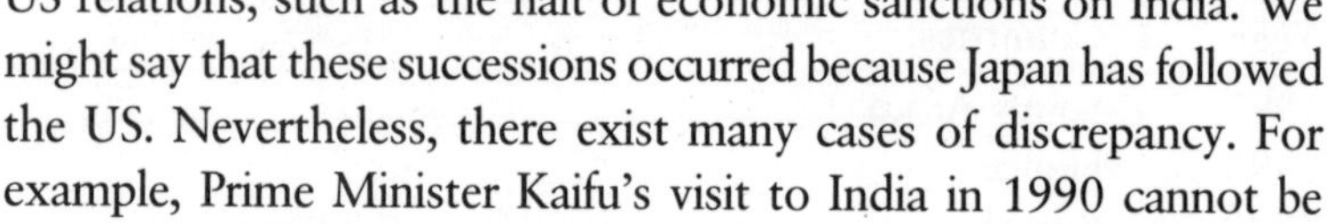

First Hypothesis

also impossible to assume that Japan's foreign policy is completely subject to US preferences. Plainly, this hypothesis is too extreme.

In the literature on Japanese foreign policy, it is sometimes argued that external pressure from the US (*gaiatsu* in Japanese) is an important factor. However, previous works on *gaiatsu* suggest that the *gaiatsu* can work not because the Japanese government obeys the US government, but because *gaiatsu* is employed in struggles of the policy making process.[23] Stated differently, even where *gaiatsu* works, it would be wrong to conclude simply that Tokyo has no autonomy in its foreign relations.

In sum, this extreme hypothesis can be dismissed because of its reliance on the assumption that Japan's foreign policy making is far from realistic, although some similarities might be explainable by it.

HYPOTHESIS TWO: URGING BY THE US

The second hypothesis is that pressure from the US defines Japan's foreign policy related to India. The second hypothesis resembles the first because both assume that Japan is subordinate to the US. However, the second one is not as extreme as the first. The US puts pressure on Japan when the dimension of Japan–India relations is important for the US. The pressure works as a trigger for Japan's India policy. It can be said the hypothesis assumes the effectiveness of *gaiatsu.*

The initiation of negotiations for Japan–India civil nuclear co-operation in June 2010 is a case that is well-suited for the hypothesis: soon after the US and France had put pressure on the Japanese government, Japan started to negotiate with India on a nuclear deal. However, this is the only case that is well explained by the hypothesis with credible evidence. The current stalemate of the nuclear co-

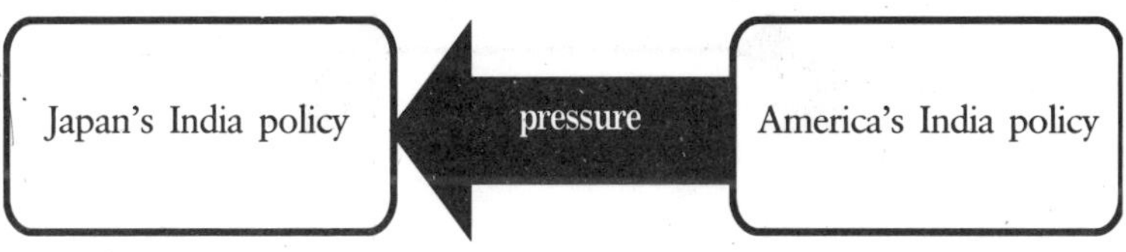

Second Hypothesis

operation negotiations, as of the end of 2011, cannot be explained by the hypothesis. Although we are able to infer that there has been some pressure from the US in some cases such as the strategic partnership, no evidence points to pressure from the US. Furthermore, by the hypothesis, it is difficult to explain other cases for which Japan–India cooperation does not seem important to the US. For example, it is difficult to imagine that the US hoped for Japan's approach to India in 2000 (when Prime Minister Mori visited India).

In summary, the explanatory power of the second hypothesis is limited at least in the respect that we seek an explanation for similarities between Japan's and America's respective India policies after the end of the Cold War.

HYPOTHESIS THREE: RATIONAL CHOICE ON COMMON INTERESTS

The third hypothesis is that Japan's and America's foreign policies related to India have turned out to be similar as a result of their respective rational decisions because Japan and the US share common interests in their relations with India. The two major factors which are regarded as shared by Japan and the US in terms of their relations with India are (1) the China factor and (2) India's rapidly growing economy. This hypothesis corresponds to the orthodox previous explanations of Japan–India relations in a sense that rational and autonomous decisions by the Japanese government are assumed.

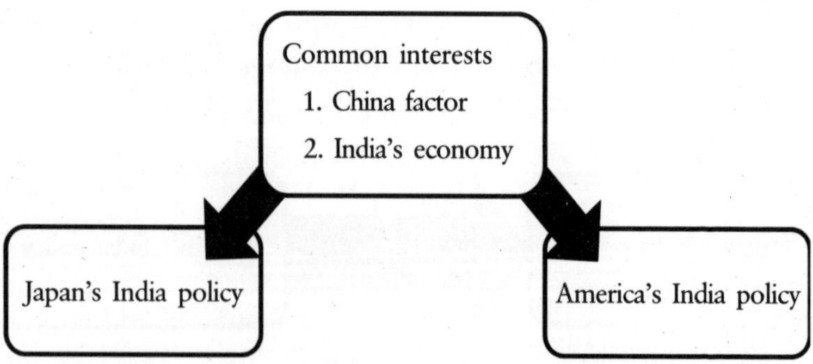

Third Hypothesis

The first possible common factor is the China factor. It can be assumed that because of the emergence of China as an assertive actor in the area, Japan and the US respectively sought closer relations with India to balance China geostrategically. In previous papers describing Japan–India relations, the China factor is regarded as a leading cause of Japan's access to India in the strategic realm. That can provide a very persuasive explanation for the developments of Japan's attempts to forge strategic cooperation with India after 2005. The argument is strongly supported by the fact that Japan–India strategic cooperation was accelerated after the anti-Japanese demonstrations in China in the spring of 2005, as Takenori Horimoto, one editor of this volume, points out.[24]

Second, the rapid economic growth of India and the expansion of economic relations can be regarded as a reason shared by Japan and the US to approach India. India sustained its high GDP growth rate in the 1990s and in the 2000s, as the graph in Figure 7.2 shows.

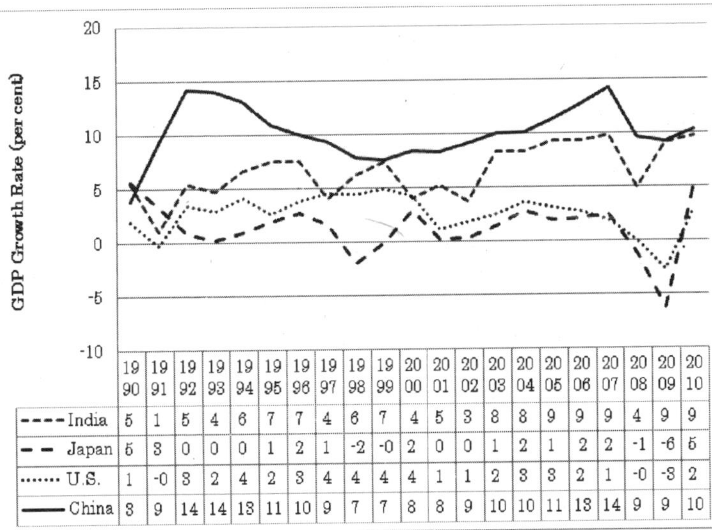

	1990	1991	1992	1993	1994	1995	1996	1997	1998	1999	2000	2001	2002	2003	2004	2005	2006	2007	2008	2009	2010
---- India	5	1	5	4	6	7	7	4	6	7	4	5	3	8	8	9	9	9	4	9	9
– – Japan	5	3	0	0	0	1	2	1	-2	-0	2	0	0	1	2	1	2	2	-1	-6	5
······ U.S.	1	-0	3	2	4	2	3	4	4	4	4	1	1	2	3	3	2	1	-0	-3	2
—— China	3	9	14	14	13	11	10	9	7	7	8	8	9	10	10	11	13	14	9	9	10

Source: Website of World Bank (http://data.worldbank.org/, accessed on 13 December 2011).

FIGURE 7.2: GDP GROWTH RATES OF INDIA, JAPAN, THE US AND CHINA IN 1990-2010.

India's growing economy has attracted much attention globally. Trade between the US and India also increased gradually during the period and has expanded rapidly especially since 2004 (Figure 7.3). Japan's trade with India has also increased, as explained earlier. Therefore, it is natural to assume that Japan and the US respectively hoped for enhanced economic links in their relations with India.

This third hypothesis is apparently well organized. Moreover, it explains both Japan's and America's India policies. Actually, each

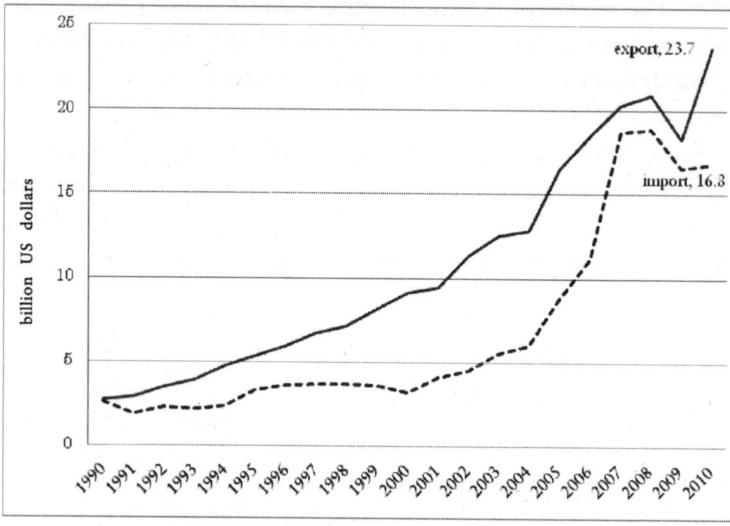

Note: Data are India's trade data with other countries in the following sources. Consequently, 'export' denotes the amount of India's export to the US, and 'import' denotes the amount of India's import from the US.

Source: (For 1990–6) International Monetary Fund, *Direction of Trade Statistics Yearbook 1997*, Washington, D.C.: International Monetary Fund, 1997; (for 1997–2003) International Monetary Fund, *Direction of Trade Statistics Yearbook 2004,* Washington, D.C.: International Monetary Fund, 2004; (for 2004–2010) International Monetary Fund, *Direction of Trade Statistics Yearbook 2011,* Washington, D.C.: International Monetary Fund, 2011.

FIGURE 7.3: INDIA TRADE WITH US.

policy initiative of both countries toward India is explainable: The economic interests can explain President Clinton's and Prime Minister Mori's visits in 2000, and the China factor can explain the agreements to the strategic partnership. However, this hypothesis is not satisfactory to resolve the research question of this chapter. Japan's India policy and America's India policy are too closely correlated for the hypothesis. An assumption of autonomous and rational decisions by both countries cannot explain the close succession of developments. For instance, it is difficult to assume that Japan, based on rational calculations of national interests, stopped its economic sanctions on India in the month immediately after the US had done so. More direct relations between Japan and the US must exist with respect to their respective India policies.

In summary, this rational and autonomous decision hypothesis cannot explain the close policy similarity, although it is able to explain each policy decision.

HYPOTHESIS FOUR: ACKNOWLEDGING OWN INTERESTS FROM OTHERS

The fourth hypothesis is that Japan has acknowledged its own national interests in fostering closer relations with India by learning

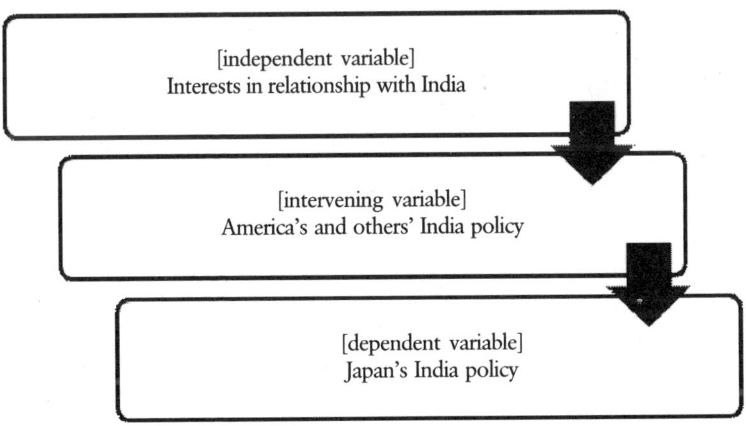

Fourth Hypothesis

from the behaviour of other countries, especially the US.[25] Interests associated with closer relations with India are regarded as independent variables. US foreign policy related to India is regarded as an intervening variable, and Japan's India policy is a dependent variable. This is a variant of the third hypothesis, in the sense that Japan's rational decisions based on its calculations of national interests are assumed. However, in the fourth hypothesis, the process of acknowledgement of the interests is considered. This hypothesis assumes that Japan acknowledges its interests in relation with India by examining other countries' relations with India.

The fourth hypothesis can explain major successions of events: halts of economic sanctions, leadership visits, and strategic partnership declarations. The US made these decisions first. Subsequently, Japan acknowledged its own interests from them and gave them due consideration. Later, Japan pursued similar policies in some cases. The initiation of the Japan–India nuclear deal negotiations is also explainable: the US and some other major countries had reached nuclear cooperation deals with India; then Japan examined its interests in producing such an agreement. Thereafter, Japan started its negotiations.

This hypothesis dovetails with the previous literature related to general Japanese foreign policy, in which a less proactive nature of Japanese foreign policy is presumed. Therefore, the hypothesis is suitable for observations by Jain that Japan's India policy has been reactive.[26] Furthermore, the hypothesis matches the so-called national character of the Japanese people. Japanese people are said to behave according to others, without their own deliberations. The way of decision of Japan's India policy assumed by the hypothesis is well matched with its alleged national character.

To summarize the section, the fourth hypothesis has greater explanatory power than others (see Table 7.5). However, it might not be fair to say that this hypothesis is better than others because it is more complicated than others. It is natural that a less parsimonious hypothesis can explain more cases closely.

TABLE 7.5: HYPOTHESES AND CASES EXAMINED IN THIS CHAPTER

	Economic sanction	Leadership visits	Strategic partnership	Nuclear deal
Hypothesis one Following the US	Suited	Partly suited	Partly suited	Not suited
Hypothesis two Urging by the US	Partly suited	Not suited	Partly suited	Partly suited
Hypothesis three Common interests	Not suited	Partly suited	Suited	Partly suited
Hypothesis four Learning from the US	Suited	Suited	Suited	Partly suited

CONCLUSION

Japan's foreign policy relative to India has resembled America's India policy in the post-Cold War era. Although it seems that Japan has followed the US, it is too extreme to infer that Japan has merely followed the US (first hypothesis) or that Japan's India policy is controlled by the US (second hypothesis). A contrasting hypothesis of Japan's autonomous calculations based on common interests is also not satisfactory to explain the close similarity of policies produced by the US and Japan (third hypothesis). The fourth hypothesis provides a modest explanation for the similarity: Japan and the US share interests, but Japan acknowledges and recognizes its own national interests in its relations with India through America's and others' relations with India. Therefore, record of Japan's India policy has come to resemble the India policy of the US.

The key element which differentiates the third hypothesis with the fourth is a perception of the interests. The third hypothesis assumes a direct link between the interests and the policy, whereas the fourth assumes the importance of the perception process. Some previous reports on Japan–India relations by a few young scholars have demonstrated consideration for this point. For instance, Harsh V. Pant of King's College London refers to a change in perceptions of individual leaders as a reason for growing Japanese–Indian co-operation.[27] Victoria Tuke, a doctoral candidate of University of

Warwick, provides a more systemic and theoretically sophisticated analysis, in which she refers to attitudes of key Japanese policymakers and Japan's domestic politics as intervening variables complementing the structural factor of the US policy.[28] These works contribute to a comprehensive understanding of the contemporary Japan–India relations. However, they cannot explain the policy similarity that this chapter specifically examines because they add factors existing within the bilateral relations: although internal factors can explain the Japan–India relations, they cannot offer a proper suggestion for the observation that not only Japan but other countries have adopted similar policies toward India.

As the interdependence between Japan and India has deepened and as the importance of Japan's relationship with India has increased, several factors are expected to be increasingly related to the development of the practical relations between the countries: global issues, regional reconfiguration of the political structure, domestic political interests, individual perceptions, and so on. However, in terms of pursuing the provision of better explanations, we should not increase the number of variables too much.[29] From this perspective, this chapter has attempted to contribute to more parsimonious and sophisticated explanations of contemporary Japan–India relations by specifically addressing similarities between Indo–Japan and Indo–US relations. Results demonstrate that Japan's India policy can be explained by external interests as independent variables and US policy relative to India as an intervening variable.

NOTES

1. 'Joint Statement towards Japan–India Strategic and Global Partnership', 15 December 2006, paragraphs 4 and 6. Retrieved from a website of Ministry of External Affairs of Japan (http://www.mofa.go.jp/region/asia-paci/india/pdfs/joint0612.pdf, accessed on 17 December 2011).
2. 'Japan–India Joint Declaration', 10 December 2001. Retrieved from a website of Ministry of External Affairs of Japan (http://

www.mofa.go.jp/region/asia-paci/india/joint0112.html, accessed on 17 December 2011).

3. Rajaram Panda, 'Changing Dynamics of India–Japan Relations: Future Trends', in Akihiro Iwashita, ed., *India–Japan Dialogue: Challenge and Potential*, Comparative Studies on Regional Powers, no. 6, 2011, pp. 9-15.
4. Michael Green, an influential Japanologist in the US, described Japan's foreign policy after the end of the Cold War as 'reluctant realism'. See Michael J. Green, *Japan's Reluctant Realism: Foreign Policy Challenges in an Era of Uncertain Power*, New York: Palgrave Macmillan, 2003.
5. For examples of this argument, see Edward J. Lincoln, 'Japan: Using Power Narrowly', *The Washington Quarterly*, vol. 27, no. 1 (Winter 2003-4), pp. 111-27, and Kyoichi Marukusu, 'Japan's Diplomacy on the Iraq War (Koizumi Seiken no Taiou Gaikou)', in Daizo Sakurada and Go Ito, eds., *Comparative Foreign Policy: The Iraq War and Seven Powers (Hikaku Gaikou Seisaku: Iraq Sensouheno Taiou Gaikou)*, Tokyo: Akashi Shoten, 2004, pp. 43-77 (Japanese).
6. Purnendra Jain, 'Japan–India Relations: Peaks and Troughs', *The Round Table*, vol. 99, no. 409 (August 2010), p. 403. The reason why Japan's India policy has been reactive is not addressed in the article.
7. Description in this section is mainly based on the following materials. A website of Ministry of Foreign Affairs of Japan, 'Japan–India Relations', February 2011 (http://www.mofa.go.jp/region/asia-paci/india/index.html, accessed on 13 December 2011); 'India–Japan Relations', a website of the Ministry of External Affairs of India (http://www.mea.gov.in/mystart.php?id=50044483, accessed on 13 December 2011); Hiroshi Inomata, 'Political and Security Cooperation between Japan and India (Nichi-In Kan no Seiji, Anzenhosho Bunya deno Kyouryoku)', *Contemporary India Forum, Quarterly Review (Gendai Indo Forum)*, no. 5 (Spring 2010), pp. 3-9 (Japanese); Jain, op. cit., pp. 406-11.
8. Website of the Ministry of Foreign Affairs of Japan, 'Japan–India Relations', February 2011.
9. Prime Minister Manmohan Singh expressed his gratitude for

the assistance in his speech in the Japanese Diet on 14 December 2006. He had earlier visited Japan in 1992 as Finance Minister.

10. After the Pokhran II nuclear tests, Tokyo temporarily recalled its ambassador in New Delhi and suspended official dialogue. See Jain, op. cit., p. 406.
11. Inomata, op. cit., pp. 4-5.
12. Website of Ministry of Foreign Affairs of Japan, 'Japan–India Relations', February 2011.
13. Inomata, op. cit., p. 5.
14. Jain, op. cit., p. 407. He also points out the influence of the US–India engagement at that time.
15. 'Japan–India Partnership in a New Asian Era: Strategic Orientation of Japan–India Global Partnership', 29 April 2005, retrieved from a website of Ministry of Foreign Affairs of Japan (http://www.mofa.go.jp/region/asia-paci/india/partner0504.html, accessed on 13 December 2011).
16. For details of the recent Japan–India strategic cooperation, see Shamshad Ahmad Khan, 'Indo–Japan Strategic Cooperation: Issues, Expectations and Challenge', in Akihro Iwashita, ed., *India–Japan Dialogue: Challenge and Potential* (Comparative Studies on Regional Powers, no. 6), pp. 19-39, and Madhuchanda Ghosh, 'India and Japan's Growing Synergy: From a Political to a Strategic Focus', *Asian Survey*, vol. 48, no. 2 (March/April 2008), pp. 282-302.
17. For President Clinton's visit to India, see Strobe Talbott, *Engaging India: Diplomacy, Democracy, and the Bomb,* rev. edn., Washington, D.C.: Brookings Institution Press, 2006, pp. 190-205.
18. 'Statement on the Next Steps in Strategic Partnership', by Prime Minister Atal Behari Vajpayee and President George W. Bush, on 13 January 2004. Retrieved from a website of Ministry of External Affairs of India (http://www.mea.gov.in/mystart.php?id=53017495, accessed on 17 December 2011). Although the statement of January 2004 says the two leaders committed the two countries to a strategic partnership in November 2001, the text of joint statement in November 2001 does not refer to the word 'strategic'. Therefore, this chapter regards the 2004 statement as the declaration of the India–US strategic partnership.

19. The joint statement in April 2005 had already mentioned the 'strategic orientation' of the Japan–India global partnership.
20. The Clinton Administration of the US in its first term (January 1993–January 1997) adopted a 'broader engagement' policy related to South Asia. But the US failed to approach India at that time. Kazutoshi Tamari, '"Engagement" in the U.S. Foreign Policy: An Analysis of America's Asia Policy in the 1990s (Gendai America Gaikou to Engagement Seisaku: 1990 Nendai America no Asia Seisakuwo Zireini)', *The Annual Bulletin of the Institute of Policy and Cultural Studies, Chuo University (Chuo Daigaku Seisaku Bunka Sougou Kenkyujo Nenpou)*, no. 11 (2007), pp. 109-25 (Japanese).
21. Jain, op. cit.
22. Reportedly, the US and France urged Tokyo to pursue a nuclear cooperation agreement with India. *Nihon Keizai Shinbun*, 9 June 2010 (Japanese).
23. For discussions related to *gaiatsu*, see Akihiko Tanaka, 'Japan's Diplomacy and International Politics: Political Science of Gaiatsu (Nihon Gaiko to Kokunai Seiji no Renkan: Gaiatsu no Seiji-Gaku)', *Kokusai Mondai (International Affairs)*, no. 348, March 1989, pp. 23–36 (Japanese), and Leonard J. Schoppa, 'Two-Level Games and Bargaining Outcomes: Why Gaiatsu Succeeds in Japan in Some Cases but not Others', *International Organization*, vol. 47, no. 3 (Summer 1993), pp. 353-86.
24. Takenori Horimoto, 'Japan's Policy Towards India: The Current Growing Japan–India Security Cooperation and the Future (Indo wo Meguru Nihon no Ugoki: Junchona Nichi-In Anzenhosho Kankei to Kongo)', in Masashi Nishihara and Takenori Horimoto, eds., *India's Emerging Military Power* (*Gunji Taikoku-ka Suru Indo*), Tokyo: Akishobo, 2010, pp. 86-98 (Japanese).
25. In conceiving the fourth hypothesis, the author was inspired by a discussion with Yukifumi Takeuchi, a visiting scholar of the Edwin O. Reischauer Center for East Asian Studies (The Paul H. Nitze School of Advanced International Studies, Johns Hopkins University, Washington, D.C.), at a seminar held in Tokyo on 24 November 2011. The author is grateful to him for his suggestion to a question from the author.
26. Jain, op. cit.

27. Harsh V. Pant, 'India–Japan Relations: A Slow, but Steady, Transformation', in Sumit Ganguly, ed., *India's Foreign Policy: Retrospect and Prospect*, New Delhi: Oxford University Press, 2010, pp. 206-25. He lists the following reasons for Japan–India engagement: first, at the structural level, a changing balance of power in the Asia–Pacific and response to the 'China Challenge'; secondly, at the domestic level, economic complementarities, trade security, the changing demographic profiles in both countries, and changing domestic political attitude in Japan; and thirdly, at the individual level, contributions by individual political leaders of both countries.
28. Victoria Tuke, 'Japan's Policy Towards India: The Implications for Japanese Foreign Policy', paper presented at Political Studies Association Conference on 30 March 2010, retrieved from a website of Political Studies Association (http://www.psa.ac.uk/journals/pdf/5/2010/880_304.pdf, accessed on 1 August 2011).
29. For the preferred explanation in the discipline of International Relations, see Kenneth N. Waltz, *Theory of International Politics,* rpt. edn., Long Grove, IL: Waveland Press, 2010, originally published in 1979, chap. 1.

CHAPTER 8

India, Japan and Maritime Security Cooperation in the Asia-Pacific

MARIE IZUYAMA

This chapter is intended to elucidate the fundamental impetus and rationale for India–Japan security cooperation, especially with respect to maritime security.

In the first part, we survey the evolution of maritime power of the respective countries to explore their motivations and objectives. Because the United States is the dominant power, relations with United States are a central issue. The author argues that symmetry prevails between Japan–US relations and India–US relations. Either US pressure or US endorsement has been a catalyst for fostering outward-looking maritime policies for Japan and India.

In the second part, the evolution of cooperative security in the maritime sphere is analysed. The author argues that non-traditional security, especially tsunami relief, has catalysed multilateral cooperation in the region. India and Japan were part of that evolution. Both have the will and capacity to share responsibility.

In the third part, we turn to Indian and Japanese relations with their maritime neighbours. What are the common features or differences between India and Japan in terms of their efforts to shape maritime regional order?

In the last part, prospects for cooperation and limits are assessed.

EVOLUTION OF MARITIME POWER

In this section, the author argues that some similar trajectory exists for India and Japan to evolve outward-looking maritime strategies. Japan expanded its maritime responsibilities during the late 1970s to the early 1980s. This expansion was the result of the redefinition and renegotiation process of the US–Japan alliance. Similarly, India altered its isolation policy around 1991 to resume interactions with foreign navies.[1] That policy change was largely triggered by proposals from the US Pacific Command.[2]

Japan

After the Second World War, Japan Maritime Self-Defense Force (JMSDF) was established as a response to strategic demand of the US, the occupier, and it was destined to work with the US from the beginning.

The Guam Doctrine of 1969, symptomatic of US disengagement, accompanied the rise of expectation from the US side that Japan take greater responsibility in the region. Simultaneously, the Japanese government confronted domestic pressure to show a cap clearly for the defence budget under the conditions of détente.

To meet this challenge, the first National Defense Program Guidelines (NDPG) were compiled as an official document in 1976. The 1978 Guidelines for US–Japan Defense Cooperation followed. The two documents opened the way for Japan to conduct joint military exercises with the US. Table 8.1 gives the evolution of USA–Japan exercises.

TABLE 8.1: EVOLUTION OF US–JAPAN EXERCISES

	1950-	1970-	1990-
Joint		1985 Joint CPX 1986 Joint field exercise	2007 BMD
Ground		1981 CPX 1981 Field exercise	
Air		1978 *Cope North* 1983 CPX 1984 Air defense	1996 *Cope Thunder*
Maritime	1955 minesweeping 1957 anti-submarine warfare	1980 RIMPAC 1988 CPX	

Note: The Table indicates starting year of major regular exercises carried on date. CPX = Command Post Exercise

Source: *Boei-handbook* (*Handbook of Defense*), various years.

In the 1980s, concomitantly with the revival of the Cold War, Japan was under pressure from the US to step up defence build-up. In response to US pressure, Prime Minister Suzuki stated that Japan ought to pursue a 'One thousand nautical mile sea-lane defense' when he visited Washington in May 1981. Finally, Prime Minister Nakasone clearly defined that the interest for the US–Japan alliance is equivalent to Japan's national interest. In January 1983, immediately before visiting the US, Nakasone pushed for a defence budget increase and also took initiative for exempting the US from the Three Principles on Arms Exports, which restricted defence equipment cooperation.[3]

After this commitment of Nakasone's, the JMSDF and US navy were able to work under a clearer division of roles and missions: JMSDF ought to be a shield for US carrier battle groups against Soviet forces. Concretely the JMSDF was blockading three straits to prevent Soviet submarine forces from entering the Pacific Ocean. In addition, JMSDF was conducting anti-submarine warfare and providing air cover against Tu-22 *Backfire* bombers.[4]

The end of the Cold War brought an end to the era of JMSDF operations in which the defence of Japan was able to fulfil a part of allied operations effectively. In the 1990s, complex security environments both in the region and beyond necessitated that the JMSDF expand its tasks. To meet post-Cold War challenges, the NDPG was revised in 1995. The 1995 NDPG stipulates the role of SDF as (a) defence of Japan, (b) response to large-scale disasters and 'situations in surrounding areas', and (c) contribution to building a stable international security environment. Response to 'situations in surrounding areas' mandated that the SDF extend logistic support to US forces in cases of contingencies on the Korean Peninsula. It should be noted that requirements for such response to traditional security overlap those for disaster response.

India

The Indian Navy has long been a junior partner in the three services of the country. One obvious reason is that India's direct threat comes historically from the north-west land mass. After transfer of power from the British, Pakistan in the west and China in the north constitute the main potential threats to India, for which the Army was obligated to respond.[5] Another reason is that the Navy was the last service to be 'Indianized', being commanded by a British chief until 1958. This might be a factor that diminishes the Navy's say in decision-making and in budgetary allocations during the nation's formative years. Allocations for Navy expenditures are almost fixed at around 15 per cent of the total defence expenditure.[6]

The Indian Navy was designed to serve the interests of the Commonwealth. One such example is that Indian Navy was conducting annual exercises off the north-east coast of Sri Lanka until 1964 along with Pakistan and Sri Lanka; sometimes Australia and New Zealand joined.[7]

After the British withdrawal east of the Suez, India never accepted the US as the British heir in the Indian Ocean region. US presence in the Indian Ocean was a cause of concern especially after a US carrier task force under the Seventh Fleet entered the Bay of Bengal in the course of the India–Pakistan war of December 1971.[8] India regarded this carrier operation as US coercive diplomacy, depriving India of freedom of action and influencing subsequent peace negotiations.[9] Through the 1970s and the 1980s, India continued to raise issues of 'great power rivalry' and 'foreign military base' in the Indian Ocean region.[10] India's concern centred around the constant upgrading of US facilities in Diego Garcia, which increased the US capabilities to intervene in the Indian Ocean littoral.[11]

To counter the presence of extra-regional navies, India pursued an 'Indian Ocean Zone of Peace' proposal. At the same time, Indian strategists started to emphasize denial power in the Indian Ocean region. India tried to develop nuclear submarine capabilities in the 1980s.[12]

However, Soviet withdrawal from Afghanistan and the end of the Cold War eased Indian concerns related to intervention by extra-regional powers. India started to interact with foreign navies, including those of Southeast Asian countries, UK, France and the US.[13] India–US defence cooperation started after Lieutenant General

Kicklighter, Pacific Command, proposed a package of military-to-military cooperation to General Rodrigues, Indian Chief of Army Staff in 1991. 'Steering Committee', a service-to-service consultative committee for each service, was established separately under the banner of the overall Defence Policy Group.[14] The first joint naval exercise was conducted in May 1992. A US–Indian naval exercise, code-named *Malabar*, was undertaken in 1995 and 1996. However, *Malabar* was halted because of India's nuclear test in 1998.

Widening Naval Operations: India and Japan under US Pre-eminence

In terms of actual operations, JMSDF had clearly diversified its activities in the 1990s. In April 1991, immediately after the Gulf War, the Government of Japan decided to dispatch minesweepers to the Persian Gulf, which constituted the first post-war overseas deployment of Japanese forces. This deployment opened the way for participation in UN peacekeeping in Cambodia (UNTAC) in 1992.

JMSDF had also got firmness and effectiveness. In March 1999, in response to an incursion by suspected North Korean spy vessels, JMSDF destroyers were authorized to use force as a maritime security operation. This was the first time that the government had issued orders for maritime security operations stipulated in Article 82 of the Self-Defense Force Law.[15]

After 9/11, instead of sending land forces to Afghanistan, Japan quickly decided to send JMSDF ships for refuelling of coalition forces engaged in Operation Enduring Freedom-Maritime Interdiction Operations (OEF-MIO). The JMSDF operation was authorized by the Anti-Terrorism Special Measures Law, a temporary law enacted in October 2001. The law was extended five times before it expired in November 2007. After the two-month halt, the JMSDF resumed similar operations under the newly-enacted Replenishment Support Special Measures Law, which also expired in January 2010.

The significance of Indian Ocean deployment is that the JMSDF proved its capability for sustainable presence in the region.[16] It has been an 'enormous value to the JMSDF by providing war zone experience', according to one analyst.[17]

Just as the 1991 Gulf War was a shock for Japan, which eventually widened the scope and geographical area of JMSDF operations, 9/11 changed the security context for India and provided the opportunity to expand military cooperation with the US.[18] As India had been exposed to Jihadist terrorism over the decade, Indian and US interests converged on counter–terrorism. India offered logistical support for Operation *Enduring Freedom* in the form of refuelling facilities, berthing facilities, search and rescue operations, and other undertakings.[19] This offer of support contrasted sharply to the Indian response to the 1991 Gulf War, when the government decision to allow US C-141 refuelling at the Sahar Airbase in Mumbai was halted because it created political turmoil.[20]

The US–India defence cooperation mechanism was rejuvenated in December 2001 by the Defence Policy Group, an institutional framework created in 1995. The US carrier *Carl Vinson* visited Mumbai in the same month.[21] A navy-to-navy steering committee was held in May 2002. As part of military cooperation for Operation *Enduring Freedom*, the Indian Navy had escorted US high-value vessels through the Strait of Malacca during April–September 2002.[22] It was against this background that the US–India naval exercise *Malabar* was held during September–October 2002 after a six year hiatus. Although *Malabar* at this stage was merely basic manoeuvring, it has developed into a multifaceted warfare exercise[23] (see Table 8.2).

TABLE 8.2: *MALABAR* EXERCISE

Date	Place	Ships participated	Aim
Sept.-Oct. 2002	Cochin	NA	Basic passing manouvres, Anti-submarine exercises, Replenishment-at-sea drills
Oct. 2003	Southwest Goa	US *Fitzerald* (DDG 62) *Chosin* (CG 65) *Pasadena* (SSN 752)	Anti-submarine War (ASW) tactics

		India *Brahmaputra* (F31) *Ganga* (F22)	
Oct. 2004	Southwest Goa	US *Cowpens* (CG 63) *Gary* (FFG 51) *Alexandria* (SSN 575) P-3C	ASW, Sea-control mission, Air defense, Surface firing, Maritime Interdiction, Visit, board, search and seizure (UBSS)
		India *Mysore* (D 60) *Brahmaputra* (F31) *Aditya* (A 59) *Shankul* (S 47)	
Sept. 2005	Southwest Goa	US *Nimitz* Carrier Strike Group *Higgings* (DDG-76)	ASW, Aviation interoperability (F 18, Sea Harrier), Air Defense
		India *Viraat* (R 22) *Gomati* (F-21)	
Oct. 2006	Southwest Goa	US *Boxer* (LHD 4) Expeditionary Strike Group	Amphibious Landing, ASW, Force Protection VBSS,
		India Navy: Western Fleet Army: 9th Battalion of the Sikh Infantry Canada *Ottawa* (FFH 341)	Surface Firings
April 2007	Philippine Sea	US *John McCain* (DDG56) *Mustin* (DDG 89) *Custis Wilbur* (DDG 54)	VBBS, surface exercises, formation steaming coordinated surface fire support, air defense exercises, ASW

		Fitzgerald (DDG 62) *Stethem* (DDG 63) *Gary* (FFG 51) *Greenville* (SSN 772) SH-60x4, P-3C India *Mysore* (D 60), *Rana* (D 52), *Ranjit* (D 53) *Jyoti* (A 58) *Kuthar* (P46)	
Sept. 2007	Bay of Bangal	US *Nimitz* (CVN 68), Kitty *Hawk* (CV 63) DDG x 6 *Chicago* (SSN 721) *Princeton* (CG59) F/A 18 India *Viraat* (R 22) 6 other ships Air Wing *Jaguar* IM, *Sea Harriers*, TU-142M surveillance Japan *Oonami* (DD 111), *Yudachi* (DD 108) P-3C x 2 Singapore Frigate: *Formidable* (68) Australia Frigate: *Adelaide*	Dissimilar Aircraft Combat Tactics (DACT) cross deck landings by aircraft and helicopters between various ships, strike and combat air patrols (CAP) by fighters operating from aircraft carriers, air defence exercises (ADEX), combined antisubmarine exercises (CASEX) Counter mechanisms to marine terrorism, piracy, human arms and drug trafficking

		Fleet oiler: *Sirius* (O 266)	
Oct. 2008	Southwest Goa	US *Ronald Reagan* (CVN 76) *Chancellorsville* (CG 62) *Gridley* (DDG 101) *Decatur* (DDG 73) *Thach* (FFG 43) *Bridge* (T-AOE10) *Springfield* (SSN 761) P-3C *Orion* India *Mumbai* (D 61) *Rana* (D 52) *Talwar* (F40) *Godavari* (F20) *Brahmaputra* (F3) *Betwa* (F37) *Aditya* (A59) *Shishumar* (S44)	Anti-submarine operations, Submarine to submarine operations, Flying operations, Cross deck embarcations, Alternating control and command
April 2009	East Okinawa	US *Blue Ridge* (LCC 19) *Fitzgerald* (DDG 62) *Chafee* (DDG 90) *Seawolf* (SSN 21) India *Mumbai* (D 62), *Ranvir* (D 54), *Khanjar* (P 47), *Jyoti* (A 58) Japan *Kurama* (DDH 144), *Asayuki* (DD 132) P-3C	ASW, Surface warfare, gunnery training, air defense, VBSS

April 2010	Southwest Goa	US *Lassen* (DDG 82) *Chafee* (DDG 90) *Shiloh* (CG 67) *Curts* (FFG 38) *Annapolis* (SSN 760) P-3 SH-60 Sea, Air and Land (SEAL) special forces detachment India *Mysore* (D-60) *Godavari* (F 20) *Brahmaputra* (F 3) *Tabar* (F 44) *Shankush* (S 45) *Sea Harriers* other fixed and rotary wing aircrafts	ASW, Surface warfare, Coordinated gunnery excercises, Air Defense, VBSS
April 2011	Philippine Sea	US *Rueben James* (FFG 57), *Stethem* (DDG 63), *Sterett* (DDG 104) nuclear powered attack submarine limited participation of *Ronald Reagan* (CVN 76) and Carrier Strike Group including Carrier Strike Group 7; Destroyer Squadron 7; Carrier Air Wing (CVW) 14; *Chancellorsville*	Liaison officer professional exchanges and embarks, communications exercises, surface action group exercise operations, formation manoeuvring, helicopter cross deck evolutions, underway replenishment, humanitarian assistance and disaster relief, gunnery exercises, VBSS, maritime strike, air defense, screen exercise, ASW

(CG 63);
Peble (DDG 88)

India

Jyoti (A 58)
Kirch (P62)
Delhi (D 61)
Ranvijay (D 55)
Ranvir (D 54)

Source: Ministry of Defence Government of India, *Annual Report*, various years; Directorate of Public Relations, Ministry of Defence, Government of India, *Sainik Samachar*; News available on home page of US navy, 7th Fleet (http://www.c7f.navy.mil/); Ministry of Defense, Government of Japan, news releases (in Japanese); *Asagumo-Shinbun* (in Japanese); *The Hindu*; *Hindustan Times.*

Whether the option was pursued under pressure or deliberate choice is not a point for this discussion. Rather, it is noteworthy to understand that the US encouraged both Japan and India to expand and enhance their maritime operations.

HUMANITARIAN ASSISTANCE/DISASTER RELIEF (HA/DR), COOPERATIVE SECURITY AND MARITIME MULTILATERALISM

Multilateral exercises in the Western Pacific

During the last decade, the Indian Navy and JMSDF have both become involved in multilateral efforts to improve maritime safety and security in the Asia–Pacific region. The US, Singapore, and Australia undertook initiatives to organize combined exercises, and the Indian Navy and JMSDF have extended their interaction through those exercises (Table 8.3).

In 2000, the US Pacific Command started to plan multilateral exercises focused on search and rescue, disaster relief, and non-combatant evacuation missions.[24] The countries in the region

TABLE 8.3: MULTILATERAL EXERCISES IN THE ASIA-PACIFIC

(a) Pacific Reach

Year	2000	2002	2004	2007	2010
Host	Singapore	Japan	Republic of Korea (ROK)	Australia	Singapore
Participants	Singapore Japan, ROK, US *Observers*: Australia, Canada, Chile, China, Indonesia, Russia, UK	Japan, Australia, ROK, Singapore, US *Observers*: Canada, China, Chile, France, India, Indonesia, UK	ROK, Australia, Japan, Singapore, US *Observers*: Canada, China, Chile, France, India, Indonesia, Thailand, UK	Australia, Canada, China, Japan, ROK Malaysia, Singapore, UK, US *Observers*: Chile, India, Indonesia, NATO, Pakistan, Peru, Russia, South Africa	Singapore, Australia, Japan, ROK, US *Observers*: Canada, China, France, India, Indonesia, Italy, Malaysia, Pakistan, South Africa, Sweden, Thailand, UK

(b) Western Pacific MCMEX/DIVEX

Year	2001	2004	2006	2011
Host	Singapore	Singapore/ Indonesia	Malaysia	Singapore/ Indonesia
Participants	(ROK) Australia, Indonesia, Japan, Singapore Thailand, US *Observers*: Canada, China, France, India, ROK Malaysia, New Zealand, Papua New Guinea, Russia, Vietnam	Singapore, Indonesia, Australia, India, Japan, ROK, Malaysia, Thailand, *Observers*: China, Canada, France, Rusia US and others	Malaysia, Australia, Indonesia, Japan, Singapore, US *Observers*: Brunei, Canada, China, India, Thailand, Vietnam, and others	Australia, France, India, Indonesia, ROK, Malaysia, New Zealand, Singapore Thailand, US, Vietnam *Observers*: China, Sweden

Source: Japan Defense Agency/Ministry of Defense, Japan, *Defense of Japan*, various years; Media stories available on website of Department of Defence, Australia, http://www.defence.gov.au/; News articles available on website of Ministry of Defence, Singapore, http://www.mindef.gov.sg/; News stories available on website of US Navy, http://www.navy.mil/

responded positively. Singapore was especially enthusiastic to host Pacific Reach 2000, a submarine rescue exercise, and Western Pacific Mine Countermeasure Exercise and Diving Exercise (MCMEX/ DIVEX) 2001. Japan had been actively participating in these multilateral exercises. Although the SDF refrains from participating in exercises which might be construed as 'collective defence', those exercises were not war exercises and therefore provoked no constitutional debates in domestic political arenas. The JMSDF hosted the Second Pacific Reach in 2002, which was the first multilateral exercise that Japan had hosted. India was also invited as an observer. Since that time, India has been sending observers to the Pacific Reach. Regarding the Western Pacific MCMEX/DIVEX, India has been regularly participating from the first exercise.

Tsunami Relief

The real test for the Indian Navy and JMSDAF robust commitments and operational capability required for disaster relief in the region came soon after December 2004 tsunami.

India conducted operation *Madad* at the eastern coast of Tamil Nadu, and operation *Sea Wave* at Andaman & Nicobar Islands. In spite of their difficulties at home, India also launched operation *Castor* in the Maldives, operation *Rainbow* in Sri Lanka, and operation *Gambhir* in Indonesia at the request of those respective governments.[25] India deployed 20,000 personnel, 40 ships, and 32 aircraft and helicopters in the affected area. The Navy alone transported 735 tonnes of relief supplies.[26]

India's quick decision can be partly explained by the low threshold in humanitarian intervention in Sri Lanka and Maldives. Some analysts also point out that India was not welcoming of the US unilateral deployment close to its coastal areas, especially in Sri Lanka.[27] India had already established its presence in Sri Lanka and the Maldives before President Bush proposed the formation of the Tsunami Core Group, comprising Australia, India, Japan, and the US based on their capabilities and resources. India accepted the proposal on 30 December.[28]

Because India understood that 'the main purpose of the coordination effort[29] is to avoid duplication of efforts, identify gaps in the relief process and find ways and means to address these deficiencies', it was easy for India to join the four-nation group without provoking command issues. The Tsunami Core Group was an exception to India's hesitant stance in relation to joining coalition operations other than those under UN command.

Japan also responded quickly. Three JMSDF ships returning from Indian Ocean replenishment missions were diverted immediately to Phuket upon request from the Government of Thailand.[30]

JMSDF ship *Kunisaki* (LST 4003) carried helicopters, which were Japan's first deployment of helicopters in disaster relief operations abroad. It was also the first joint operation by maritime, ground, and air SDF forces, which became a stepping stone for transforming the SDF into more jointly active forces.

US–India Cooperation in Disaster Relief

India's capability in disaster relief was highly appreciated by the United States.[31] Although it was not accorded the level of attention of the level of a nuclear deal, the US–India Disaster Relief Initiative was announced on 18 July 2005, when US President Bush visited Delhi. It was stated that 'US and India will strengthen their military capabilities to respond effectively to future disasters by conducting joint and combined military exercise'. The US and India also agreed to cooperate in helping to build disaster response capabilities in other countries.[32] The Disaster Relief Initiative was later integrated into the Indo–US Framework for Maritime Security Cooperation announced in March 2006.[33]

Regarding the US maritime strategy, the 2004 tsunami reinforced the direction towards cooperative strategy.[34] Particularly, India's Navy emerged as an indispensable partner for the cooperative strategy. India came forward to the idea of commitment to ensure 'a secure maritime domain' and to support 'existing multilateral efforts'.[35] When the US deployed the hospital ship *Mercy* in 2006, which was later established as an annual mission *Pacific Partnership*, Indian medical officers joined.[36] The purpose of *Pacific Partnership* is to build partner capacity and to improve disaster-response readiness.[37] Indian officers partially participate in *Pacific Partnership*, in which the US Pacific Command sends a hospital ship or an amphibious ship to countries in the Pacific.[38]

Once India's role and responsibility in disaster relief were recognized, strengthening of her capabilities in areas such as amphibious operations was legitimized. The USS *Trenton*, an amphibious landing ship, was transferred to India in 2007 under the Foreign Military Sales Programme.[39] It became the first US ship to join the Indian fleet. The bilateral amphibious exercise *HABU NAG* commenced in 2006. The counterpart on the US side was Task Force 76, a forward-deployed amphibious expeditionary strike group based in Okinawa, Japan. During *HABU NAG 2010*, several Indian officers observed amphibious operations on board the USS *Essex* (LHD 2) and landed on Okinawa.[40]

SHAPING MARITIME REGIONAL ORDER

Southeast Asia in Indian Maritime Strategy

The preceding section explained that India is much more forthright in partnering with the US and other regional countries than might be expected from diplomatic statements or Indian media coverage. What is India's own rationale for engaging the region?

Recent studies on Indian security policies elucidate India's strategic moves in Southeast Asia. Scott, in his enquiry into India's 'extended neighbourhood' concept, argues that India is seeking strategic denial, especially eastward and southward in the Indian Ocean region.[41] Brewster sees India's ambition to play a direct security role in Southeast Asia.[42] Holmes and Yoshihara observe an analogy of the British Raj in India's regional policy, which is to create a geographic buffer.[43] India's maritime interest is clearly stated in its maritime doctrine, in which the Strait of Malacca is included among primary areas of interest as one of the choke points leading to the Indian

Ocean. Beyond Malacca, the South China Sea and other areas of Western Pacific are defined as secondary areas of interest.[44]

All of those are very recent trends. Although India enjoys one or other historical ties with each Southeast Asian country including support for anti-colonial struggles or common positions in Non-Aligned Movement, her relations with the region as a whole were not so much structured strategically until setting of the 'Look East' policy in 1992. India became a Sectoral Dialogue Partner of ASEAN in 1992, a member of ARF in 1995, and a full dialogue Partner of ASEAN in 1996. The ASEAN–India summit was set in 2002 to accommodate compensation for India's exclusion from ASEAN plus three.

Regarding naval contact, India's gateway for an eastward turn was Singapore, which started bilateral exercises as early as 1994. However, a certain amount of anxiety prevailed within ASEAN over India's naval expansion eastward. To allay that anxiety, India launched a forum of regional navies for building friendship and mutual understanding in 1995. The biennial forum, called MILAN, has been held in Port Blair, Andaman Islands, which is now the headquarters of India's integrated command. MILAN developed into multilateral exercise involving seven navies and observers from three countries.[45]

MILAN is an example of India's will to take a leading role in shaping the maritime regional order. However, India is cautious not to be regarded as a hegemon. Because naval presence is sensitive especially for Indonesia and Malaysia, India plays a limited role, as in cooperative patrols (COPRAT) with Indonesia, since 2002. India has also conducted coordinated patrols with Thailand since 2005.[46]

Southeast Asia in Japan's Maritime Strategy

Southeast Asia has not been the primary area of interest for Japan's traditional security, which is defence of the 'surrounding sea'. Rear Admiral Takei, JMSDF, proposed that the Taiwan–Guam–Tokyo triangle should be the vital area of interest for the defence of the surrounding sea. Southeast Asia came to this picture only in the context of freedom of the seas.[47] Although Japan is heavily dependent on the Strait of Malacca for its energy imports, the Lombok Strait might serve as a substitute route in case of contingency.[48] Rather than an immediate security interest, Southeast Asia is important for Japan to mobilize support for a multilateral regional security framework.

The end of the Cold War compelled Japan to review its defence policy, which had been single-mindedly dependent on its alliance with the US. Prime Minister Hosokawa, the first non-Liberal Democratic Party prime minister, appointed an advisory group to submit a report on defence review. The Higuchi Report vigorously proposed multilateral security cooperation as a new approach for securing Japan.[49] Under the circumstances of the US reducing its forward presence in the Philippines and Korea, Japan was contemplating a mechanism to embed itself into the regional and global security order. The ideas advanced in the Higuchi Report constitute the origin of multilateralism in Japan's contemporary defence policy. Some analysts characterize this multilateralism as a 'hedge' to alliance.[50] Japan has also started to invest in an ASEAN-centred security framework such as ARF, and later, ASEAN plus three.

The area yielding the most success for Japan's initiatives has been that of anti-piracy. Japan has initiated conferences among coast guards in the region in 2000. The conference developed into the 'Heads of Asian Coast Guard Agencies Meeting', the first of which was hosted by Japan in 2004. Japan also undertook efforts to institutionalize regional cooperation for anti-piracy. Following Prime Minister Koizumi's proposal at the Japan–ASEAN summit in November 2001, negotiations for 'Regional Cooperation Agreement on Combating Piracy and Armed Robbery against ships in Asia (ReCAAP)' started. It was eventually adopted at the conference in Tokyo in November 2004. Among the 16 negotiating parties including 10 ASEAN states, China, Korea, Japan, Bangladesh, India and Sri

Lanka, 14 states became contracting parties by 2007. Norway, the Netherlands, and Denmark joined later.[51]

The central feature of ReCAAP is information sharing. ReCAAP agreed to establish an information sharing centre in Singapore [Article 4(3)]. To share information about incident or imminent threat of piracy and armed robbery, and to cooperate in rescue, arrest or seizure, ReCAAP also stipulated that each contracting party should designate a focal point responsible for communication with the centre (Articles 9 and 10). Other cooperative efforts in areas such as extradition, mutual legal assistance, capacity building, and joint exercises shall be pursued bilaterally among contracting parties (Articles 12–15).

It is evident that Japan's efforts at anti-piracy cooperation in Southeast Asia are civilian-focused.[52] Japan's Coast Guard, which is under the administrative auspices of the Ministry of Land, Infrastructure, Transport and Tourism, is not part of the defence forces. Therefore it is easier to carry forward proactive diplomacy. The JMSDF and Ministry of Defense are not involved in the ReCAAP process. A salient advantage of Japan's Coast Guard status as being a 'civilian' organization is that it can use Official Development Assistance (ODA) for assisting maritime security and safety agencies in Southeast Asian countries. Under the banner of 'capacity building', Japan's Coast Guard has been providing training and equipment for law enforcement to Malaysia, Indonesia and Philippines. Under the ODA schemes, Japan transferred three patrol vessels to Indonesia in 2007.[53]

The Japan Coast Guard and Indian Coast Guard started anti-piracy exercises in 2000, prior to negotiation for ReCAAP. However, without an Indian commitment in ReCAAP, coast guard-to-coast guard cooperation could not have advanced so rapidly. A Memorandum of Cooperation was signed by heads of two coast guards in November 2006. The memorandum stipulates sharing information on preventing and responding to acts of crimes at sea such as piracy and armed robbery, carrying out search and rescue operations at sea, and exchange of technical assistance for prevention and protection from natural disasters like tsunami.

Compared with Japan's Coast Guard, the JMSDF has been extremely shy at having bilateral service-to-service interactions. Although Japan's Ministry of Defense has had defence dialogue schemes with Singapore and Indonesia since 1997, and with Vietnam since 2001, no navy-to-navy staff talks with ReCAAP countries have been pursued except for those with India. Bilateral naval exercises have not been conducted except with Korea and India.

CONCLUSION: IMPLICATIONS FOR INDO–JAPAN COOPERATION

This chapter has specifically addressed cooperative trends in the regional maritime security order and the position of India and Japan in such trend. Because the Indian Navy and JMSDF interact not only in multilateral exercises in the Western Pacific but also in actual operation for responding to tsunami and other disasters, HA/DR is expected to provide a good platform for Indo–Japan maritime security cooperation. In addition, the case of anti-piracy efforts in Malacca shows that Indo–Japan cooperation can bear fruit if they share a clear regional vision.

However, to advance security cooperation, lack of convergence on fundamental strategic perceptions should be sorted out. There is a noteworthy lack of a trilateral reference point to the US forward presence in the region in the Japan–India Joint Declaration on security cooperation signed in 2008.[54] That important lack contrasts with the Japan–Australia Declaration, which affirms 'the common strategic interests and security benefits embodied in their respective alliance relationships with the United States', and commits to 'strengthening trilateral cooperation'.[55] With this convergence, Japan and Australia proceeded to perform bilateral exercises in 2009, two years after the trilateral exercise.[56] Moreover, the Japan–Australia Acquisition and Cross-servicing Agreement (ACSA) was signed in 2010 between the Japan Self-Defense Forces and the Australian Defence Force.[57]

The other side of the same coin is incongruity with regard to 'that large continental entity situated within the geo-political arc of Asia'.[58] According to an Indian analyst, the Indian strategic community is divided into two broader lines. One includes those who believe that cooperation with Japan will counterbalance China. The second includes those who think China should be included in a cooperative security framework.[59]

Because the policy-making mainstream in Japan believes that US military presence in the Asia–Pacific region is not only securing Japan but also assuring regional countries by functioning as deterrence and crisis response,[60] it is natural that Japan designs Indo–Japan cooperation *in tandem* with India–Japan–US trilateral cooperation.

Conducting exercises with foreign countries other than the US demands domestic legal and political clearance. It also requires that Japan explain to its neighbours its intentions to hold such exercises. Humanitarian operations pose less of an obstacle. For example, Japan conducts bilateral salvage exercises with Korea and Russia.

If Japan and India define the purpose of exercises as promoting overall security in the regional complex, then particular area for exercises should be identified. Such functional approach was behind the first bilateral exercise conducted on 9 June 2012.[61] Now that there is a convergence of interest in the safety of sea lanes as a public good for the region, the next step for Japan and India is to develop familiarity with each other's operational concept as a step to fulfil their shared responsibilities in the region.

NOTES

1. Rahul Roy-Chaudhury, *India's Maritime Security*, New Delhi: Knowledge World in association with Institute for Defence Studies and Analysis, 2000, p. 175.
2. Roy-Chaudhury, *India's Maritime Security*, op. cit., pp. 177-8.
3. Akihiko Tanaka, *National Security of Japan* (in Japanese), Tokyo: Yomiuri, 1997, pp. 289-98.
4. Narushige Michishita, 'Evolution of Sea Power for Japan Maritime Self-defense Force', (in Japanese) Kyo-ichi Tachikawa et al., eds., *Sea Power,* Tokyo: Fuyo-shobo, 2008, pp. 247-50.
5. David Brewster, *India as an Asia Pacific Power,* London and NY: Routledge, 2012, p. 26.

6. Ministry of Defence, *Annual Report*, various years.
7. Roy-Chaudhury, *India's Maritime Security*, pp. 175-6.
8. Ministry of Defence, *Annual Report 1971-72*, p. 9; *1972-73*, p. 8.
9. S.N. Kohli, *Sea Power and the Indian Ocean: with Special Reference to India*, New Delhi: Tata McGraw-Hill Publishing Co., 1978, p. 19.
10. Ministry of Defence, *Annual Report* refers to this point up to 1987-8 version.
11. Ministry of Defence, *Annual Report 1973-74*, p. 2; *1985-86*, p. 2.
12. For Indian submarine capabilities, see G.V.C. Naidu, *Indian Navy and Southeast Asia*, New Delhi: Knowledge World in association with Institute for Defence Studies and Analysis, 2000, pp. 38-40, 54-7.
13. Naidu, *Indian Navy*, pp. 96-8; Roy Chaudhury, *India's Maritime Security*, pp. 175-80.
14. Jyotika Saksena and Suzette Grillot, 'The Emergence of Indo-US Defense Cooperation', Gary K. Bertsch, et al., eds., *Engaging India: US Strategic Relations with the World's Largest Democracy*, New York and London: Routledge, 1999, pp. 157-8; Dipankar Banerjee, 'An Overview of Indo-US Strategic Cooperation', Sumit Ganguly et al., eds., *US-Indian Strategic Cooperation into the 21st Century*, London and New York: Routledge, 2006, pp. 68-70.
15. The National Institute for Defense Studies, *East Asian Strategic Review* 2000, pp. 95–101; Japan Coast Guard, *Annual Report 2000* (*Kaijo-hoan-hakusho*), available on http://www.kaiho.mlit.go.jp/info/books/h12haku/2bu.htm (Japanese version) http://nippon.zaidan.info/seikabutsu/2000/00671/contents/024.htm (English version).
16. Author's interview to the former Chief of Staff, JMSDF, 17 November 2011.
17. Richard Tanter, 'Japan's Indian Ocean Naval Deployment: Blue Water Militarization in a "Normal Country"', *The Asia–Pacific Journal: Japan Focus*, http://japanfocus.org/-Richard-Tanter/1700, accessed on 5 December 2011.
18. Raja Mohan, *Crossing the Rubicon: The Shaping of India's New Foreign Policy*, New Delhi: Viking, 2003, p. 235.

19. Ministry of External Affairs, *Annual Report 2001-02*, p. 66.
20. J.K. Baral and J.N. Mahanty, 'India and the Gulf Crisis: The Response of a Minority Government', *Pacific Affairs*, vol. 65, no. 3 (Fall, 1992), pp. 374-9.
21. Raja Mohan, *Crossing the Rubicon*, p. 235.
22. Ministry of Defence, *Annual Report 2002-03*, p. 26.
23. Donald A. Camp, 'US-India Maritime Security Cooperation', N.S. Sisodia et al., eds., *India-US Relations: Addressing the Challenges of the 21st Century*, New Delhi: Magnum Books, 2008, p. 189.
24. Ministry of Defense, Japan, *Defense of Japan*, 2001, p. 230.
25. Indian Navy, Press Briefing, 'Relief Operations', 4 January 2005, <indiannavy.nic.in/TSUNAMI-PRESSBRIEFING.ppt>, accessed on 25 January 2010.
26. Ministry of Defence, *Annual Report 2004-05*.
27. *Outlook*, 31 January 2005, available at http://www.outlookindia.com/article.aspx?226372, accessed on 25 January 2010.
28. Ministry of External Affairs, India, Press Briefing, 'On Relief Efforts in the Wake of Tsunami', 30 December 2004.
29. India carefully avoided the term 'core group' and uses 'coordination group' instead.
30. Ministry of Defense, Japan, *Defense of Japan*, 2005, p. 316.
31. See statement of Secretary of State Rice at joint press briefing with Indian External Affairs Minister Natwar Singh, 16 March 2005, available on http://www.america.gov/st/washfile-english/2005/March/20050316140204ndyblehs0.3364832.html, accessed on 29 February 2012.
32. http:///state.gov/p/sca/rls/fs/2005/49730.html, accessed on 12 October 2008. http:///usinfo.state.gov/sa/Archive/2005/Jul/18-714325.html, accessed on 12 April 2006.
33. John H. Gill, 'US–India Military-to-Military Relations: Changing a Course to the Future', Sisodia et al., eds., *India–US Relations*, p. 176.
34. For background of the US strategy and disaster relief, see Shigeru Suzuki, 'US Military's Disaster Relief Operation and Civil Activity Abroad: Diplomatic and Strategic Background for Operation Tomodachi' (in Japanese), National Diet Library, Japan, *Reference*, September 2011.

35. Indo–US Framework for Maritime Security Cooperation, March 2006.
36. Donald A. Camp, 'US–India Maritime Security Cooperation', Sisodia, *India–US Relations,* p. 192.
37. US Marine Corps, US Navy and US Coast Guard, 'Naval Operations Concept 2010', p. 47.
38. US Department of Defense thinks India's regular participation is desirable. Department of Defense, 'Report to Congress on US-India Security Cooperation', November 2011, p. 7.
39. http://articles.timesofindia.indiatimes.com/2007-01-19/us/27870677_1_indian-navy-uss-trenton-ship, accessed on 24 January 2012.
40. http://www.navy.mil/search/display.asp?story_id=39670; http://www.navy.mil/search/display.asp?story_id=56358; http://www.indianexpress.com/news/mod-clears-joint-amphibious-exercise-at-us-b/685653/, accessed on 24 January 2012. see also, David Brewster, *India as an Asia Pacific Power,* London and NY: Routledge, 2012, p. 54; Department of Defense, 'Report to Congress', 2011, p. 3.
41. David Scott, 'India's 'Extended Neighborhood' Concept: Power Projection for a Rising Power', *India Review,* vol. 8, no. 2, April-June 2009, pp. 138-9.
42. Brewster, *India as an Asia Pacific Power,* ch. 9.
43. James R. Holmes, Andrew C. Winner and Toshi Yoshihara, *Indian Naval Strategy in the Twenty-first Century,* London and NY: Routledge, 2009, pp. 153.
44. Integrated Headquarters, Ministry of Defence (Navy), India, *Indian Maritime Doctrine,* 2009, pp. 65-8.
45. http://indiannavy.nic.in/Milan%202008.htm, accessed on 29 January 2012; Brewster, *India as an Asia Pacific Power,* p. 105; *Indian Express,* 5 February 2010.
46. Ministry of Defence, India, *Annual Report 2004-05,* p. 202; *2005-06,* p. 37.
47. Tomohisa Takei, 'JMSDF in the New Maritime Era' (in Japanese), *Hatou,* November 2008.
48. Energy Agency calculates that the Lombok route requires three additional days amounting to $99,000 per one tanker (VLCC). Agency for Natural Resources and Energy, 'Survey on Oil

Transportation' (in Japanese), February, 2006. http://www.meti.go.jp/committee/materials/downloadfiles/g60214a08j.pdf.

49. Takeshi Fukuda, 'Three Turning Points in US-Japan Security Cooperation' (in Japanese), National Diet Library, Japan, *Reference*, July 2006, pp. 159-61.
50. Gaye Christoffersen, 'Japan and the East Asian Maritime Security Order: Prospects for Trilateral and Multilateral Cooperation', *Asian Perspective*, vol. 33, no. 3, 2009, p. 110.
51. http://www.recaap.org/AboutReCAAPISC.aspx; http://www.mofa.go.jp/mofaj/gaiko/kaiyo/kaizoku_gai.html accessed on 17 January 2012.
52. Yoichiro Sato, 'Southeast Asian Receptiveness to Japanese Maritime Security Cooperation', Asia–Pacific Center for Security Studies, September 2007, available on www.apcss.org .
53. http://www.mofa.go.jp/mofaj/gaiko/oda/shiryo/kuni/08_databook/pdfs/01-01.pdf; http://www.mofa.go.jp/policy/terrorism/state0703.html .
54. Sourabh Gupta, 'Japan–India Maritime Security Cooperation: Floating on Inflated Expectations?' *East Asia Forum*, 11 May 2010, http://www.eastasiaforum.org/2010/05/11/japan–india–maritime-security-cooperation-floating-on-inflated-expectations/, accessed on 29 January 2012.
55. 'Japan–Australia Joint Declaration on Security Cooperation', 13 March 2007.
56. The first Japan–Australia bilateral naval exercise was held in September 2009. The second was held in 2010.
57. Ministry of Foreign Afairs, Japan, Press Release, 19 May 2010, http://www.mofa.go.jp/announce/announce/2010/5/0519_02.html.
58. B. Raman, 'Maritime Security Concerns of Japan and Prospects of India–Japan Cooperation', Chennai Centre For China Studies, *C3S Paper* No.335, 18 August 2009, http://www.c3sindia.org/india/752, accessed on 29 January 2012.
59. Shamshad Khan overviewed Indian strategic thinking. Shamshad Ahmad Khan, 'Indo-Japan Strategic Cooperation: Issues, Expectations and Challenges', in Akihiro Iwashita, ed., *India-Japan Dialogue: Challenge and Potential*, paper no. 6, Comparative Studies on Regional Powers, Slavic Research Center, Hokkaido University, Japan, July 2011.

60. See 'National Defense Program Guidelines for FY 2011 and Beyond', Approved by the Security Council and the Cabinet on 17 December 2010.
61. *Asagumo Shinbun* (in Japanese), 14 June 2012. http://www.asagumo-news.com/news.html, accessed on 30 August 2012.

CHAPTER 9

Prospects and Challenges for Expanding Japan–India Economic Relations

MAKOTO KOJIMA

INTRODUCTION

Thanks to vigorous economic growth under economic liberalization and its Look East policy, introduced after 1991, India has deepened its economic relations with East Asian countries. A remarkable expansion of India's trade is apparent with ASEAN countries, China, and Korea since the beginning of the 2000s, with only Japan–India relations being apparently left behind. Indo–China bilateral trade has expanded remarkably to become more than four times greater than Japan–India bilateral trade.

The first Indian boom occurred in the mid-1990s, and disappeared after India conducted nuclear tests in 1998. Although India has become the largest recipient of Japanese ODA since 2003-4, both bilateral trade in goods and Japan's foreign direct investment (FDI) into India had almost been stagnant until quite recently. With major Indian exports to Japan dominated by products of mineral oils, gems and jewels, marine products (mainly shrimp) and iron-ore, India and Japan have not yet formed such dynamic international division of labour as is apparent among East Asian countries. Japan's cumulative FDI into India is so far greater than that of Korea, but as far as electronics appliances are concerned, Japanese companies have been overwhelmed by Korean companies in the Indian market.

Both India and Japan are highly complementary economies that have yet to be fully exploited. Japan has abundant capital and is highly advanced in technological skills and product development while India is endowed with a huge market and abundant human resources. Japan is outstanding in terms of its manufacturing abilities, whereas India presents advantages in IT services and bioinformatics. Recently, however, a new tide has been observed in Japan to expand Japan–India relations based on mutual complementarities, which gathers momentum also under the strengthening of strategic and global partnership between the two countries.

In this article, possibilities and challenges of future Japan–India bilateral relations are explored, particularly addressing recent new developments in the fields of trade, FDI, IT offshore investment, and human resource exchange.

JAPAN–INDIA MERCHANDISE TRADE ON A MODEST GROWTH

Before Second World War, India had been Japan's major trade partner, accounting for 10–15 per cent of Japan's foreign trade at least until 1937. Major imported products from India were cotton and pig iron. Even after the war, India remained an important trade partner of Japan's, accounting for 2-4 per cent of trade until 1965. In the post-war era, iron-ore replaced pig iron as a major imported product from India, and Indian iron ore played a critical role in the remarkable post-war development of the Japanese steel industry at least until Japan started to import iron-ore, on a large scale, from Australia and Brazil. Thereafter, under the closed inward-looking regime, India had been long struggling with stagnant industrial development and was largely left behind by the global tide. Japan, however, joined OECD members in 1964, and has ridden on the track of high economic growth, becoming an economic superpower. It was since these times that Japan and India became economically estranged from each other.

India's major trade partners in the 1950s had been the UK and the US; in the 1970s the USSR and Japan also became major trade partners along with the US and the UK. This arrangement implied that economic relations between East Asian countries and India had been generally weak except for those with Japan.

Along with the introduction of economic reforms in 1991, India adopted an outward-oriented policy to develop its own economy by making use of the tide of globalization. More specifically, India intended to strengthen economic ties with East Asian countries, an emerging global growth centre, under the Look East policy. Despite pursuit of the Look East policy, Indian trade with Japan has long remained stagnant.

Although total India–Japan bilateral trade amounted to US $4.19 billion in 1996-7, it had shrunk to US $3.64 billion in 2000-1 and US $3.66 billion in 2001-2 (Figure 9.1). It was only in 2003-4 that bilateral trade started to show an upward trend: US $5.36 billion in 2004-5, and US $13.82 billion in 2010-11. Improved bilateral trade, however, has been largely overshadowed in comparison to other bilateral trading relations such as those of India–ASEAN, India–China and India–Korea. India–Japan bilateral trade was surpassed by India–China trade in 2002-3, and even by India–Korea trade in 2005-6. In this connection, as of 2010-11, India–China and India–ASEAN trade have increased 4.6 times and 4.2 times, respectively more than that with Japan. Japan's share in all India trade has decreased from 5.9 per cent in 1997-8 to 2.2 per cent in 2010-11, along with a significant decline of Japan's rank in terms of total amount of trade

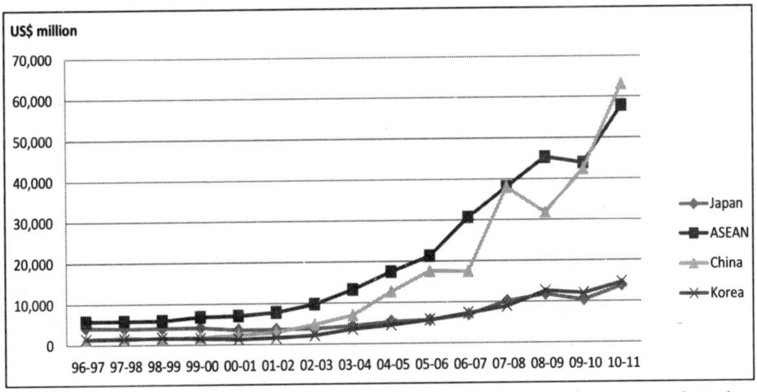

Source: Ministry of Commerce and Industry, Government of India, Export and Import Data Bank.

FIGURE 9.1: TRENDS IN INDIA'S TRADE WITH EAST ASIA.

from third to twelfth. India's share in Japan's total amount of trade, in contrast, remained at only 0.6 per cent during 2010-11.

Japan–India trade has almost constantly shown Japan's surplus, and the sluggish bilateral trade was possibly a reflection of major commodities traded on both sides: imports from Japan were composed of, first and foremost, machinery and components, iron and steel products, consumer electronics, auto and components, precision instruments, and so forth, and India's exports to Japan exclusively concentrated on lower-value added marine products and jewels and ornaments, of which commodities did not reflect the current India's competitive and dynamic industrial structure. Recently, however, because of increased petroleum products from India, which are becoming the most important Indian exports to Japan, Japan–India bilateral trade has shown signs of increasing since 2006-7 with an average annual growth rate of 19 per cent between 2005-6 and 2010-11. Even so, India–China bilateral trade fairly outperformed, recording 29 per cent annual growth during the same period.

The Japan–India Comprehensive Economic Partnership Agreement/Economic Partnership Agreement (CEPA/EPA) came into effect in August 2011. Tariffs were scheduled for elimination on 90 per cent of Indian and 97 per cent Japanese goods over ten years, compared with around 75 per cent of Indian goods in the case of India–Korea CEPA. Japan is expected to export more auto parts and steel products exports to India, and to import more agricultural and marine products from India.

Auto components, iron and steel products, electric and electronics parts, and general machinery are included in concessionary import items on the Indian side. For example, iron and steel products (cold and hot rolling steel plates, alloy steel, and galvanized sheet iron) are currently subject to 5 per cent tariff rates, which are scheduled to be eliminated within five years so that favourable effects on bilateral trade are expected in the near future. Regarding automobile components, the tariff rates for gearboxes and diesel engines, currently 12.5 per cent, will be reduced by half within 6–8 years, while for electric and general machinery, the tariff will be eliminated completely within 10 years. Regarding concessionary import items on the Japanese side, the tariff rate for almost all goods in industrial and mining industries imported from India will be eliminated immediately, together with the rates for durian, asparagus, shrimp, and lumber, while the tariff rate for other agricultural and marine products will be diminished to zero within 7-10 years.

The treatment of generic medicine imported from India deserves special attention. Previously, it had been actually quite difficult for India to export generic medicines to Japan, where quite restrictive measures were instituted for the import of generic medicines. However, increased imports of generic medicines from India can be expected as the national treatment, on the side of Japan, is accorded for applications for registration and other approvals required for the release of generic medicine. Furthermore, some improvement has been made for the mobility of human resources, including Yoga instructors, English teachers, and Indian cuisine masters. It is expected that India–Japan bilateral trade will be more than doubled to $25 billion by 2014 under the CEPA/EPA.

Before the Japan–India CEPA/EPA, India–ASEAN FTA had already come into effect in January 2010. India has increased its import machinery from ASEAN, with imports of parts or components showing a remarkable increase. Actually, in 2010, seven items out of top ten imported machinery products comprised various machine-related parts, including semiconductors and thermionic tubes, office equipment parts, auto parts and components, internal combustion engines, and superheating/cooling equipment.[1] This trend indicates that India has apparently incorporated itself increasingly into the East Asian regional production network, where large quantities of machine-parts are imported and exported within the region. Actually, according to a survey of the Japanese companies' activities in Asia–Oceania conducted by JETRO, many Japanese companies located in Singapore and Thailand selected India as the most important country for their operations and export destination in the coming three years.[2]

It is noteworthy that while exports from East Asian countries to India have expanded, finished products exported from India destined to EU and the US have also shown a marked increase,[3] indicating that India, while implementing a multi-directional diplomacy, has also been incorporated into the East Asian production network as an important production and exporting hub. It can be reasonably inferred that such a tendency will be accelerated with the Japan–India EPA coming to fruition.

NEW HORIZONS FOR JAPANESE INVESTMENT INTO INDIA

It is in the field of investment rather than trade where we can witness a more dynamic trend in recent Japan–India economic relations. Japanese foreign direct investment (FDI) into India reached a peak of US $434 million in 1997, but it decreased after that in the wake of India's nuclear experiments in 1998. Japan ranked fifth, accounting for 5 per cent of the total accumulated volume of FDI inflows into India since April 2000 to November 2011. It was as recently as 2007 that Japan's FDI into India began to show conspicuous expansion. Japan's FDI into India increased to US $1,562 million in 2010-11 and furthermore in 2011-12, ranking 3rd after Mauritius and Singapore (Table 9.1).

Faced with stagnant markets in economically advanced countries and aggravated investment environments in China where wages are rising and industrial policies are becoming more restrictive and unpredictable for foreign companies, India has become more attractive in Japanese business circles. Until recently, Japanese companies had a negative image of India's investment environments that constituted a sense of 'psychological distance' from India. However, Korean companies' successes in gaining a large share of consumer electronics markets indicate that what Japanese companies identify as areas of concern, i.e. adverse investment environments, are not necessarily critical factors that would deter Korean or Singaporean companies.

Convinced, at long last, that India offers a huge domestic market and that it will grow to be a leading economic power, Japanese companies have been committed to India increasingly. The number of Japanese companies in India has increased from 248 in January

TABLE 9.1: SHARE OF TOP INVESTING COUNTRIES INTO INDIA: FDI INFLOWS

(US $ million)

Ranks	Country	2005-6	2006-7	2007-8	2008-9	2009-10	2010-11	2011-12 April-Nov.	Share of Total Inflows April 2000-Nov. 11 (%)
1	Mauritius	2,570	6,363	11,096	11,208	10,376	6,987	7,822	41
2	Singapore	275	578	3,083	3,454	2,379	1,705	3,775	10
3	USA	502	856	1,089	1,802	1,943	1,170	805	7
4	UK	296	1,878	1,176	864	657	755	2,571	6
5	Japan	208	85	815	405	1,183	1,562	2,489	5
Total Inflows		5,546	15,726	24,579	27,309	25,834	19,427	22,635	

Source: Ministry of Commerce and Industry, Government of India, Fact Sheet of Foreign Direct Investment (FDI)

2006 to 438 in January 2008, from 550 in October 2008 to 627 in October 2009, from 725 in October 2010 to 812 in October 2011 (Figure 9.2). Vigorous Japanese investment into India can also be confirmed by the FDI outflow data maintained by the Government of Japan. Japan's FDI into India increased steeply from 178.2 billion yen in 2007 to 542.9 billion yen in 2008 and 344.3 billion yen in 2009,[4] indicating that India became one of the three most important destinations of Japan's FDI into Asia, comparable to China and ASEAN, although it showed a tendency to decline thereafter (Figure 9.3).

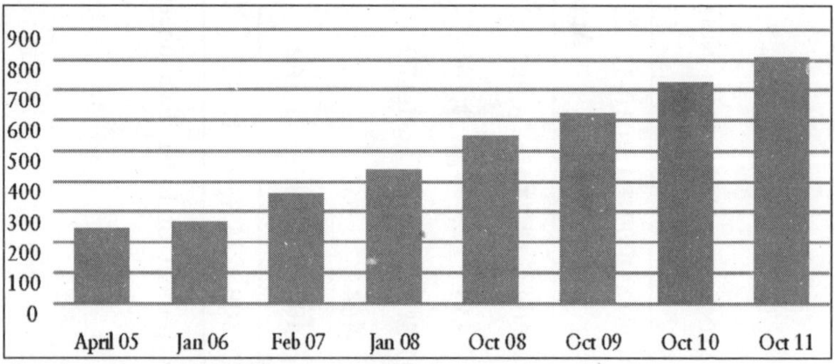

Source: Japanese Embassy in India.

FIGURE 9.2: NUMBER OF JAPANESE COMPANIES INVESTING IN INDIA.

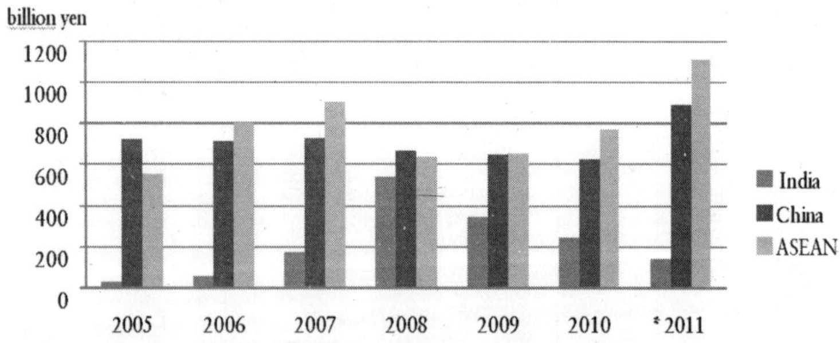

Note: *2011 (January-November).

Source: Minister of Finance, Government of Japan, Japan's Balance of Payments: Outward and Inward Direct Investment

FIGURE 9.3: JAPAN'S OUTWARD DIRECT INVESTMENT IN INDIA, CHINA AND ASEAN (CALENDER YEAR).

New developments in increasing Japanese FDI in India can be summarized as follows:

First, Japanese companies have entered increasingly into a wider range of manufacturing sectors, making inroads into the huge market. In the past, Japan's FDI into India had been lopsided in the automobile sector. According to the FDI inflow data maintained by the Government of India, the top sector receiving FDI from Japan from 1991 until 2005 was the transportation industry (60.4 per cent), followed by electrical equipment (7.2 per cent), service sectors – financial and non-financial – (3.7 per cent), ceramics (2.2 per cent) and textiles (2 per cent).[5] In recent years, however, not only automobile assemblers and auto-parts suppliers, but also other companies in various fields including steelmakers, pharmaceutical companies, and construction machinery producers have begun to make their presence known in India. Regarding the automobile sector, following Suzuki, all major Japanese assemblers have positioned India as the strongpoint for production of small cars and recently sport utility vehicles (SUVs) in their global strategy. Nissan and Toyota have newly released remarkably low-priced cars geared for emerging countries.

A firm presence of Japanese automobile assemblers and auto-parts makers strongly induces other companies engaged in steel production and logistics to come to India. All major Japanese steel producers have tied-up with their Indian counterparts to produce sheet iron for automobiles or to set up blast furnaces in India, with Nippon Steel forming an alliance with Tata Steel, Sumitomo Metal Industries with Bushan Steel, JFE Steel with JSW Steel, and Kobe Steel with SAIL. Logistics companies, including Nippon Express, Hitachi Transport System and Itochu, have already started their operations in India, and shipping companies, including Mitsui O.S.K. Lines, are ready to engage with marine transportation of automobiles exported from India to Europe. In the construction machinery sector also, both Komatsu and Hitachi Construction Machinery are now reinforcing their production in India.

Regarding the electronics appliances sector, where Japanese companies have lagged far behind Korean companies, Panasonic and Sony have become determined to make a strenuous effort to catch up with LG and Samsung with a firm commitment from top management. Panasonic Electrical Works, currently merged with Panasonic, succeeded in expanding its sales network by acquiring Anchor Electric in 2007. Panasonic has steadily expanded its share in the Indian electronic appliances market from less than 2 per cent in 2010 to 5-6 per cent in 2011, further aiming to expand its share from 10 per cent in 2012 to 25 per cent in 2018 to be the largest electric appliances company in the Indian market. Sony, using its own production base in Malaysia, outstripped the Korean companies of LG and Samsung in the sale of flat panel display TVs in 2010. Sony has no factory in India.

Other promising and newly-expanding areas for Japan's FDI into India include pharmaceuticals and products necessary for daily life. Currently, Japanese pharmaceutical companies are keen to establish strongholds in India, aiming to either strengthen their cost competitiveness or to enter the Indian market. Daiichi Sankyo acquired Ranbaxy Laboratories, the largest pharmaceutical company in India, in 2008. Eisai set up its own factory in Andhra Pradesh in 2010 to produce its main generic medicines, which will be exported to Japan and the USA. Fujifilm has recently tied-up with Dr. Reddy's to set up a joint venture in Japan for producing generic medicines. Takeda Pharmaceuticals, the largest Japanese pharmaceutical company, also has a keen eye to invest in India. It is also to be noted that many leading Japanese companies have newly started to enter into India in various fields of goods that are used daily, including foods, stationery, cosmetics, sanitary goods, and other products.

Second, both the Japanese government and private companies are now more willing to commit themselves to infrastructural development in India. Poor conditions in infrastructure used to constitute the most formidable barrier deterring Japanese companies from investing in India. However, given that India intends to invest as much as $1 trillion into infrastructural development during its

Twelfth Five Year Plan, the Japanese companies have come to realize that it will surely provide major business opportunities for them. Some Japanese companies are keen to be suppliers of mechanical equipment, notably generation turbines or rolling stock in Ultra Mega Power Projects or the Dedicated Freight Corridor. Mitsubishi Heavy Industries set up two joint venture companies with Larsen & Toubro to produce supercritical pressure boilers and turbines in 2007, with Hitachi subsequently tying-up with BCE Energy Systems, and Toshiba with Jindal South West (JSW). The Delhi–Mumbai Industrial Corridor (DMIC) and Dedicated Freight Corridor (DFC) between Mumbai–Delhi are among the priority areas of Japanese government-sponsored investment into India, along with the newly-mooted Integrated Industrial Region in southern India. Obsessed with risk-aversion, strong hesitation has prevailed among the Japanese construction companies against entering Indian markets, which constitutes an impediment to the progress of the DFC. However, a new trend is emerging. Kajima Construction, the leading Japanese general contractor, has recently decided to enter India to construct a factory for Ford Motor Co. Regarding those infrastructural developments for which management aspects are important, Japanese companies are more likely to tie up with Singaporean or Australian companies because they are not experienced in these areas.

Third, Japanese financial institutions such as commercial banks, insurance and security companies, have also come to approach the Indian market aggressively. This has never occurred before. Until recently, the Indian subsidiaries of Japanese commercial banks used to furnish funds only to Japanese companies operating in India. However, given that infrastructural development projects require a huge capital demand and knowing that Indian companies are active in their fund-raising in global capital markets, Japanese financial institutions have come to recognize the Indian market as an important target, furnishing funds to Indian companies. For example, the Bank of Tokyo-Mitsubishi UFJ has announced intensification of its investment into India as a region of strategic importance, from the current 700 billion yen to 1 trillion yen by 2014, financing not only

Japanese companies but also public enterprises related to infrastructural development. Mizuho Corporate Bank has announced a tie-up with International Finance Corporation to finance infrastructure projects, while Sumitomo Mitsui Banking Corporation has acquired a 4.5 per cent stake in Kotak Mahindra Bank in 2011. In the field of insurance, Tokyo Marine & Nichido Fire Insurance Group had already formed a joint venture with the Indian Farmers Fertilizer Cooperative Limited in 2000, while Nippon Life Insurance Company has recently signed a Memorandum of Understanding (MoU) to acquire a 26 per cent stake in Reliance Capital Asset Management. In the field of securities, Nomura Asset Management Co. purchased a 35 per cent stake in LIC Mutual Asset Management Company, a subsidiary of Life Insurance Corporation of India (LIC) in 2009 to form a joint venture, while Mizuho Securities Co. entered into a strategic alliance with Tata Capital to promote investment banking activities and securities businesses in 2010.

Lastly, we can point out a new trend in the Japanese investment into India, not only in the field of FDI, but also in the field of portfolio investment. Japanese investors have increasingly turned to buying Indian stocks in their financial portfolios via brokerage firms, thanks to a favourable expansion of the Indian economy. Given that domestic interest rates remain at low levels, Japanese people are increasingly turning to foreign markets for their investment. Actually, Indian stocks are getting no less popular than Chinese stocks. Consequently, Japanese portfolio investment into India has increased conspicuously since 2005, although some reversal of trends has occurred under the global financial turmoil.

IT OFFSHORE INVESTMENT

With India's image as an IT power established, and Indian people's mathematical ability gaining higher esteem, elementary books on Indian mathematics have popped up among best-sellers, and the Indian International schools in Tokyo have attracted attention among parents who are enthusiastic about their children's education. Currently, Japanese people are facing up to the grim fact that young people are increasingly shying away from science studies and that their mathematical ability is declining under the promotion of less stringent educational guidelines across the country.

Japan is globally ranked the second largest IT market with an estimated turnover of $100 billion. Japan is renowned as an extremely competitive nation in manufacturing industries and hardware production. Today, however, hardware and software are merging, and the importance of software in the manufacturing industry has increased especially in leading-edge sectors so that Japan's strength in hardware manufacturing is expected to decay without software development capabilities. Japan now faces an acute shortage of IT engineers to meet these demands. Such a phenomenon has become accentuated since 2007, when many IT engineers belonging to the baby boomer generation began to retire. As for 2007, Japan had a total capacity of 907,990 IT engineers, and was therefore short of 501,000 IT engineers it needed, including 360,000 professionals.[6] According to a survey made by the Information-Technology Promotion Agency of 3,000 IT companies in Japan, the percentage of those IT companies which felt a quantitative shortage of IT engineers declined from 75.6 per cent in 2007 to 48.8 per cent in 2008 attributable to the recession triggered by the Lehman shock, but as many as 85.5 and 87.0 per cent of them acknowledged a qualitative shortage of IT engineers in 2007 and 2008, respectively.[7]

Generally speaking, Japanese companies are inclined to in-house procurement. Moreover, they are rather cautious about overseas IT offshore investment. When looking offshore, they prefer to turn to China, although numerous advantages apply to using Indian IT capabilities. India enjoys good esteem in high-quality control/management capability, a wide range of IT skills covering open to mainframe environments and rich global experience, and its intellectual property regulations are more reliable than those of China. It is no secret any more that Japanese major automobile assemblers outsource some of their embedded software to Indian IT companies. However, Japanese companies overall have not sufficiently tapped Indian IT capabilities. As for the destination of Japan's IT offshore investment, still 80 per cent of Japanese companies have outsourced to China and 25 per cent to India (see Figure 9.4). For India, Japan accounts only for less than 2 per cent of its total software and IT services exports. Main reasons for Japan not using India fully include language barriers and cultural misunderstanding, scarcity of Indian residents in Japan, scarcity of globalized human resources on the side of Japan, and different software development style – characterized as an *integral approach* rather than a modular one – including ambiguity in requirement specifications among Japanese companies.

Many major Indian IT companies, including TCS, Infosys, and Wipro have come to Japan since the early 1990s, but they are still struggling to penetrate the Japanese market. They set up their subsidiaries in China later than Japan, where they have a much larger presence than in Japan. Taking the example of TCS, its employees in Japan still amount to fewer than 500, while its employees in Chinese subsidiaries exceed more than 1500 in 2011. To break the deadlock, they recently showed their intentions to increase their share in the Japanese IT market through mergers and acquisition or by setting up a joint venture.[8] Furthermore, we must incorporate consideration of the temporary aftermath of the Great Eastern Japan Earthquake in March 2011, which reduced the number of Indian IT engineers working in Japan from around 15,000 to 7,000. Many Indian IT engineers have not yet returned to Japan.

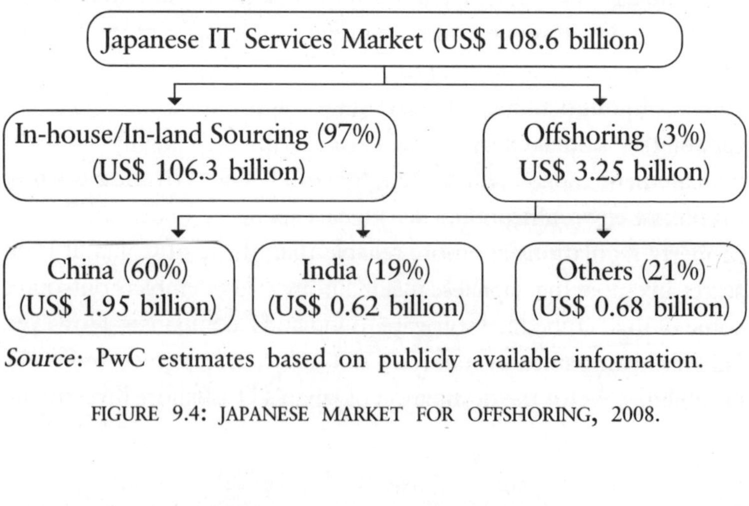

Source: PwC estimates based on publicly available information.

FIGURE 9.4: JAPANESE MARKET FOR OFFSHORING, 2008.

Indian IT companies are struggling to expand their activities for customers in Japan, but some new trends are visible in Japanese IT offshoring to India. Some hesitation among Japanese companies remains with respect to outsourcing to Indian IT companies, but it is noteworthy that some leading Japanese IT companies are becoming more aggressive in tapping Indian IT capability directly. Japanese IT giants, both NTT Data and Fujitsu, have already set up their own IT captive centres in India through the acquisition of American IT companies. NTT Data intends to expand its IT engineers in India to 10,000 within a year, while Fujitsu plans to expand its IT engineers to 5,000 in three years, with an aim of providing offshore services for Japanese companies. As for Japanese subsidiaries of IBM and Accenture, they are already increasingly using Indian IT resources through offshoring to their Indian counterparts. Sony India Software Center, an R&D hub in Bangalore, has increased its employees by three times to 1000 in the past three years. Currently, it is no exaggeration to say that Japanese IT companies are increasingly under pressure to tap Indian IT capability if they truly seek to become global entities.

HUMAN EXCHANGES

The promotion of human exchange is vital for improvement of mutual understanding and thereby consolidating further expansion of Japan–India relations. It is noteworthy that there are as many as 3 million Indian–Americans, most of whom are professionals, playing an indispensable role in deepening and cementing ties between India and the USA. Regrettably, the level of people-to-people exchange between India and Japan is far from satisfactory in any channel, which marks a remarkable contrast with that between Japan and China (Table 9.2). Regarding the level of student exchange, it must be noted that the number of Chinese students remaining in Japan amounted to almost 88,173 in 2010, while Indian students were only 546, who are outnumbered not only by Bangladeshi and Sri Lankan students staying in Japan, but also by Indian students staying in China.[9] Improving scholarship and Japanese language training

TABLE 2: HUMAN EXCHANGES AMONG JAPAN, INDIA AND CHINA

Categories (A)	Japan-India (B)	Japan-China (C)	Ratio (C)/(B)
No. of Japanese Visitors (2009)	124,219	3,317,500	1:27
No. of Foreign Vistors to Japan (2010)	66,900	1,427,100	1:21
No. of Foreign Students in Japan (May 2010)	546	86,173	1:158
No. of Japanese Residents (2009)	4,018	127,282	1:32
No. of People Learning Japanese Language (2009)	18,000	827,000	1:48
Sister/Friendship Cities	5 pairs	337 pairs	1:67
No. of Direct Flights (Summer 2010: Airliners)	17 per week	556 per week	1:32

Source: Japanese Embassy in India, quoted from Hiroshi Hirabayashi, 'Japan–India Relationship: The Past and the Future', *Contemporary India Forum*, no. 12, 2012 (in Japanese).

schemes for Indian students, increasing the number of lectures given in English at Japanese universities, and providing attractive career paths for Indian graduates to apply for expanded employment opportunities in Japanese companies are urgently needed to attract more Indian students to Japan.

We must also devote attention to the fact that current human exchanges between Japan and India are even lagging behind those of India and Korea. The number of Indian visitors to Korea and vice versa amounted to around 70,000 in 2009, and the number of Korean residents in India amounted to 8518 in 2010, compared with 4,018 Japanese residents in India in that year.[10]

Currently, Japanese companies are desperately in need of young people who are qualified in promoting businesses in emerging economies. Some Japanese MNCs, including JFE Steel, IHI, and Toshiba, which fully recognize the necessity of globalized personnel to brush up their English communications skills and enhance multicultural understanding, have started to send a certain number of their employees to India for training. The timing is good now, entering this new phase of Indo–Japan relations, for us to consolidate our relations especially through acceleration of people-to-people exchanges.

STRATEGIC AND GLOBAL PARTNERSHIP

Before full-fledged closer economic relations are established, both Japan and India have progressively formed strategic and global partnership amid growing concern over geopolitical issues. Since Prime Minister Manmohan Singh visited Japan in December 2006, and a strategic partnership was formed between the two countries, both prime ministers have agreed to visit each other annually. India is the first case for Japan to make an official promise of mutual visitation, while for India it is the second case after Russia. Along with the prime minister's mutual visitation, strategic dialogue by foreign ministers, national security dialogue by the defence ministers, and other various ministerial level of exchanges including economic policy dialogue between Japan's Minister of Economic and Trade Industry and India's Minister of Industry and Commerce, are held annually, and current governmental exchanges might represent the most active period ever seen in the history of Japan–India relations. Based on the strategic partnership, both governments have come to forge close cooperation in the spheres of economics and national security.

Both governments share a common goal of becoming permanent members of the UN Security Council, and India has been therefore perceived by Japan as a critical partner in fulfilling their goals together. China's emergence as a global political power, which represents a future destabilizing factor for Japanese foreign policy, has also increased India's importance as a diplomatic trump card for Japan in the Asian region. Japan, wishing to take more weight on the ASEAN + 6, adding three countries, i.e. India, Australia and New Zealand to the ASEAN + 3 (Japan, China and Korea), took the initiative in convening the East Asian Summit including the membership of India under the

ASEAN+6 framework, which might surely reflect Japan's national security perspective. In this connection, the East Asian Summit started officially in December 2005. The US and Russia formally participated in November 2011.

In the economic sphere, a long-awaited Japan–India CEPA/EPA was finally signed in February 2011. It came into effect in August though a new upsurge in India–Japan economic relations is to be expected. Prime Minister Noda's visit to India in December 2011 also brought in its wake strengthening of bilateral relations in the fields of economy and national security. The Japanese government pledged to offer a total amount of US $4.5 billion loans in the next five years for implementing the Delhi–Mumbai Industrial Corridor and Dedicated Freight Corridor, and arranged economic cooperation for constructing road and port facilities, especially in southern India, where many Japanese companies are expected to operate. In addition, during Noda's visit, both leaders signed an agreement to increase the maximum dollar currency swap arrangement five times up to $15 billion from the previous limits, which is expected to mitigate the negative effects of a weakening Indian rupee. Regarding rare earth minerals, which are critical resources especially for auto components manufacturers, the Japanese government has reached an agreement with India, the second largest producer after China, to launch a collaborative development project which will help Japan alleviate negative effects of overdependence on China. Currently, China officially restricts exports of rare earth minerals, which has caused severe damage and anxiety to the Japanese auto industry. In the fields of logistics and national security, primarily to preserve sea lanes in the Indian Ocean, both governments agreed to conduct joint military exercises between the Indian Navy and the Japanese Self-Defense Forces, with the intention of coping with troublesome piracy of Somalia and the growing Chinese influence in the Indian Ocean. The exercise is planned to start from 2012.

Amid steadily progressing formation of the Japan–India strategic partnership, it is important at this point in time for both parties to make an all-out effort at deepening mutual economic dependence either through strengthening Japanese companies' FDI into India or IT offshore investment. These efforts might contribute to building a robust ground for additional development of bilateral relations. To enhance active economic exchange, so-called 'psychological distance' that most Japanese companies have in mind should be removed through various public–private partnership channels including official development assistance (ODA) and human exchange programmes. We must recall the fact that broad-based human exchanges constitute a prerequisite condition leading to the successful development of America's IT offshoring to India and Japan's FDI to China.

PROSPECTS AND CHALLENGES

The Japanese economy has been strained in the aftermath of the massive earthquake and tsunami in March 2011, accompanied by radiation leakage from Tokyo Electric Power Company's Fukushima No. 1 nuclear power plant. The aftereffects of the Great East Japan Earthquake on India–Japan economic relations cannot be ignored. Japanese manufacturers were obliged to reduce their production in India, because Japanese domestic supply chains were damaged abruptly, but the tide of Japan's FDI into India seems to be irreversible. Currently, Japanese companies are at a crossroads. Faced with a stagnant market in Japan, many Japanese companies are under pressure to go global, devoting great attention to rising emerging economies. Under domestic supply chains damaged by the earthquake and record high yen appreciation, Japanese companies are pressured further to reallocate their production facilities to emerging economies, which provides excellent opportunities for additional acceleration of Japanese FDI into India.

Furthermore, negotiations for Japan–India Nuclear Agreement were suspended following the severely unprecedented accident at the Fukushima No. 1 nuclear power plant. Japanese technologies are indispensable for the construction of nuclear power plants, with the Japan Steel Works Ltd. playing a dominant role in producing reactor pressure vessels throughout the world. Nevertheless, negotiations for the Japan–India Nuclear Agreement are expected to resume, given bilateral mutual trust that has been firmly established between both governments under strategic and global partnerships.

The following two tasks should be addressed for additional expansion into India–Japan economic relations. First, the greatest efforts possible should be taken under the basis of public-private partnership on both sides to enhance the Delhi–Mumbai Industrial Corridor along the right line, which will further consolidate Japan–India collaboration and engender huge economic benefits for both countries. Second, human exchange should be promoted using every possible channel, which will be a springboard for additional expansion of bilateral relations.

NOTES

1. Ryuichi Ushiyama, 'India–ASEAN Relations: Production Network Being Progressively Formed between India and ASEAN', in Japan Center for Economic Research, ed., *India in the World: Leading to Expanding Asia*, JCER, 2011 (in Japanese).
2. To put it more precisely, in the case of Japanese companies located in Thailand (644 companies replied), India ranked 1st (21.8 per cent), followed by Japan (14.4 per cent), and Indonesia (14.3 per cent); in the case of Japanese companies in Singapore (141 companies replied), India ranked 1st (28.4 per cent), followed by Indonesia (19.9 per cent), and China (12.8 per cent). See JETRO, Survey of Actual Activities of Japanese Companies in Asia and Oceania, 2010 October 2010 (in Japanese).
3. Intermediate products exported from eastern Asia to India had been expanding from US$ 5.89 to US $41.89 billion during 1999-2009, while finished goods exported from India to EU and the USA increased from US $5.89 to US $19.67 billion, and US $5.47 to US $11.88 billion, respectively. See Ministry of Economy and Industry, Government of Japan, White Paper on International Economy and Trade 2011, p. 101 (in Japanese).
4. The steep surge in Japanese investment into India in 2008 reflects the fact that Daiichi Sankyo gained a majority control of Ranbaxy Laboratories for 490 billion yen and NTT DoCoMo bought a

26 per cent equity stake in Tata Teleservices for 250 billion yen.

5. Governments of Japan and India, *Report of the India-Japan Joint Study Group*, 2006, Chapter 4.
6. Association of IT Services Industry, White Paper on IT Services Industry 2010 (in Japanese).
7. Information-Technology Promotion Agency, Japan, *IPA/SEC White Paper 2008 on Software Development Projects in Japan: Digest Edition.*
8. TCS set up a joint venture with Mitsubishi Corporation in February 2012, aiming to expand the revenue in Japan from the current fewer than $100 to $500 million within 4-5 years.
9. Indian students in China were already as numerous as 5694 in 2006. Currently it is estimated to increase to around 9,000, including numerous students studying in medical courses. Indian medical candidates choose to study in China, attracted by lower education fees and wider entrance acceptance.
10. Shigesaburo Kabe, 'Relations between India and North-East Asia (Korea and Taiwan): Vigorous Expansion of Korean and Taiwanese Companies in India', in Japan Center for Economic Research, ed., *India in the World: Leading to Expanding Asia*, JCER, 2011 (in Japanese).

CHAPTER 10

India–Japan Economic Partnership: Scope and Prospect

SRABANI ROY CHOUDHURY

The era after the Second World War initiated a new world order. The historical bond with India as a birthplace of Buddhism (*Tenjiku*) and the association during the war led to a warm relationship between these two nations. India's abstinence from signing the San Francisco Peace Treaty, followed by signing the bilateral Treaty of Peace and Amity with Japan in1952[1] paved the way for a friendly and supportive partnership between both the nations at the political as well as the economic front. Japan at that time was keen in forging this relationship as India was a source of iron-ore and India as a vast country emerging from colonial rule and trying to put together an economic growth plan had great potential for Japan.

However, India was soon to decide towards following a policy of sustainable development with strong import substitution which essentially saw doors closed to foreign investment, although operations on the trade front continued, albeit under strict control. Thus, when Japan had its economic success and spread its manufacturing base to most Asian economies, India could not profit by it. The year 1991 was the turning point for India as having incurred bad debt it was forced into opening up its economy. In this hour of need as balance of payment position of India came under severe pressure, it was Japan who came to India's rescue and was the major contributor to the bailing out process.

The liberalized Indian economy with a new thirst for economic growth, found Japan an ideal teacher for its economic plan. Japan, by then, was the second largest economy having proved to the West its authority in the manufacturing sector. It was being commended as an Asian Giant, with its unique style of management. Thus, India initiated a fresh new bilateral economic relation urging Japanese companies to come to India. It also started de-regulating its markets to enable more foreign investment and trade. Under Prime Minister Narasimha Rao, India embarked on a 'Look East' policy by which it desired to attract the ASEAN countries and also Japan.

Economic prospects since then and even now, looks very encouraging for both these nations. This paper focuses on the period 2000[2] onwards and the thrust is to understand the three aspects of economic relations – trade, foreign direct investment and overseas development assistance (ODA) and estimates their current position *vis-à-vis* the other contending nations. The bilateral agreement of comprehensive economic partnership, signed in 2011, is then discussed with the intention of highlighting the opportunities that both the nations can construct given the broad platform that this agreement has created.

TRADE

Post-Second World War, Japan in its first round of economic development had benefited from imports of iron-ore from India. Though having mutual benefit, India–Japan trade did not gain the momentum that was expected. Figure 10.1 shows a year by year comparative data of India's export and import from the year 1998 to 2010. A look at the figure gives a rather dismal view of exports and imports between India and Japan. The major export to Japan from India continues to be iron-ore followed by marine products, agriculture products and gems and jewellery and main imports from Japan are heavy machinery, value-added iron and steel, organic chemicals, surgical equipment, plastic and rubber. From 2006 onwards exports to Japan has increased with a visible drop in 2008-9. However by 2010 it had again climbed to the 2007-8 level. The dip was mainly because of the strong recession that occurred world over in which Japan was one of the worst affected. But imports continued unabated from Japan to India, as India unaffected by world recession

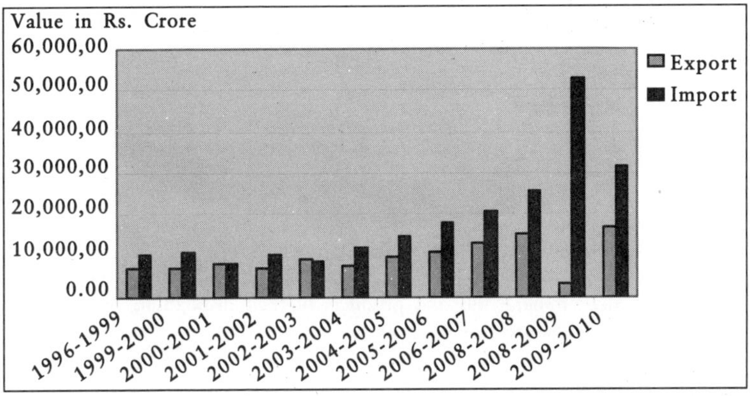

Source: Export Import Data Bank, Ministry of Commerce & Industry, GOI, commerce.nic.in

FIGURE 10.1: INDIA–JAPAN TRADE STATISTICS.

grew at 6.5 per cent. Among the imports the major contribution came from auto components as the automobile market in India faced great demand.

If one were to look at the commodity basket of imports and exports (Figure 10.2), the composition reflects that India is mostly exporting primary sector products which have little weight in the Japanese import basket. The largest share is of mineral fuels and ore followed by marine products with organic chemicals a poor fourth (3.42 per cent). The share of Japan in India's export shrank from 6 per cent in 1995 to below 2 per cent in 2010-11.

The imports from Japan also are little to applaud about. Nuclear reactors, boilers, etc., is the single most commodity imported from Japan. The rest are divided between a whole lot of products and among those which are exported to Japan (where there is some value addition) and then returned back to India, export and import of iron-ore is one such item that has figured in this category from the post-Independence period of India. Thus, composition of imports by India does not reflect a growing economy in which machinery and machine tools should have been a majority in the basket. If one has to look at the import partners, China has been at the first position for nearly a decade now and has flooded the Indian market

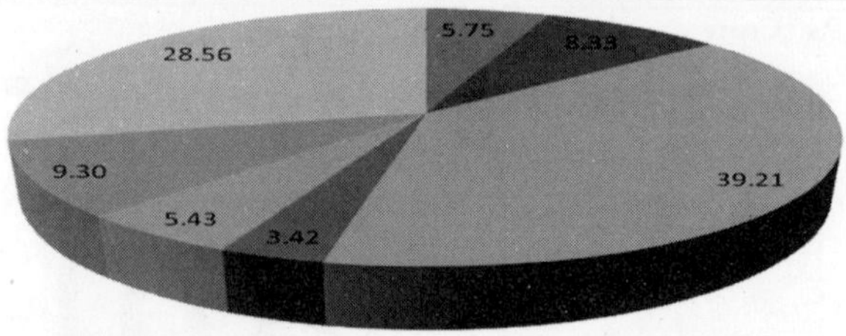

- Fish and crustaceans, molluscs and other aquatic invertibrates
- Residues and waste from the food industries; Prepared animal fodder
- Mineral fuels, mineral oils and products of their distillation; Bituminous substances; Mineral waxes
- Organic Chemicals
- Natural or cultured pearls, procious or semi-precious stones, pre-metals, clad with pre-metal and articles thereof; imt. jewellery; coin
- Iron and steel
- Others

FIGURE 10.2: SHARE OF DIFFERENT ITEMS IN TOTAL EXPORTS OF INDIA TO JAPAN (%) 2010-11.

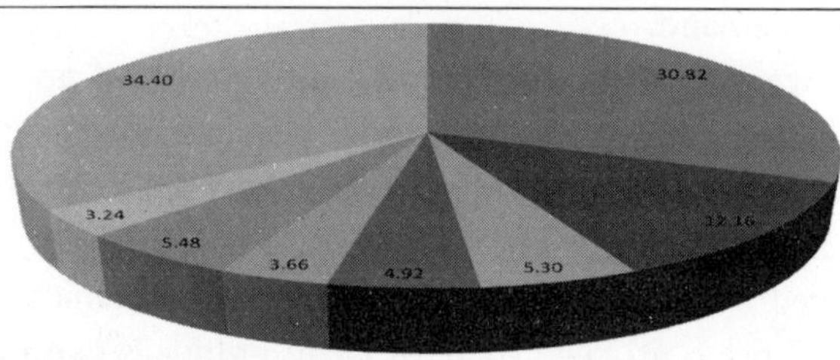

- Nuclear reactors, boilers, machinery and mechanical appliances; parts thereof
- Iron and Steel
- Optical, photographic cinematographic measuring, checking precision, medical or surgical inst. and apparatus parts and accessories thereof
- Organic Chemicals
- Articles of iron or steel
- Vehicles other than railway or tramway rolling stock, and parts and accessories thereof
- Plastic and articles thereof
- Others

Source: Export Import Data Bank, Ministry of Commerce & Industry, GOI, commerce.nic.in

FIGURE 10.3: SHARE OF DIFFERENT ITEMS IN TOTAL IMPORTS OF INDIA FROM JAPAN (%) 2010-11.

with cheap products. Other than the USA the other three countries are basically oil providers. However, India's imports from Japan has shown some improvement in the first half of 2011-12 with a sharp growth of 32 per cent , and Japan's position in India's imports has moved up from 16th position to 14th.

A look at the main trading partners of India (Figures 10.4 & 10.5) reveals that Japan does not figure among the first four countries, which it was till the year 2000. In fact, post-2000, Japan has steadily lost its position to other countries and today stands at 14th position. This deterioration that one witnesses in trade partnership between Japan and India is mainly because while other nations, especially China and Korea, has taken advantage of India's open market, Japan though a long-term trade partner did not pay attention to India and thus was not able to divert its commodity basket according to India's needs. As far as Japan is concerned, just around 0.6 per cent of Japan's global trade in merchandise[3] is with India, thus making it insignificant.

A trade relationship is a barometer for economic conditions and plays a strong role in establishing a bond between two nations. Moreover, it is usually from close trade ties that investment between the countries take place. Further, it is also an indication that small

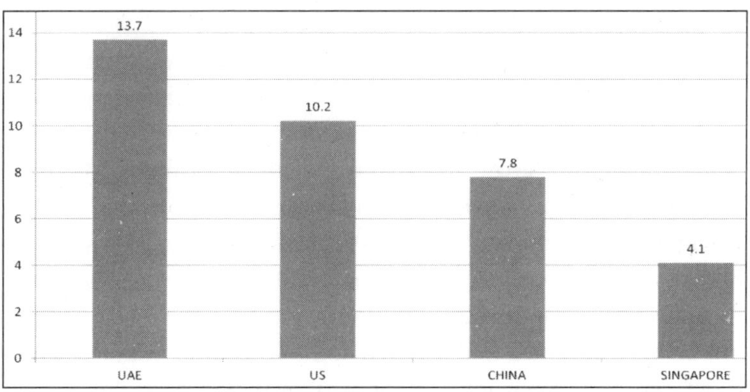

Source: Export Import Data Bank, Ministry of Commerce & Industry, GOI, commerce.nic.in

FIGURE 10.4: INDIA'S EXPORT PARTNERS IN 2010-11: SHARE IN TOTAL EXPORTS.

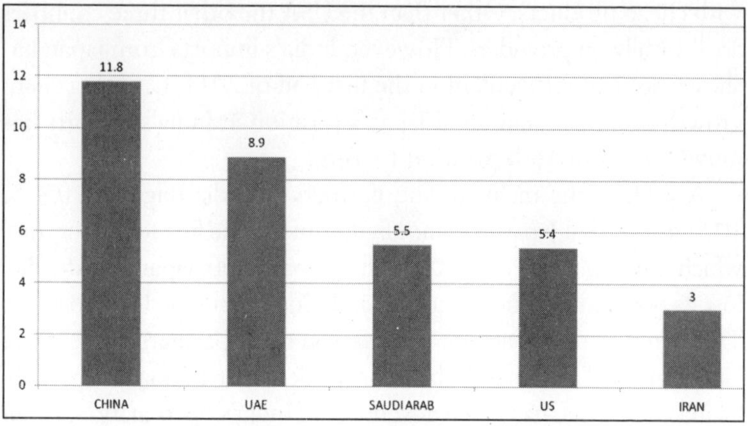

Source: Export Import Data Bank, Ministry of Commerce & Industry, GOI, commerce.nic.in

FIGURE 10.5: INDIA'S IMPORT PARTNERS IN 2010-11: SHARE IN TOTAL EXPORTS (%).

and medium enterprises of Japan who are the main body of Japanese exports have not explored the Indian market. The apathetic trade relation between these two nations does not echo the sentiments often promoted by the diplomatic arena.

FOREIGN DIRECT INVESTMENT

Foreign direct Investment (FDI) from an industrialized country to a developing country is an indicator of growth and vibrancy of the developing nation. FDI helps the developing nation with the crucial capital required to grow and also helps inflow of intangible assets like technological knowledge. The multinational corporations' reasons for entry into developing countries is motivated by market seeking, efficiency seeking, resource seeking, or created asset-seeking behaviour.

India opened up its economy to the world in the 1990s. In the late 1980s also, India had allowed some foreign investment albeit under scrutiny. Then investment was restricted to technological transfer, and participation of the foreign company in managing the company or establishing joint venture was prohibited. An exception was the Maruti-Suzuki venture where the Government of India was a major stakeholder. Some Japanese companies like Sanyo and Honda had by then entered the Indian market and established relationship on the basis of technology transfer. As India cautiously opened up sectors for foreign players, companies like Honda in automobiles, Sanyo in electronics, and Hitachi in consumer durables ventured into India. This was in 1993. Initially allowed around 40 per cent stake, these companies set-up joint ventures with Indian partners and conducted its business. As the Indian economy liberalized and allowed more equity participation, these Japanese companies, having tested Indian waters increased their equity participation. All this prove that the investment climate in India was favourable.

In 1996, in the second round of liberalization, some Japanese companies like Toyota that had shied away in the first round, came to India. With the Indian domestic market growing at nearly 2 per cent every year and a high level of disposable income available for consumerism, it is difficult for Japanese companies, which on the other hand, are facing stagnation in their domestic economy, not to look at India as their country of choice.

However, a close look at some macro data shown in Figure 10.6, throws up some questions that need to be addressed to enable India to become a key destination. If one takes a close look at the

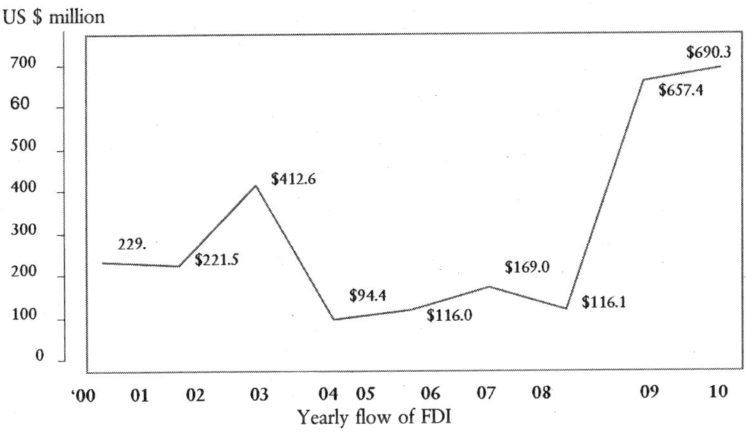

Source: Compiled from data from Ministry of Commerce, India.

FIGURE 10.6: FOREIGN DIRECT INVESTMENT FROM JAPAN INTO INDIA.

graph below one can see that the major take off of Japanese investment into India has happened in the last two business cycles (i.e. 2008-9, 2009-10). With some upswing witnessed in the period between 2002 and 2005 it tapered to a nominal level in the period of 2005-8. This was more due to the external environment as the world went through recession in which Japan was severely affected. Some of the spurts that one observes in the figure are often related to a large investment done by a single company. For instance, the peak in 2002-3 is essentially due to Mitsubishi Chemical's strong investment in Haldia. Thus, this only reflects that Japanese investors did not make use of the 'Look East' policy of India and the enthusiasm that one encounters today is only limited to the last two years.

Looking at the number of Japanese companies having business operations in India, as shown below in Figure 10.7, one can see a steady growth since 2005 and after 2006 it has remained above 1 per cent year on year. According to latest available statistics, Japanese companies have made actual investments of US $4.083 billion between April 2000 and May 2010. The top sectors (Table 10.1) attracting Japanese FDI is automobiles followed by service

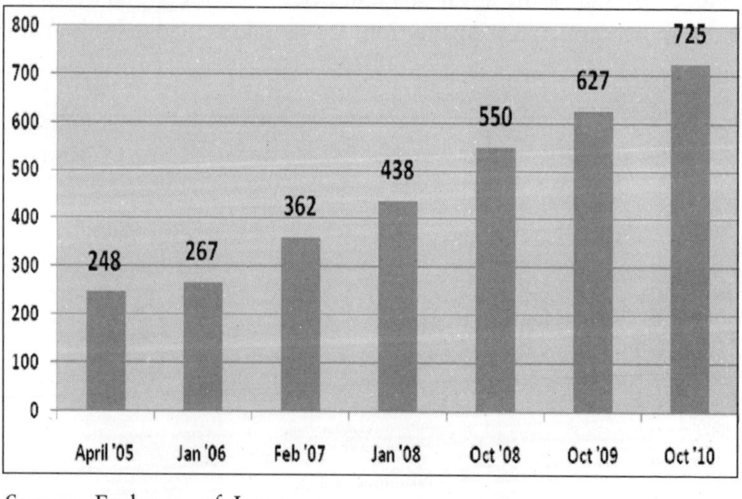

Source: Embassy of Japan.

FIGURE 10.7: INFLOWS OF JAPANESE COMPANIES.

TABLE 10.1: TOP SECTORS ATTRACTING FDI INFLOW FROM JAPAN APRIL 2000–JANUARY 2011

Rank	Sector	% of FDI inflow from Japan
1	Automobile industry	27
2	Services sector	14
3	Electrical equipment	11
4	Industrial machinery	7
5	Trading	7

Source: Ministry of Commerce dipp.nic.in

sector consisting of both financial and non-financial sector with industrial machinery coming in fourth. Considering Japanese are known for their precision machines and machinery, it continues to baffle Indian business at the lack of interest shown by this sector.

A comparison of the top investing countries' share in Indian FDI as shown in Table 10.2.

It is surprising that a newly-industrialized country like Singapore[4] is ahead of Japan. Before the year 2005 Japan was ranked fourth and by 2010, countries like Singapore and the Netherlands had relegated it to the sixth position. However in the two quarters April 2010-September 2011, Japan's cumulative share in FDI has shot up to 4.8 per cent and improved its position to fifth in the total ranks.

TABLE 10.2: TEN TOP INVESTING COUNTRIES IN INDIA 2000-2010

Rank	Country	% Share in FDI inflow
1	Mauritius	43.68
2	Singapore	8.94
3	USA	7.67
4	UK	5.58
5	Netherlands	4.09
6	Japan	3.27
7	Cyprus	3.08
8	Germany	2.60
9	France	1.45
10	United Arab Emirates	1.20

Source: Ministry of Commerce dipp.nic.in

Thus one may infer here that though Japan shows promise of being a strong investor in India, in reality it has yet to take concrete steps to actually show its presence. Further, if one is to make a comparison of Japanese outflow of FDI from 1996 to 2010 approximately around the time that India opened up its economy, one can assume that in the first half of the 2000s Japanese FDI shifted from the US to Europe. In the second half of the 2000s, it found destination in Asia, Oceania and Central and South America. The data in Table 10.3 shows that as part of the shift towards Asia, India's share rose from 0.5 per cent in the first half of 2000s to 3.4 per cent in the second half, hence proving that India is yet to come under Japanese business purview. Contrarily, China continues to be the most favoured destination, considering that its political relationship with Japan is not as cordial as that with India.

TABLE 10.3: DIRECTION OF JAPAN'S OUTWARD FDI, 1996-2010

Region	1996-2000	2001-5	2006-10
Asia	*27.7*	*26.6*	*29.0*
ASEAN	15.1	9.1	10.8
Singapore	3.1	1.7	3.0
China	5.4	12.2	9.5
South Korea	1.8	2.1	2.0
India	1.3	0.5	3.4
Europe	*20.8*	*29.9*	*26.6*
UK	8.7	12.2	6.9
Netherlands	10.1	8.5	10.7
North America	*36.0*	*27.6*	*21.9*
US	35.4	25.9	20.9
Oceania	*2.2*	*3.7*	*6.6*
Australia	1.6	3.0	6.3
Central & South America	*12.8*	*11.7*	*14.7*
Brazil	2.1	2.0	4.2
Cayman Islands	8.0	7.5	9.0
Middle East	*0.5*	*0.2*	*0.6*
Africa	*0.4*	*0.6*	*0.7*
South Africa	0.4	0.2	0.4
World	*100.0*	*100.0*	*100.0*

Source: JETRO, 2011.

OVERSEAS DEVELOPMENT ASSISTANCE (ODA)

Economic relations between a developing nation and a developed nation are never complete without a discussion on overseas development assistance (ODA) that is given out by the developed nation. Japan's initial venture into Asian economies mainly the ASEAN countries saw a two-pronged strategy of giving ODA which encouraged FDI flow. Often, it was seen that ODA facilitated gaps that made it difficult for FDI to operate. On the other hand, ODA was often tied with respect to technological know-how and other requirements by ensuring that a Japanese company implemented the project. This overtime drew a lot of criticism and thus, today most of the ODA is dispersed in a more egalitarian manner.

Since Independence, India has been a recipient of Japanese aid. Historically India was the first country to get aid from Japan and it forged a bond between the nations. Since most of the ODA was Japanese aid in those days, it also gave business to and supported the continuation of the major Japanese trading company offices in India. Some projects that have qualitatively changed India during the period prior to the liberalization of the Indian economy were the Bombay High Deep Sea Drilling Project in which Japan provided the first offshore jack-up drilling rig and its success led to reducing India's dependence on oil, several fertilizer projects that ensured the 'Green Revolution' programme could be implemented and led to India becoming self-sufficient in food grain production and also Vishakhapatanam Outer Harbour Project and Cochin Shipyard Project which facilitated sea logistics.

Post-liberalization ODA from Japan continued to impact lives of Indians in more ways. Today, Japan ODA focus rests on:

- Development of economic infrastructure mainly in the area of power and transportation.
- Poverty reduction mainly through agriculture and rural development.
- Environmental protection through afforestation and improvement of quality of water.
- Assisting to improve health and medical care.[5]

Japan gives three types of aid – Yen loans, Grant Aid Cooperation and Technical Cooperation. Figure 10.8 shows clearly that Yen loan is the most common form of aid from Japan and grant-aid and technical aid form only a miniscule part of the aid basket. If one were to examine the break-up between the grant-aid and technical aid given to India in the same period (Figure 10.9), it is encouraging to note that grant aid is decreasing and technical aid is on the increase in the last few years. This augurs well for a country like India which today needs the knowledge, understanding and skill development to become production efficient in areas in which technical aid is being given. The major projects that Japan today is undertaking in India continue to be in the area of infrastructure. The Delhi-Mumbai Industrial Corridor (DMIC) and the Delhi-Mumbai Freight Corridor (DMFC) aimed at connecting ports in Gujarat to green field manufacturing zones in India would probably impact the Indian population most. Other important projects include North Karanpura Super Thermal Power Project (1): 15.916 billion yen, Delhi Mass Rapid Transport System Project (IV): 19.292 billion yen, Ganga Action Plan Project (Varanasi): 11.184 billion yen and Uttar Pradesh Buddhist Circuit Development Project: 9.495 billion

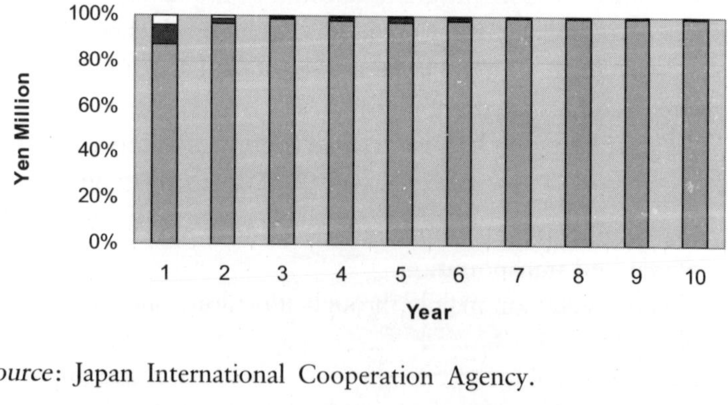

Source: Japan International Cooperation Agency.

FIGURE 10.8: OVERSEAS DEVELOPMENT ASSISTANCE FROM JAPAN TO INDIA 2000-2009.

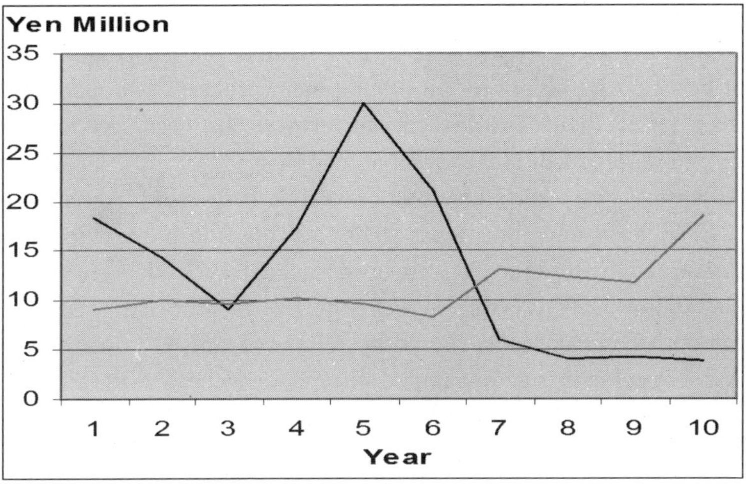

Source: Japan International Cooperation Agency.

FIGURE 10.9: PERCENTAGE CONTRIBUTION BY GRANT AID AND TECHNICAL COOPERATION 2000-9.

yen. The recent visit of Prime Minister of Japan His Excellency Noda in December 2011 and the promise of a *shinkansen* line all prove that Japan would like India to overcome its infrastructure issues and fast track its developmental process.

COMPREHENSIVE ECONOMIC PARTNERSHIP AGREEMENT (CEPA)

The above discussion throws up a myriad of issues to which solutions are not easy to come by. If one goes by the trade statistics it shows that India-Japan trade relations have not made many inroads, in fact to a great extent it has only deteriorated in the current decade. As far as FDI is concerned, it has picked up momentum in the last half of the decade and there is a definite alignment between both the business partners to use this route for mutual growth and prosperity. Nonetheless, the desirous quantum is yet to find a place. The ODA is essentially a catalyst to help ensure that the externalities are made conducive for economic growth of developing countries. India with an average growth of 7 per cent needs this assistance to help build both physical resource in form of infrastructure as well as human resource to facilitate the growth programme. But ODA alone can at best be a harbinger to the development process. A broader and deeper trade as well as investment relations are necessary to give momentum to bilateral economic relations.

India–Japan Comprehensive Economic Partnership Agreement (CEPA) was signed in August 2011 and comes into operation at a time when the entire world is engaged signing Free Trade Agreements and Economic Partnership Agreements. It is an important milestone for both the nations as the entire region of ASEAN, North-East Asia have already signed many such agreements both at the bilateral level and multilateral level. To India, this agreement assumes more significance because one, it is the first time that India has concluded a bilateral agreement with an industrialized country; and two, it is also the first truly comprehensive agreement concluded by India as it goes far beyond the other agreements, given the wide range of issues it covers. To Japan, it is probably one of the many such agreements but its importance lies in the fact that with this agreement Japan moves beyond the geography of East Asia. Moreover, since trade between these nations has been slipping and investment has not been as desirable, an agreement is expected to give a boost in the positive direction.

The move for such an agreement was initiated on 15 December 2006, with a Joint Ministerial statement announcing the launch of negotiations for the conclusion of an economic partnership agreement (EPA)/CEPA. A Joint Task Force (JTF) was set up to facilitate this. The endeavour of the JTF was to establish an India-Japan EPA/CEPA which would not only trade in goods but also trade in services, measures for trade promotion facilitation and liberalization of investment flows, measures for promoting economic cooperation in identified sectors and other areas for a comprehensive economic partnership between India and Japan. After long and tenacious rounds of negotiations lasting over four years, the India–Japan CEPA document was signed on 16 February 2011 in Tokyo. As a prerequisite to diplomatic *modus operandi*, India and Japan exchanged diplomatic notes informing each other of the legal procedures necessitated for bringing the Agreement in force on 30 June 2011. On 1 August 2011, the CEPA between Japan and India became operational. It took nearly five years of negotiations to conclude this agreement. The India–Japan CEPA is the third such agreement that has been concluded between India and other nations (similar agreements were signed with Singapore in 2005 and with Korea in 2009).

The Agreement has 15 chapters, 147 articles, covering goods, services, rules of origin, movement of natural persons, telecom, financial services, investment, intellectual property rights, government procurement, sanitary and physio-sanitary measures, customs procedures and cooperation in other services. The agreement not only covers trade in goods but also trade in services, measures for trade promotion facilitation and liberalization of investment flows, measures for promoting economic cooperation in identified sectors and other areas for a comprehensive economic partnership.

The Objective of CEPA is to:

- Liberalize and facilitate trade in goods and services between India and Japan
- Increase investment opportunities and strengthen protection for investments and investment activities in both the countries
- Ensure protection of intellectual property and promote cooperation in the field thereof
- Promote cooperation for the effective enforcement of competition laws in each Party
- Improve business environment in each country
- Establish a framework to enhance closer cooperation in the fields agreed in the Agreement
- Create effective procedures for the implementation and application of this Agreement and for the resolution of disputes

The CEPA aims to reduce or eliminate tariffs over the next ten years on over 90 per cent of goods traded between two countries. A list of 802 items which enjoy exemption/concession have been notified vide *Customs Notification 69/2011–Cus,* dated 29 July 2011.[6] The pact is expected to provide access to the $5-trillion-GDP in the Japanese market. About 94 per cent of the tariffs between Japan and India will be eliminated within 10 years (about 97 per cent by Japan and about 90 per cent by India) on a trade value basis. By 2014 one expects to find some difference in the composition as well as volume of both trade and investment as a result of this agreement.

Though it is early to conclude the quantum of difference that this agreement is expected to make, some exposition that can be made are that some sectors that was out of reach for India because of entry barriers (like pharmaceuticals) will be accessible. Textile products including readymade garments sector would be able to compete on a fair play basis. A bigger difference would be seen in the service sector as greater access for contractual suppliers, professionals such as accountants, researchers, tourist guides and management consultants who will now be able to provide their services in Japan. Not only computer engineers but a whole range of engineering services such as mechanical, electrical, construction, industrial, design engineers and project management specialists would be able to access the Japanese market. Instructors and yoga practitioners, classical music and dance practitioners, chefs and English language teachers have found a mention in the agreement. From Japan's viewpoint, the CEPA is significant because, India has made commitments for liberalization in its telecom, financial and distribution sectors. The agreement will not only augment but also facilitate more investment flow from Japan to India as it provides an atmosphere conducive for Japanese companies to establish their manufacturing base in India. Japan's business community will get access to the huge Indian market for their manufactured goods and can take advantage of India's growing market resources, especially its human resources.

CONCLUSION

India today is poised to become a destination for investment. Many factors are aligned to make it so. Primarily, the Indian domestic market is booming with a growth potential of at least 2 per cent every year. Although 70 per cent of the population of India resides in rural areas, with the technology boom, it is seen that rural India also desires products once thought to be limited to the urban sector. The upper middle class has been exposed to international brands and over time they have an understanding of the value of quality over price that used to be a major driver for consumerism. Thus a new breed of consumers is emerging in the Indian market. Telecommunication is also integrating rural India and narrowing the urban-rural divide. Second, the human resource is also expected to vastly improve due to attempts made by the Government of India towards better education and progressively more skilled manpower will become the order of the day. Given the size of the Indian population, manpower is bound to remain cheaper than most other nations. In the first growth phase India had jumped on to the services sector. Of late, there has been an attempt to return to the manufacturing sector. Efforts to build a strong and vibrant manufacturing sector so as to encompass a larger mass and make the development process more meaningful to the population at large is on the agenda. India is emerging as a technical pool as it provides talented low cost software engineers. Information Technology (IT) can become the strategic enabler. India is a natural partner for innovation led high-end products. A large section of the population of India speaks English and a substantial number is being added every year making India a choice destination as an IT enabled services (ITES) provider. Third, infrastructure development of both roads and railways are becoming critical to enable fast movement of goods within as well as between the manufacturing hubs and ports. India has recognized the dire need for infrastructure development and has been working towards finding solutions. India is positioned geographically between the East and the West. With a highly skilled, IT enabled workforce that is comparatively inexpensive, it can end up becoming an 'eco-strategic' location where innovation and R&D activity can be conducted to serve clients in the Eastern part of the world as well as the Western part of the world.

Japan on the other hand faces a serious issue of on-going recession domestically. Many of its companies are reeling under losses because of the current world recession. India with a domestic market orientation would naturally be a good destination for Japanese businesses. Further, Japan's strength lies in its strong technological capability which has its base in the small- and medium-scale sector, giving rise to an opportunity that can hardly be ignored by the Japanese, as India has a large medium-scale sector which are in need of technology tie-ups. Infrastructure development is another strong forte of Japan and with DMIC and DFC on the anvil it gives Japanese companies an enormous opportunity to make inroads into India. The new consumers though in niche products are finally valuing quality, the major driving force for Japanese products. Thus the time is probably most opportune for high end Japanese electronics and cosmetics to reach out to this market. Today, Japan faces the fastest ageing society in the world and this essentially means a smaller working population. Thus reliance on the global market will become a necessary option. The working age population in India stands at 4 million graduates and is expected to add another 200 million by 2030. As discussed earlier in this paper, India with its increasingly skilled population can be the destination for Japanese companies and its service industry giving Japan an opportunity to regain its economic viability. China which was a favoured destination so far for Japan was essentially an export-oriented economy, which in turn led to uncertainties at the time of world recession. India is still a rather domestic market-oriented economy and thus companies can insulate themselves by being in business in India. Further, the southern Indian coast which is very close to the current auto-parts and electronic component hub located in Malaysia and Indonesia can be integrated to form a powerful trio and enable growth of low cost automobiles for the world at large. Japan's GDP growth rate might be poor, still it remains a capital and technology rich country and India on the other hand is hungry for the same. Thus a huge complementary market is present in these sectors too. With Europe going through an economic crisis, solution to which could take a while, Japan at this juncture can ill afford to ignore India.

India and Japan have different economic needs and interestingly, each country's needs could be addressed by the other. Given such complementarities in area of economics, it is time that both the nations keep the focus which has been gained in the past decade and culminated in CEPA and make headway into future of prosperity.

NOTES

1. The first treaty signed on terms of equality by Japan after regaining sovereignty.
2. Wherever felt desirous, previous years have also been included in the discussion.
3. Exports as well as imports.
4. Mauritius investment does not count because this country has a special tax regime which allows for foreign companies to leverage on this. Thus most of the investment from Mauritius is routed through other countries and does not reflect the true picture.
5. As reflected in JICA's website.
6. Comprehensive Economic Partnership Agreement Between The Republic of India and Japan.

REFERENCES

A report entitled 'Recent Trend and Prospects of FDI in India by Bonghoon Kim'. Available through email at gators@maxtin.co.kr.

Anand, Jaideep and Andrew Delios (2006), 'Competing Globally: How Japanese MNCs Have Matched Goals and Strategies in India and China', *Columbia Journal of World Business*, 51-62.

Annual Issue of SIA Newsletter (2001), 'FDI Synopsis on Japan' Department of Industrial Planning and Promotion, New Delhi India.*

Bala, Komaraiah J. (2003), 'India-Japan Business Relations in the 21st Century', in *Japan's Role in South East Asia*, ed. M.D. Dharamdasini, New Delhi: Lancer Books.

Bearnish, Paul W., Andrew Delios, and Don Lecraw (1997), *Japanese Multinationals in the Global Economy,* Cheltenham, UK: Edward Elgar Publishing.

Bhalla, A.S., 'Sino-Indian Liberalization: The role of Trade and Foreign Investment', *Economics of Planning*, Netherlands: Kluwer Academic Publisher, 1998, pp. 151-73.

Badar, Alam Iqbal (1997), 'FDI Inflows Scenario is not Bright One', *Monthly Commentary*, 14-18 May.

Delios, Andrew and Paul W. Bearnish (2004), 'Joint Venture Performance Revisited: Japanese Foreign Subsidiaries Worldwide', *Management International Review*, 44(1): 69-91.

——, (1999), 'Geographic Scope, Product Diversification and the Corporate Performance of Japanese Firms', *Strategic Management Journal*, 20(8): 711-27, 1999.

Delios, Andrew, Ajai Singh Gaur and Shige Makino (2008), 'Political Hazards, Experience and Sequential Entry Strategies: The International expansion of Japanese Firms, 1980-1998', *Strategic Management Journal*, 20(8): 711-27.

Delios, Andrew and Witold J. Heinsz (2000), 'Japanese Firm's Investment Strategies in Emerging Economies', *Academy of Management Journal*, 43(3): 305-23.

Esho Hideki (2001), 'The Japanese Response to India's New Economic Policy', in *Economic Liberalisation in India: Japanese and Indian Perspective* ed. K.V. Kesavan, New Delhi: ICSSSR.

Guha, Ashok and Amit Ray (2000), 'Multinational Versus Expatriate FDI: A Comparative Analysis of the Chinese and Indian Experience', *Working Paper No. 58*, ICRIER, New Delhi.

IBEF's Report on 'India–Japan: A Little Japan in India', November 2007, Available at www.ibef.org.

IBM reports entitled 'Indians View their Automotive Future', IBM Institute for Business Value.

JBIC's Report by Shiro Izuishi entitled Commentary: Trends of Japanese Foreign Direct Investment in Fiscal 1999. Available at www.doingbusiness.aol

Jetro White Paper on 'Outward Foreign Direct Investment', Various Issues.

Kumar, Nagesh (ed.) (2002), 'Liberalization and Japanese Foreign Direct Investments in India', in *Building a global Partnership: 50 Years of India-Japan Relations*, ed. Kesavan, New Delhi: Lancers Book.

Li, Wei (2003), 'A Road to Common Prosperity-Examination of an FTA between India and China', *RIS Discussion Paper 49*, Research and Information System for the Non-Aligned and Developing Countries (RIS), New Delhi, India.

Mathiyazhagan, Maathai K. and Dukhabandhu Sahoo (2008), 'Do Foreign Investment Inflows Benefit the Major Sectors in India?' 2: 25, Institute of South Asian Studies, ISAS, Singapore. Accessed on 24 January 2008, Available at www.isaas.

Makino, Shige, Paul W. Bearnish and Natalie Bin Zhao (2004), 'The Characteristics and Performance of Japanese FDI in Less Developed and Developed Countries', *Journal of World Business,* 39(4): 377-92.

Nagraj, R. (2003), 'Foreign Direct Investment in India in the 1990s: Trends and Issues', 38: 1701-12, *Economic Political Weekly Review.*

Oskarsson, Patrick (2005), 'India Attraction: Profitable Multinationals as Subsidy Junkies: A Study of Incentives for Foreign Direct Investment India', Finnwatch, Finland.

Press Note No. 1 (2005), Department of Industrial Planning and Promotion, New Delhi, India. Available on www.dipp.go.in.*

SIA Newsletter (2007), 'FDI Synopsis on Japan', Department of Industrial Planning and Promotion, New Delhi India. Available on www.dipp.go.in.*

Siddhartan, N.S. (2006), 'Regional Differences in FDI Inflows: China-India Comparison', Research Paper, Institute of Economic Growth, Delhi University.

Srivastava, Sadhna and Ramkishen S. Rajan (2004), 'What Does the Economic Rise of China Imply for ASEAN and India? Focus on Trade and Investment Flows' Accessed on 28 January 2008, Available on Keha_Ch09.qxd 20/07/04.

WEBLIOGRAPHY

Comprehensive Economic Partnership Agreement between the Republic of India and Japan (2011), Ministry of Commerce, Government of India, Accessed 2 February 2012, URL: http://commerce.nic.in/trade/ijcepa_basic_agreement.pdf.

Export Import Data Bank, Department of Commerce, Government of India, (Online: Web), Accessed 28 January 2012, URL: http://commerce.nic.in/eidb/default.asp.

FDI, Statistics, Department of Industrial Policy and Promotion, Government of India (Online: Web), Accessed 29 January 2012, URL:http://dipp.nic.in/English/Publications/FDI_Statistics/FDI_Statistics.aspx.

FDI, Ministry of Finance, Government of Japan (Online: Web), Accessed 29 January 2012, URL:http://www.mof.go.jp/english/international_policy/reference/itn_transactios_in_securities/fdi/index.html.

Japanese Trade and Investment Statistics, Japan External Trade Organization, (Online: Web), Accessed 29 January 2012, URL:http://www.jetro.go.jp/en/reports/statistics/.

Trade Statistics of Japan, Ministry of Finance, Government of Japan, (Online: Web), Accessed 29 January 2012, URL:http://www.customs.go.jp/toukei/info/index_e.htm.

CHAPTER 11

Present Status of Japanese Studies in India: Prospects and Problems

P.A. GEORGE

The first decade of the twenty-first century has seen a dramatic change in the world economic scenario as the centre of economic activities drifted to Asia from the West. Rise of China as a super economic power pushing Japan aside to the third position and gradual rise of India in terms of economic strength have jeopardized the traditional world economic order centred on the US and Europe. If this trend should continue uninterrupted for the coming one decade or two, no doubt the three Asian economic giants, China, Japan and India, would control the world economy by the end of the first quarter of this century. In other words, it means that we are now at the threshold of a new Asian Age, thereby envisaging a new world order. This being the background, it is pertinent enough to discuss now about the present state of Japanese Studies in India, its future prospects and problems.

As we are all aware, during the second half of twentieth century, Japanese studies, including the Japanese language education had shown unprecedented growth throughout the world especially, in America and Europe. In various developed countries, Japan has been studied as a whole, giving great weight to all aspects of Japanese studies – not just the language. However, in Europe, especially, in France and other mainland countries, Japanese studies is in the brink of collapse now mainly due to two reasons. First of course is the financial crunch caused by global economic slump and depression. Mostly funded by the state governments, the universities and educational institutions in these countries where Japanese studies or Japanese language education programmes are offered are being sidelined for more economically viable courses, such as science and technology, information technology, business management, international trade and various other fields of study pertaining to the service sector and so on, which would bring immediate result and contribute to the overall economic development of the country. Educational institutions are forced to generate funds from various sources in order to sustain the *status quo* of area studies and foreign language learning. The second major reason for the withering of Japanese Studies in European countries could be traced from the sudden and dramatic rise of China as an economic power to be reckoned with, which in turn weakened the significance of Japanese Studies in Western countries gradually while giving unprecedented popularity to Chinese Studies and Chinese language education.

In countries in the developing world, including India, though recently Japanese language education has been given high leverage, initiative to proliferate Japanese studies by the state, academic institutions or individual level has been almost absent henceforth, though the changing world order and economic and political situation in this part of the world call for a large-scale proliferation of Japanese Studies. Fortunately, now the governments of both India and Japan recognize the need for a strong Indo–Japan Global Partnership and increasing level of strategic cooperation; which in turn gives an impetus for Japanese Studies and Japanese language education in India. More and more scholars and researchers are showing interest in specializing in one of the many fields of Japanese studies. It is a welcome change.

INDIA'S CONTACT WITH JAPAN

Though India was known to the Japanese people right from the introduction of Buddhism to Japan in the sixth century from China through Korea, it was only indirect, superficial information about Tenjiku, the Western Paradise. As Buddhism spread throughout the country during the Nara and Heian periods in Japan, Japanese people began to look towards Tenjiku, the land of Buddha, with reverence and nostalgia. For a common Japanese believer, Tenjiku was a place lying beyond this ephemeral world which he called the Western Paradise. Tenjiku was not only a source for hope and inspiration for the Japanese but also a source for their spiritual experience and eternal salvation. But on the contrary, back in India nobody knew about even the existence of Japan until the modern period. In fact, people of India did not even distinguish the Japanese and Korean people from the Chinese in the ancient times, and that may be the main reason why Indians were so ignorant about the Japanese people and their culture. Even now in rural India people do not distinguish Japanese, Korean, or Vietnamese from Chinese.

One exception to this was the Indian Buddhist monks of ancient times who visited China as a part of their mission to propagate Buddhism. These monks predominantly from the peninsular India came to know about the country called 'Wa' (Japan) during their sojourn in China. Some of them must have crossed over to Japan through the Korean peninsula in the early periods of propagation of Buddhism in the Far East. A south Indian Buddhist monk called Bodhidharma was one of them, who is said to have visited Japan during the seventh century and presided over the eye opening ceremony of the Great Buddha of Todai-ji temple at Nara. However, none of the Indian monks who crossed over to Japan, or for that matter to China, are believed to have returned to their mother country, India. Hence, for the people back in India there was no way to get information about Wa or Japan.

Indians came in direct contact with Japan and the Japanese people only by the second half of the Meiji period. Of course, there had been occasional contact and visit from the Japanese side even during the Tokugawa (Edo) period, but hardly any Indian reciprocated during the medieval or early modern period. Some of the early Indians who showed special interest on Japan towards the end of the nineteenth century and beginning of the twentieth century were either business entrepreneurs, spiritual leaders or government officials from erstwhile princely states of India. Among them were Jamshedji Nusserwanji Tata (visited Japan in 1893), Swami Vivekananda (1893), M. Visvesvaraya (1898 and 1909), Rabindranath Tagore (first visit

1913) and Syed Ross Masood (1922).[1] However, these Indians were attracted to Japan as they were inspired by its extraordinary economic growth after the Meiji Restoration in 1868 and the Japanese people's endurance power and fighting spirit which made them victorious in the Japan–China War in 1895 and Russo–Japan War in 1905.

Tagore's close association with Okakura Tenshin opened the door for him to know more about the Japanese language, culture and art. Okakura Tenshin visited Kolkata in January 1902, with a mission to meet Swami Vivekananda and invite him to the religious conference scheduled to be held at Kyoto. In fact, prior to that in 1890 Swami Vivekananda had a brief sojourn in Japan on his way to Chicago for attending the World Parliament of Religions in 1893. Ernest F. Fenollosa, a renowned professor of Economics and Philosophy at the University of Tokyo during the later period of Meiji was Okakura's professor and an ardent admirer of Swami Vivekananda. Hence, he was instrumental in the mutual meeting of Okakura, Swami Vivekananda and Tagore.[2]

Tagore introduced Japanese language, art and culture into the curriculum of Vishwa Bharati (Santiniketan) University in the beginning of the 1920s and brought several Japanese language teachers and artists from Japan to teach in the university. Perhaps, this may be considered as the beginning of Japanese Study in an academic institution in India though it did not last long because of Japan's engagement in militarism/imperialism in the 1930s and later its participation in the Pacific War. Hence Japanese Studies as an academic field of study in real sense in India began only after the end of the War and India's Independence from British colonial rule.

This paper will look into the status of Japanese Studies in India first and then discuss the future prospects. Finally, it will discuss the problems which might hinder the growth of Japanese Studies hereafter.

THREE COMPONENTS OF JAPANESE STUDIES

When we talk about Japanese studies in India, we often think only in terms of Regional (Area) Studies. This is not the right perspective.

'Japanese Studies' should mean not only regional or area study but also culture study and language study. In other words, Japanese Studies in India has three equally important components like in any other foreign country, namely: (i) Area Studies, (ii) Culture & Literature Studies, and (iii) Language Studies. These three components together constitute Japanese Studies, and the term 'Japanese Studies' in this paper refers to all these three categories.

GROWTH OF JAPANESE STUDIES IN POST-INDEPENDENT INDIA

India had established its diplomatic relations with Japan in 1952. There was a spurt in the number of institutions with academic programmes related to Japanese Studies ever since. The first of such kind was the introduction of Japanese language teaching in the School of Foreign Languages under the Defense Ministry of India in 1954. This was followed by the establishment of the Indian School of International Studies and the introduction of PhD (research) programme in Japanese Studies along with the introduction of Japanese language teaching in 1955.

The signing of Indo–Japan Cultural Exchange Agreement in 1957 was another turning point again in the field of Japanese Studies in India. The Japanese Embassy in New Delhi began a Japanese language course for Indian public in its Cultural and Information Centre along with its Consulate in Kolkata in 1958. This had given a rare opportunity to the Indian citizens living in and around Delhi and Kolkata to come across the language and culture of Japan without much financial burden on them.

India signed the 'Memorandum on Promotion of Japanese Studies in India' with Japan in October 1969. Soon after that the University of Delhi introduced Japanese Studies, Area Studies as well as Japanese language teaching together in one department. Similarly, in Jawaharlal Nehru University also Japanese Studies flourished as a result of incorporation of the erstwhile Indian School of International Studies into JNU's School of International Studies and introduction of Japanese language teaching into School of Languages in 1973. Thereafter for about two decades Japanese Studies in India kept moving horizontally as it mainly remained within the academic premises of University of Delhi and JNU only.

It is also noteworthy here that the Japanese Studies and language programmes introduced at the governmental and university level did not find many takers initially, as there was hardly any scope for good jobs in the 1970s and early 1980s. Though Japan and India established their diplomatic relation in 1952 after the Second World War, and began to cooperate closely in various fields, including trade and economic relations and grassroot level cultural exchanges after the signing of Cultural Exchange Programme in 1956, it did not progress smoothly as was expected initially. There were various reasons for this downward trend in the relationship which touched rock bottom during the period of rapid economic growth in Japan in 1960s and 1970s.

Japan's increasing dependency on America for defense and security related matters after the ratification of US–Japan Security Treaty in 1960 may be considered as one of the major reasons for India drifting away from Japan. Because, the basis for India's foreign policy during the Cold War era was non-alignment and India was basically against the polarization of power and politics into two blocs, the capitalist bloc led by the USA and the so-called socialist bloc led by the erstwhile USSR. But at the same time, though India considered itself as a leader of the third bloc, i.e. the group of non-aligned countries, in all practical purpose it tilted towards the Soviet bloc which disappointed the Japanese. Hence, there emerged a feeling of distrust between Japan and India, and ultimately they drifted away from each other. It is an irony that this distrust and psychological barrier which emerged during the period of Cold War still stand as impediments in the way of Indo–Japan relations even in the twenty-first century.

Nevertheless, India's 'Look East' policy and opening of its market in the 1990s has opened a new chapter in Indo–Japan relations. The cloud that enwrapped the Indo–Japan relations during the Cold War slowly began to fade and a new age of friendship and mutual rediscovery began with the initiative of the former Japanese Prime

Minister Yoshiro Mori. In that sense, Prime Minister Mori's visit to India in 2000 was a turning point yet again in the history of Indo–Japan relations. In the summit meet, both India and Japan for the first time recognized the significance of 'Indo–Japan Global Partnership in the 21st Century' for creating a peaceful, prosperous new Asia and world. Thereafter the Prime Ministers of both the countries have been reiterating their commitment to strengthen the Indo–Japan Strategic and Global Partnership, the need for quantum increase in cultural, academic and people-to-people exchanges and to substantiate the Japan–India strategic partnership, in every subsequent summit meets carried out regularly every year, either in Japan or in India.

THE EIGHTFOLD INITIATIVE OF 2005

When we discuss about the growth of Japanese Studies in India, it is necessary to look into the contents of the famous 'Eightfold Initiative' proclaimed jointly by prime ministers of India and Japan, Manmohan Singh and Koizumi Junichiro, respectively in 2005, which would become the lifeline of Indo–Japanese relation and cooperation in the new Asian age. Following are the eight topics of priority highlighted in this initiative:

1. Enhanced and upgraded dialogue architecture, including strengthening of the momentum of high-level exchanges, launching of a High Level Strategic Dialogue and full utilization of the existing dialogue mechanisms.
2. Comprehensive economic engagement, through expansion of trade in goods and services, investment flows and other areas of economic cooperation, and exploration of a Japan–India economic partnership agreement.
3. Enhanced security dialogue and cooperation.
4. Science and Technology initiative.
5. Cultural and academic initiatives and strengthening of people-to-people contacts to raise the visibility and profile of one country in the other.
6. Cooperation in ushering a new Asian era.
7. Cooperation in the United Nations and other international

organizations, including cooperation for the early realization of UN reforms, particularly Security Council reform.

8. Cooperation in responding to global challenges and opportunities.

Item five of the Eightfold Initiative, 'cultural and academic initiatives and strengthening of people-to-people contacts to raise the visibility and profile of one country in the other' is the initiative which brings hope to the future state of Japanese Studies in India.

PRESENT STATUS OF JAPANESE LANGUAGE EDUCATION IN INDIA

The factors which helped rapid spread of Japanese language education and Japanese Studies in India are considered to be opening of Indian Market and Liberalization of Indian Economy in the 1990s and strengthening of Indo–Japan Economic cooperation, rapid advancement of Japanese companies into Indian market and sudden increase in the number of Japanese joint venture companies, along with the 'Look East' policy of the Indian government, 'Indo–Japan Partnership in the New Asian Age' and 'Eightfold Initiative' and IT boom. As already mentioned above, based on item no. 5 of the Eightfold Initiative, India and Japan in principle had agreed to work together to promote Japanese Studies, especially, Japanese language education in India, on a large scale. The target set in 2005 was to produce at least 30,000 Japanese knowing Indian citizens by the end of 2010. It was a highly ambitious target. Though we failed to achieve this target, there has been almost a twofold increase in the number of Japanese language learners in India during four years between 2006 and 2010. One of the reasons for this sudden increase in the number of Japanese language learners in India is the introduction of Japanese in to the CBSE's (Central Board of Secondary Education) syllabus as a third language from 2006. Now there are around 40 schools in and around the national capital region offering Japanese language as the second or third optional language.

According to a survey conducted by the Japan Foundation in the beginning of 2010, there were 173 schools, universities and educational institutions in India teaching Japanese language, 18,373 learners and 491 teachers altogether. The number of Indian students studying Japanese in 2003 was only 11011. This has increased to 18,373 in 2009, an increase of over 70 per cent within a short span of three years. There has been over 60 per cent increase in the number of institutions during this period and over 31 per cent increase in the number of Japanese language teachers. India's rank in the list of 20 countries with the highest number of students studying Japanese was 16th in 2009 as against 20th in 2003. However, compared to the gigantic figure of 9,64,014 students learning Japanese language in South Korea in 2009, which tops the list, India's 18,373 is a miniscule number, especially when the size of population of both the countries is taken into consideration.

Table 11.1 shows the number of Japanese Language Institutions by region, Table 11.2 shows Japanese Language Education in Primary and Secondary Schools, Table 11.3 shows Japanese Language Education in Higher Education, Table 11.4 shows Japanese Language Education in non-academic institutions, and in Figure 11.1, Learners of different levels are shown. These data are provided by the Japan Foundation, New Delhi Office.

Presently there are about 175 institutions in India offering Japanese language courses both in the primary, secondary and higher levels of education. They include both public and private institutions. Traditionally, north India is the hub of Japanese Studies, be it Japanese language education or Japanese Area Studies, and still it maintains its top position in terms of number of institutions, students and

ABLE 11.1: NUMBER OF JAPANESE LANGUAGE INSTITUTIONS BY REGION JF-ND

Region	Primary/ secondary	Higher education	Private schools	Total
North	40	8	9	57
East	4	4	7	15
South	4	14	34	52
West	7	4	58	49
Total	55	30	88	173

teachers. Especially, research in Japanese Area Studies is mainly carried out only in University of Delhi and JNU, both of which are situated in Delhi. South India and west India also showed remarkable increase but the eastern part of the country is lagging very much behind the other three regions in terms of number of schools as well as number of learners and teachers.

There has been a fivefold increase in the total number of learners, almost threefold increase in the number of schools and approximately fourfold increase in the number of teachers of Japanese language in the Primary and Secondary schools in a short span of three years (from 2006-9, Table 11.2). In the case of higher education, increase in every category has been almost threefold as understood from Table 11.3. As against this, the increase in non-academic institutions during this period has been very nominal (Table 11.4). Another characteristic noticed is that the total number of teachers is more in higher education sector though the total number of learners is less than primary and secondary education. Out of total 491 Japanese language teachers in India in 2009, only 91 teachers are native Japanese speakers, all others are Indian teachers.[3]

TABLE 11.2: JAPANESE LANGUAGE EDUCATION IN PRIMARY AND SECONDARY SCHOOL JF-ND

Year	No. of learners	No. of Schools	No. of Teachers
2003	446	5	5
2006	1,001	20	21
2009	5,455	55	70

TABLE 11.3: JAPANESE LANGUAGE EDUCATION IN HIGHER EDUCATION (JF-ND)

Year	No. of learners	No. of Schools	No. of Teachers
2003	653	11	31
2006	1,444	13	36
2009	4,142	30	95

TABLE 11.4: JAPANESE LANGUAGE EDUCATION IN NON-ACADEMIC INSTITUTIONS JF-ND

Year	No. of learners	No. of Schools	No. of Teachers
2003	4,347	46	20
2006	8,566	73	312
2009	8,776	88	326

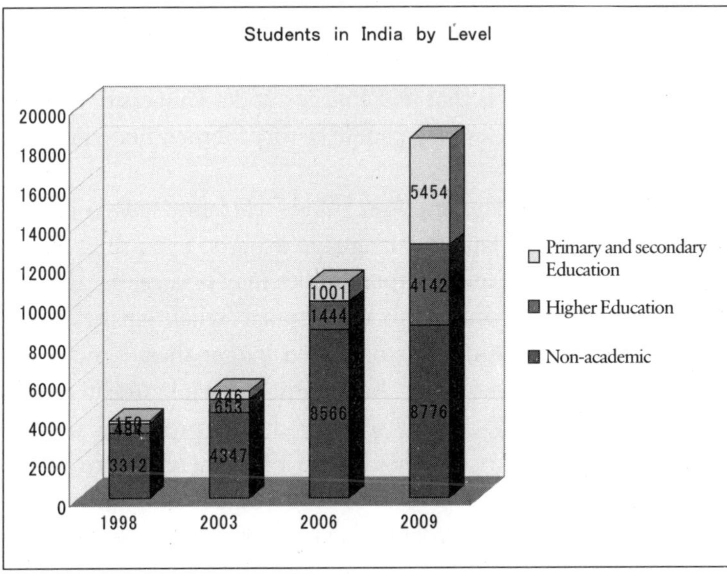

FIGURE 11.1: LEARNERS OF DIFFERENT LEVELS (JF-ND).

AREA STUDY ON JAPAN IN INDIA

The scope of Japanese Area Studies in India at present is not wide. In fact, it is not enough to meet the requirement and demand of the time. What is required is a wide range of research in diversified fields of Area Studies by hundreds and thousands of scholars throughout India. Universities in every state and region of the country should introduce Japanese area study programmes along with language and culture studies. For that first of all we need dedicated support and funding not only from Indian government but also from the Japanese government and other funding agencies like the Japan Foundation.

Though item 5 in the Eightfold Initiative, gave an impetus to the language studies, it hardly did any contribution to improve Area Study or Culture Study so far. Hence, irrespective of several rounds of bilateral summits between India and Japan, these fields of study remained in a stagnant state. No other university or academic institution, besides JNU or University of Delhi has introduced any course or programme on Japanese Area Studies or Culture Studies. The only consolation is that few colleges under University of Delhi are offering some courses on Japanese history for their undergraduate programmes.

There are very few Japanese Area Studies scholars in India compared to a large number of Japanese language experts. Even the scholars of Japanese Literature and Culture Studies may outnumber the area study scholars. But contrary to the popular belief, Japanese Area Studies in India has a long history, even longer than some of the European and Asian countries. In fact, the erstwhile Indian School of International Studies is said to have already produced six PhD scholars in Japanese Area Studies before it was merged in to School of International Studies of JNU in 1970. I would like to take up here JNU for a case study, in order to have an idea of Japanese Studies held in India.

JAPANESE AREA STUDIES IN JNU

As mentioned above, Japanese Area Studies in India began in 1955 when the Indian School of International Studies was established. This institution was later merged with the School of International Studies when JNU was established in 1969 and a Centre for East Asian Studies was created for the study of China, Japan and Korea. In fact, there has been a surge in the field of Japanese Area Studies in India in the beginning of the 1970s after the signing of Memorandum on Promotion of Japanese Studies in India in October 1969 between India and Japan. University of Delhi also created the Department of Chinese and Japanese Studies soon after the signing of this Memorandum and introduced programmes of Japanese Area Studies and Japanese language teaching simultaneously. Unfortunately, due to the low profile of relationship between India and Japan during the Cold War period as mentioned earlier, the area study on Japan both in University of Delhi and JNU remained in stagnation for a long period. This situation has not changed much even in this age of renewed and rejuvenated Indo-Japan relationship.

The major fields of study at present in Japanese area studies in the Centre for East Asian Studies (CEAS), JNU, are Japanese International Relations and Diplomacy, Japanese History, Politics, Economy, Trade, Japanese Management, Japanese Education System, etc. A total of 75 scholars have finished their M.Phil. from 1970 to 2006 as against just 26 PhDs between 1959 to 2006. This is an indicator of the fact that very few scholars are going in for further research in Japanese Area Studies after M.Phil. In other words, it reveals not only the lack of popularity of Japanese Area Study in India, but also shows the state of stagnation caused by various factors which I would like to discuss when I talk about the factors which hinder Japanese Study as a whole and Japanese Area Study in particular in India.

Out of 26 scholars who obtained Ph.D. degrees on Japanese Area Studies from Centre of East Asian Studies in SIS until 2006, 15 have researched on Japan's Diplomacy and Foreign Policy, four have studied Japanese economy, one each had conducted research on topics related to Japanese culture, literature, religion, Japanese defense, Japanese history and comparative study on industrial relations in Japan and India. As against this, the major research topics in M.Phil. are Japanese politics, Japan and international politics, Japan's foreign policy, diplomacy and international relations, Japanese economy, education system, nuclear non-proliferation and Japan, US–Japan relations, Japanese management system, various social and environmental problems and so on.

From the above statistics it could be inferred that majority of scholars in Japanese Area Studies opt for specializing in Japan's Diplomacy and Foreign Policy. Very few people go in for research in Japanese history, politics, economics, culture and religion or other topics related to social sciences and humanities. It seems there are two reasons for this imbalance. The first and foremost reason is the abundant availability of research and reference materials in English for the most favoured research topics of Foreign Policy and Diplomacy. One need not surf through the original Japanese texts and documents in the case of this field. Though it makes the work of the researcher easier, his ideas will be overwhelmingly influenced by the Western outlook on Japan, and the end product of his research will be lacking originality.

The second reason is the researcher's inability to read through the original source materials written in Japanese as most of the Area Studies research students in India do not possess sufficient knowledge of Japanese language. Sound knowledge of the language of the country is essential for meaningful research on topics pertaining to its history, society, politics and other fields of social sciences and humanities. Just working knowledge or superficial knowledge of the concerned language is not sufficient. For meaningful Japanese Area Study, learning of Japanese language by the research scholars until they achieve enough proficiency to read and comprehend original Japanese source materials should be made mandatory and environment for learning the language should be created. The present system of learning the language only for two semesters (two or three hours a week) is extremely insufficient as it imparts only the elementary knowledge of the language.

JAPANESE LITERATURE AND CULTURE STUDIES IN JNU

The Centre for Japanese, Korean and North East Asian Studies (CJKNEAS) in the School of Language, Literature and Culture Studies (SLL&CS) in JNU offers a M.Phil./Ph.D. programme in Japanese literature and culture studies. CJKNEAS has already produced four Ph. Ds since 1982 and around ten M.Phil. degree holders since the introduction of M.Phil. programme in 2006. Prior to 2006, CJKNEAS had pre-Ph.D. course, in place of M.Phil., leading to admission to Ph.D. programme. However, very few students get themselves admitted to the M.Phil./Ph.D. programme in literature and culture studies as most of the students of B.A. and M.A. of Japanese language leave the university soon after their graduation for joining highly lucrative jobs available in plenty. Even those students with a bent for research are drawn away by the power of money.

Major topics of research in Japanese literature and culture studies are ancient/classic literature, setsuwa/monogatari literature, literature of Meiji period, Buddhist Thought and religion, ancient, modern and contemporary art, folklore studies, education system, comparative linguistics and Japanese society and culture, etc. The research scholars of Japanese literature and culture studies have good command over the Japanese language as they get into the field of research after completing their master course in Japanese language. But if insufficient proficiency of Japanese language is a negative factor for the researchers of area studies, sufficient proficiency of Japanese language is a negative factor for the scholars in literature and culture studies in JNU because most of them leave the university after completing their M.Phil. to do higher studies in Japan as they get scholarships very easily thanks to their proficiency in the language. Hence, hardly any scholar remains in literature and culture studies for doing Ph.D., which is a major problem.

MAJOR FACTORS WHICH HINDER THE DEVELOPMENT OF JAPANESE STUDIES IN INDIA

First of all, lack of government policy may be highlighted as the main reason why in India Japanese Studies is not flourishing. Though the Indian government has identified Japanese language education and Japanese studies in the country as a priority field since the signing of the Eightfold Initiative, its effective implementation is not carried out perhaps due to the government's priority for other fields of study or shortage of funds. Another important reason why scholars in India do not opt for Area Studies in general and Japanese Studies/Area Studies in particular is the lack of job opportunity. Sending experts of regional studies and foreign languages as diplomats in embassies or officials in foreign affair departments is a common practice in Western countries including America and in some of the developed countries of Asia. However, this practice is seldom done in India. Hence, fields such as foreign language learning and area studies have not become popular among the career oriented Indian youth. In some of the advanced countries, people learn Japanese language and opt for Japanese studies out of their sheer interest in the culture and society of the country. This trend is almost nil in present-day India.

A second major reason is lack of access to learning institutions. Presently, Japanese is taught only in few universities or private institutions and all these institutions are concentrated in cities like Delhi, Pune, etc. Urban Indians have a better access but very few would opt for learning it as most of the career-oriented youth consider learning a foreign language below their dignity. In other words, there is a negative perception to learning foreign languages among our youth. They are ignorant about its vast scope and immense opportunities. The significance of Japanese language in the changing global scenario, where Information Technology and Virtual World have become the catchwords of the day, should be highlighted and publicized through newspapers and visual mass medias, so that more and more Indians will take up Japanese Studies as their field of specialization.

Third, meaningful area study can be conducted only if a research scholar or a student has high level of proficiency in the language of the country or region he opts for his specialized study. Most of the Japanese area studies scholars in India do not possess sufficient knowledge of Japanese language, which is a fact. Unfortunately, students who excel in learning Japanese language often opt for corporate jobs soon after their graduation, creating a vacuum in the area of culture studies and regional studies. This is again different in Western countries, where renowned area/regional study scholars began their Japanese studies by learning the language first.

Besides the above-mentioned points, shortage of qualified Japanese language teachers in the primary and secondary school levels, lack of interdisciplinary approach in Japanese language teaching in universities, non-implementation of unified or equivalent syllabus for same programme of study in different educational institutions, discrepancy in the evaluation system, lack of mutual respect, acceptance, understanding, coordination and cooperation among scholars of language, literature and culture studies and area studies, etc., also hinder the overall growth of Japanese Studies in India.

SIGNIFICANCE AND NECESSITY OF JAPANESE STUDIES IN THE NEW ASIAN AGE

Japanese Studies in the twenty-first century should be diversified and expanded, taking into consideration the increasing significance of Japan to India in this age of globalization and changing geo-political equations and balance of power in Asia. Increase in the quantum of bilateral trade between the two countries during the last few years and the recent signing of Free Trade Agreement, strategic cooperation, joint military exercise, etc., have strengthened the present bilateral tie between India and Japan. At the same time, this improvement in our relations with Japan is a clear pointer to the future state of affairs in the later part of twenty-first century, when India and Japan cannot remain isolated or alienated any more. In such a situation, there is a need for diversifying Japanese Studies to meet the demand of the time. In other words, Japanese studies scholars should not restrict their research only to the traditional themes like Japan's history, diplomacy and foreign relations, industrial relations and work culture, management system, employment system, Japan's modernization, nationalism, militarism and imperialism, etc. What is required at this hour is Japanese Studies in a comparative perspective. Japan's economic, political, international and diplomatic relations with other countries of the Asian region and world should be studied in a comparative context.

In addition to that, an ageing population, shrinking birthrate, problems related to traditional 'ie' system, marriage, education system, juvenile crimes, Japan's sub-culture, soft culture, environmental problems, natural disasters, study of its literature and culture in comparative perspective, etc., can be some of the topics for Japanese area /culture studies in the future.

NOTES

1. For more details on this subject, please see, Gita A. Keeni, 'Study of Japanese Language at Viswa-Bharati, Santiniketan: Its Past, Present and Future Prospects', in P.A. George, ed., *Japanese Studies: Changing Global Profile*, Northern Book Centre, New Delhi, 2010.
2. Please see Sushila Narsimhan, 'Japanese Studies in India: Major Trends and Challenges', in P.A. George, ed., *Japanese Studies: Changing Global Profile*, Northern Book Centre, New Delhi, 2010.
3: Please see, P.A. George, 'Status of Japanese Language Teaching in India: Current and Future Trends', in Rajaram Panda and Yoo Fukazawa, eds., *India and Japan: Blossoming of a New Understanding*, The Japan Foundation New Delhi and Lancer Books, New Delhi, 2004, for a detailed description of State of Japanese Language Education in India.

REFERENCES

George, P.A., ed., *Japanese Studies: Changing Global Profile*, New Delhi: Northern Book Centre, 2010.

George, P.A. 'Prospects of Japanese Language Education in India: Present and Future', *World Focus*, vol. XXX, January 2009, pp. 23-6.

George, Pullattu Abraham, *Ajia shinjidai no nichiin kankei to indo ni okeru nihon kenkyu (Indo-Japan Relations in the New Asian Age: State of Japanese Studies in India)*, in Shirahata Yozaburo and Liu Jianhui, eds., *Japanese Studies: Past, Present and Future: Breaking New Ground for Research in Japanese*, International Research Center for Japanese Studies, Kyoto, 2009, pp. 55-64.

Panda, Rajaram and Yoo Fukazawa, eds., *India and Japan: Blossoming of a New Understanding*, New Delhi: The Japan Foundation and Lancer Books.

Present Condition of Overseas Japanese-Language Education: Survey Report on Japanese Language Education Abroad 2009, The Japan Foundation, Tokyo, Japan, 2011.

CHAPTER 12

Problems of Youth Employment in India and Japan: A Call for a Joint Comparative Study

MAYUMI MURAYAMA

INTRODUCTION

This paper is a rudimentary step taken in the expectation that its results will engender future joint research related to the issues of youth employment and unemployment in India and Japan.

Three possible scopes of research can be used to assess India and Japan, or any set of two countries: one deals with bilateral relations (most papers compiled in this book might be categorized as such), two mutually conducted studies [i.e., studies of Japan or Japanese conducted by Indians (see Chapter 11) and studies of India and Indians done by Japanese], and finally comparative studies assessing India and Japan. My proposed research belongs to the third category.

A cursory review of the comparative studies between India and Japan presents some characteristics of research of this type.[1] First, several popular topics are examined by more than single authors, namely political systems, economic development processes, infrastructure investment, and status and condition of women. Other topics pursued by single studies include comparison of consumer organizations, homeless population, the IT sector, forest use and management, industrial entrepreneurship development, human resource management, policy finance, and so on.[2] Second, almost every study has been conducted by a single author. Therefore, unless an author has an equal amount of knowledge and understanding about both countries, which is rare, the comparison necessarily entails a degree of tilt towards one of the two countries.

Another feature of comparative studies between India and Japan is that, although the exact number is difficult to count, there are rather few if we consider the production of numerous studies of the first and the second types of research described earlier. One reason is related to the logic of conducting comparative research: conducting comparative research requires that certain conditions of comparability be met, such as availability of comparable datasets and justification of making a comparison, whether India and Japan can be worthy of being compared to draw some meaningful findings and conclusions from the exercise. In contrast to India and China, who have recently presented a popular set of comparison as two emerging economic giants, India and Japan seemingly lack in commonality, whether in terms of structure, institutions, or history, around which similarities and differences of the two countries can be assumed to be more clearly manifested.

Comparative method – its assumptions, aims, selection of comparable fields or objects, subjectivity of researcher, its effectiveness and so forth – has long been subjected to criticism; there is no agreement about the best comparative method among scholars, as explained by Andre Béteille.[3] Nevertheless, according to Béteille, 'our deepest insights into society and culture are reached in and through comparison' and we can make our comparisons illuminating and fruitful only after we 'improvise, and (to) exercise our judgement as well as our imagination'.[4] Béteille is also of the view that 'there is nothing wrong in comparing institutions that exist in widely dissimilar contexts, provided one keeps in mind the dissimilarity of their contexts'.[5]

Drawing on the proponents of comparative method as summarized by Béteille, I also add the instrumental value of comparative method as a tool of action research. Herein, I propose to conduct a joint study of the particular issue of youth unemployment by Indians and Japanese including not only scholars but also young people themselves. Several motives underlie the proposal. First is the importance of the topic not only for the two countries but also as a worldwide concern, as discussed below. Second, a joint team comprising members of both countries would lend more depth and width to a cross-national study than a single individual could do. Finally, through the very process of joint research, we would be able to elucidate one another and common issues, in addition to their similarities and differences. On that basis, we could work together to search for solutions of the problems, not a zero-sum game of a kind, where a gain of a country or a party means a loss for another, but more inclusive and sustained ones.

Before entering the discussion, *youth* should be defined. No fixed definition of *youth* exists throughout the world. The International Labour Organization (ILO) refers to the age group of 15-24 as youth in their reports or main statistics.[6] This age range is generally used in many other countries. However, different definitions are also used depending on the purpose of identifying particular group of population. For instance, India's National Youth Policy of 2003 includes the age group of 13-35 years, and the survey on the employment condition of young people conducted by the Ministry of Health, Labour and Welfare of Japan defines employed youth as those between 15 and 34 years of age.[7] Additionally, the National Sample Survey (NSS) of India includes people aged 15-29 years as youth.[8] The ILO definition is adopted in this paper unless otherwise described.

Figure 12.1 presents the age distribution of the populations of India and Japan. Although the demographic compositions differ greatly between India and Japan, the shares of youth population are non-negligibly high at 18.4 per cent and 12.5 per cent respectively (15-24 years) and 26.5 per cent and 20.2 per cent (15-29 years). Therefore, the conditions and problems related to young people have profound implications for all society in each country.

YOUTH UNEMPLOYMENT AS A GLOBAL CONCERN

In the recent past, I observed young people's struggle for job search in both India and Japan. As a Japanese person, I assumed it a norm that students start the *shuukatsu* (shortened form of *shuushoku katsudou*, meaning job hunting) before graduation and that most of them start working immediately after graduation. An important

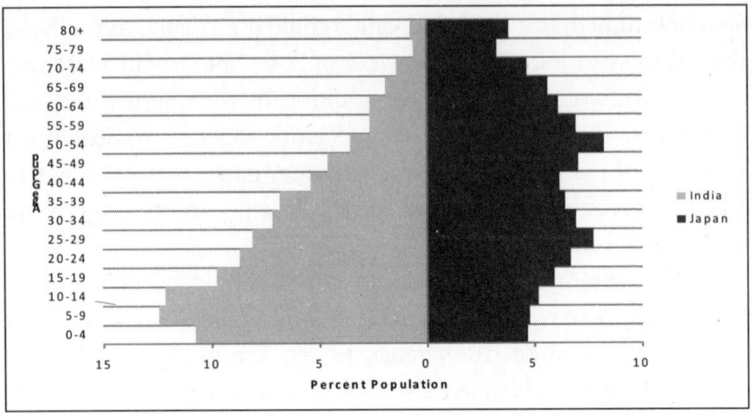

Source: Compiled from Population Census of India 2001 and of Japan 2000.

FIGURE 12.1: INDIA (2001) AND JAPAN (2000): SHARE OF AGE-WISE POPULATION.

problem embedded in this system is that the duration of *shuukatsu* has been increasingly lengthened: *shuukatsu* now starts one and a half years before graduation (for college and university students) depriving students of valuable time for learning and subjecting them to the mental stress attributable to a prolonged job-hunting process.

However, the two categories of young people I met in Delhi presented quite different pictures. One group of youth belonged to mostly economically better-off and academically stronger young people who were completing Bachelor of Arts courses at a prestigious college of University of Delhi. The other group comprised young people who resided in a resettlement colony in Delhi, many of whom were engaged in income-generating work of some kind while being enrolled in correspondence courses to obtain a degree from the same university. Although their socio-economic conditions differed widely, for both groups of young people in Delhi, that transition from school to work was individual practice. There was no across-the-board system of transition such as that practised in Japan. Notwithstanding the differences in the environment that surround the young people in India and Japan, however, it is true for the young people of both countries that they are compelled to endure a fairly long period of stress and uncertainty seeking rewarding employment.

Difficulties that young people face in finding a job are not limited to India and Japan. Severe implications of the youth unemployment have been more often observed elsewhere in the world.

In the UK, youth (16-24 years) unemployment reached a record high of the 1.02 million during July-September 2011. One in five young people was out of work. The main reason behind the surge of unemployment is the deterioration in the job market because of pressures from the Eurozone debt crisis. However, it is important that the job crunch is more keenly felt among young people because they account for about 39 per cent of all unemployed people.[9] Given this background, and the still-fresh memory of riots which broke out in the UK in August, 2011, severe unemployment problems among young people might constitute an underlying cause. The unemployment rate among people younger than 24 years old was almost 20 per cent. A Japanese media company reported that decreased employment opportunities are attributable to the shift of manufacturing factories overseas, followed by the economic downturn after the financial crisis.[10] Youth unemployment is regarded as a major cause of popular uprisings in the Arab world, as well.[11]

Let us summarize the global trend of youth unemployment based on the ILO report.[12] At the end of 2010, there were an estimated 75.1 million unemployed young people in the world; the youth unemployment rate stood at 12.7 per cent.[13] Since 1991, when the measurement of youth unemployment began, the youth unemployment rate remained at 11.1-13.2 per cent, the lowest in 1992 and the highest in 2002. According to the ILO reports, youth unemployment differs from that of overall unemployment in several regards. One, the unemployment rate is substantially higher among young people than among adults (25 and older). In terms of the world average, the youth unemployment rate is almost three times higher than the adult unemployment rate (2.8 times in 2010), with some regional variations. For instance, it is higher in Southeast Asia and the Pacific region (4.9), South Asia (4.5), and the Middle East

(4.1), but lower in Sub-Saharan Africa (2.0). Although not all reasons for higher unemployment rate for young people are negative, in general, young people are the first to be laid off (first-out) and last-in in times of surplus labour competing for a limited number of jobs. This tendency was confirmed also as an impact of the global economic crisis during 2008-9.

A second feature of youth unemployment is that young people suffer disproportionately from deficits in gainful employment, measured in terms of working poverty and employment status. For instance, in 2008, young people accounted for 18.1 per cent of the total globally employed but 24 per cent of the so-called *working poor* (with per capita expenditure of less than US $1.25 a day). Young working poor people are most concentrated in the agricultural sector. Additionally, young people are more likely than adults to engage in unpaid contributions to family work.

Succinctly put, it might be said that 'youth are not just disadvantaged in terms of accessing work, but also in finding productive work that provides sufficient income to escape poverty'.[14]

In relation to differences in youth unemployment in developed and developing countries, ILO reports state that whereas in most OECD countries, the unemployment rate is higher among less educated youth, in developing countries, the opposite is true. The reasons are the following: generally, higher education reduces the risk of unemployment and increases the chances of getting full-time or longer-term employment. However, in developing countries, the supply of highly educated young people has outpaced the supply of jobs to accommodate them. Moreover, they are more likely to belong to better-off households that can provide better or longer support for their job search.[15]

In addition to those generalized patterns of youth unemployment, a regional feature specific to South Asia (along with Sub-Saharan Africa) is that, in sharp contrast to the other regions where the absolute size of youth labour force is on decline, in South Asia and Sub-Saharan Africa, the annual growth of the youth labour force shows little or no likelihood of slowing at least until 2015.[16]

YOUTH UNEMPLOYMENT IN JAPAN

With those facts in mind, we can examine the situations of youth unemployment in India and Japan. Although the data are slightly outdated, Table 12.1 presents unemployment rates of both young people and adults in the two countries for comparison.

The following observations can be made from Table 12.1: (1) youth unemployment rates are substantially higher than adult unemployment rates in both countries as elsewhere, (2) the youth unemployment rate has risen, except during the decline of 2000-5 in Japan, and (3) as far as this simple comparison is concerned, the youth unemployment problem is more severe in India than it is in Japan. Not only is the unemployment rate among young people higher in India than in Japan but also differentials between youth and adult unemployment rates are much wider in the case of India.

It is noteworthy, however, that the degree of severity of the problem is largely specific to the social contexts and individual as well as social perceptions about the issue. Figure 12.2 depicts that both adult and youth unemployment rates in Japan began to rise in the early 1990s and that the rise of the youth unemployment rate has been much steeper than that of adults. As described earlier, both rates declined after their respective peaks in 2002 to around 2007-8, and positive change was greater in the case of the youth unemployment rate. The improvement is attributable to a prolonged economic recovery that started in 2002 and to the gradual retirement of the first baby-boomers born after Second World War. Nevertheless, after the economic crisis, youth unemployment surged again from

TABLE 12.1: YOUTH AND ADULT UNEMPLOYMENT RATES IN INDIA AND JAPAN (PER CENT)

Year	Youth unemployment rate		Adult unemployment rate	
	India	Japan	India	Japan
1994	8.3	5.5	2.2	2.5
2000	10.1	9.2	2.6	4.2
2005	10.5	8.7	2.6	4.0

Source: Compiled from ILO Key Indicators of the Labour Market.

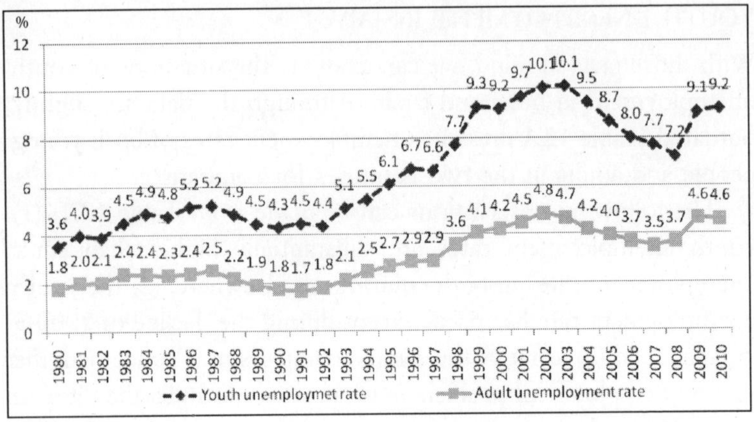

Source: Compiled from ILO Key Indicators of the Labour Market.

FIGURE 12.2: TREND OF YOUTH AND ADULT UNEMPLOYMENT RATE IN JAPAN.

7.2 per cent to 9.1 per cent during 2008-9. It was the highest annual increase followed by 1.8 per cent point increase recorded during 1998-9 when the Asian financial crisis that occurred in 1997 and domestic economic recession led to massive reductions in employment.

Until the early 1990s, Japan's youth labour market was characterized by the rapid transition of school leavers into stable employment and low unemployment and low job turnover. These patterns were sustained with a combination of strong demand for youth labour as cheap and potential workers and with a unique school-to-work transition system in which schools were linked directly to firms, which provided placement support for their students.[17] Under the general practice of lifetime employment, firms provide intensive on-the-job training to new recruits and a workplace-based social security system.

The system began to collapse in the early 1990s when Japan was hit by economic recession. That period coincided with the time when the children of the first baby boomers entered the labour market, thereby creating an imbalance in the demand and supply of labour. As presented in Figure 12.2, youth unemployment rose from a steady 4-5 per cent through the early 1990s to 10 per cent over the decade.

Inescapably tied to the indigenous factors described above were accelerated global competition and neo-liberalistic policy reforms taken by the government, which led to increasing fluidity in employment. That result implies that not only the quantity of jobs available for youth has decreased but that the quality has also deteriorated. Although the data are not strictly coherent, a general trend is apparent from Figure 12.3 by which the share of non-regular employment among young people increased rapidly in the latter half of the 1990s.

In 2010, 30 per cent of young workers aged 15-24, excluding students, were engaged in various non-regular forms of employment such as part-time, *arbeit* (temporary worker), dispatched workers from temporary labour agency, and contract employees (Table 12.2). These jobs are characterized as low income, with limited career prospects and fewer skill-development opportunities. A substantial gap in social insurance coverage is also apparent between

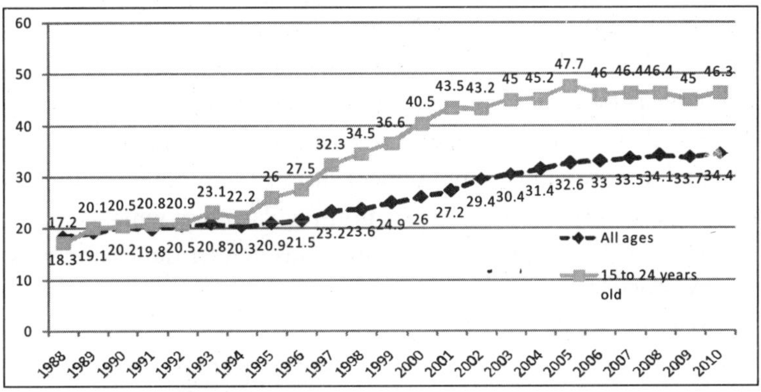

Note: Since 2002 there have been some changes in survey methods and reference period; therefore, data before 2002 and after are not strictly comparable.

Source: Compiled from *Historical Data 10: Employee by age group and type of employment – Whole Japan*, Statistics Bureau, Ministry of Internal Affairs and Communications.

FIGURE 12.3: CHANGES IN THE SHARE OF NON-REGULAR EMPLOYMENT AMONG YOUNG AND TOTAL WORKERS (PER CENT)

TABLE 12.2: SHARE OF NON-REGULAR EMPLOYMENT BY AGE GROUP AND GENDER IN JAPAN, 2010 (PER CENT)

	M+F	Male	Female
All ages	34.4	18.9	53.8
15-24 years old	46.3	43.1	49.6
Excluding students	30.4	25.1	35.4
25-34 years old	25.9	14.0	41.4
35-44 years old	27.4	8.1	53.7
45-54 years old	30.7	8.1	57.7
55-64 years old	44.2	28.9	69.0
65 years old or more	68.9	68.6	69.7

Source: Compiled from *Historical Data 10*: *Employee by age group and type of employment – All Japan*, Statistics Bureau, Ministry of Internal Affairs and Communications.

young regular workers and young non-regular workers, i.e., unemployment insurance, public health insurance, and employee pensions. Furthermore, mobility between non-regular employment and regular employment is extremely limited. Consequently, once a young person fails to obtain regular employment after leaving school, there is a considerable risk of a young person remaining trapped in non-regular employment. It must also be noted that, as Table 12.2 shows, the share of non-regular employment among females is high across all age groups. This gender dimension must be investigated further.

Referring to the pre-1990s situation, Yuki Honda notes seemingly smooth cyclical relations in which resources were put in among the three social spheres: family, education, and work. Based on life-term employment and salary increase according to the seniority system, one could establish and maintain a family. That person in turn put resources and motivations for children's education so that the supply of the future generation of labour can be secured.[18] Even then, there were dropouts from the system; the system itself entailed many problems. Nevertheless, today, what differs from the earlier times is that probably most people have become aware that we can no longer rely upon the earlier system to ensure the economic and social security of individuals and the society as a whole. The issue of youth unemployment has played an instrumental role in spreading this awareness.

YOUTH UNEMPLOYMENT IN INDIA

India presents a different set of circumstances and outcomes. The analytical approach used here is a limited review of the literature and statistical data to compensate for a lack of experiential knowledge of the author about youth unemployment or *shuukatsu* in India.

G.K. Chadha reports that although the youth unemployment problem is one of the few policy concerns that are common to both developing and developed economies, differences exist in emphasis: whereas the transition of youth from school to work is a public policy concern in developed countries, it is a switch-over from school to work for younger group of young people (15-19 years) under economic pressure that has been the major emphasis of policy concern in developing countries.[19] In developing countries, youth unemployment has been regarded in a framework resembling that used to examine child labour issues. If it is so, then lessening the labour participation of adolescents (15-19 years), rather than facilitating proper employment for young people must have been viewed the way to redress the problem. Whether this was the reason or not, the problem of youth unemployment was not assigned its due importance according to the seminal work by Pravin Visaria. His work, published in 1998, was presented as a country study of the ILO's Action Programme on Youth Employment.[20] According to Visaria, although youth unemployment was recognized even in the First Five Year Plan (1951-6), the problem was not afforded adequate attention. In addition, the National Youth Policy of 1988 formulated on the occasion of International Year of the Youth acknowledged the importance of eradication of unemployment among young people, but little action was initiated to implement the objective.

Apparently, it was not until the late 1990s and early 2000s that youth unemployment began to be addressed more or less seriously.

Two elements caught the attention of the government and researchers: one was the continuing increase of the labour force; another was the economy's inability to create appropriate employment despite accelerated GDP growth in the post-reform period. Based on this awareness, two task forces were formed by the Planning Commission to examine the current employment and unemployment situation and to suggest strategies for employment creation and the target set by the government.[21] The reports described unemployment among educated young people as a core of the problem, stating that 'it creates a sense of despair across a wide section of the population including not only the educated youth but their parents and families'.[22] Also in 2000, the Indian Society of Labour Economics took up the topic of youth unemployment in India as a main theme of its annual conference.[23] Behind the interest lay also the concern for a 'youth bulge' brought by the demographic structure and change. Youth unemployment in this context is regarded as implying that the bulge will not bring a so-called demographic dividend but rather anarchy as social impact of growing quantities of young unemployed people.[24]

The literature related to the problem of youth unemployment in India seems to present two distinct approaches: The first group of literature includes studies undertaken to measure the level of youth unemployment based on macro-level data.[25] Variables such as states, residence (rural–urban), gender, educational level, marital status, economic well-being, and social and religious categories were also analysed for the assessment of their respective relations to youth unemployment.

Following are the major findings:

First, the unemployment rates in both rural and urban areas were substantially higher among young people than among people aged 15 and over. The predominant share of young people in all unemployed people indicates that the problem of unemployment is largely a problem of youth unemployment. Furthermore, marginalization of young people in the Indian labour market has worsened, as evidenced by the increase of youth share among all unemployed people.[26]

Second, the youth employment rate is significantly higher among urban young people than among their rural counterparts for both males and females. The conditions in rural areas, however, might indicate underemployment of rural young people.[27]

Third, according to Chadha, who disaggregated young people into three age groups – 15-19, 20-4 and 25-9 years – and compared their unemployment rates with those of other age groups, the urban unemployment problem disappears only when the job-aspirants enter their thirties. Consequently, 'search efforts for good job openings continue as long as the job-seekers are still in their late twenties'.[28]

Fourth, unemployment among 'educated' people or those who have passed the high-school certificate examination (matriculates) or more educated people is generally emphasized as a problem. Furthermore, the unemployment level is higher among educated females than among educated males.[29]

The general feature of youth unemployment drawn from previous studies remains the same in the latest NSS data (2009-10), too.[30] Table 12.3 presents the following trends: (1) the unemployment rate is around 2.5 times higher for young people compared with the entire working persons; (2) the unemployment rate is higher in urban areas both for young people and for all working persons; (3) the unemployment rate increases generally with the level of education, and (4) among educated young people, the unemployment rate is higher for females than it is for males. It is particularly high for educated female young people in rural areas. In addition, the survey found that the unemployment rate in the usual status was highest in Kerala, followed by Jharkhand and Assam, whereas Bihar followed by Assam and Kerala exhibited the highest youth unemployment rate in urban areas.

Examining long-term trends, during 1993-4 and 2009-10, youth unemployment rates have increased for both males and females in rural areas but they have decreased in urban areas (Figure 12.4). The decrease is highest for urban male young people.

Visaria listed the following reasons for youth unemployment: (1) lack of training for work; (2) acceleration of population growth

TABLE 12.3: YOUTH AND ADULT UNEMPLOYMENT RATES BY RESIDENCE, EDUCATION AND GENDER IN INDIA 2009-10

	Rural				Urban			
	Male		Female		Male		Female	
	15-29	15-59	15-29	15-59	15-29	15-59	15-29	15-59
Not Literate	2.2	0.5	0.0	0.0	3.8	1.1	2.6	0.7
Literate up through primary	2.9	1.1	1.4	0.5	4.1	1.7	2.0	0.9
Middle	4.0	1.9	3.9	2.3	5.4	2.6	8.1	4.1
Secondary	5.0	2.2	6.8	4.7	5.9	2.2	20.5	11.3
Higher Secondary	7.8	3.7	22.2	15.2	10.9	4.7	19.1	11.8
Diploma/certificate	21.4	9.5	46.6	33.6	12.8	5.4	17.9	9.7
Graduate and above	16.6	6.5	30.4	20.5	13.8	4.3	24.7	12.9
Educated (Secondary & Above)	8.3	3.7	17.8	11.8	10.3	3.8	22.5	12.3
All	4.7	1.8	4.6	1.8	7.5	3.0	14.3	6.2

Source: Compiled from Statement 6.5, NSSO, *Employment and Unemployment Situation in India, 2009-10*. It is based on 'usual status (ps+ss)'.

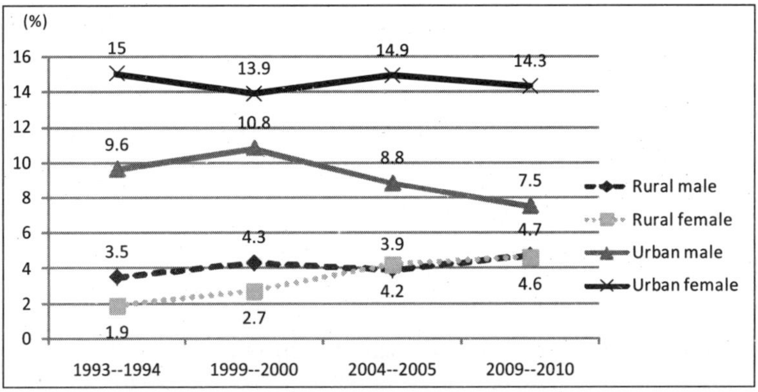

Note: It is based on usual status (ps+ss). See National Sample Survey Organization, *Employment and Unemployment in India, 2009-10*, pp. 16-18.

Source: Compiled from Statement 6.4, NSSO, 2009-10, p. 160.

FIGURE 12.4: CHANGES IN YOUTH (15-29 YEARS) UNEMPLOYMENT RATES, INDIA.

and mortality decline; (3) expansion of education, which has changed the nature of work sought by the young people; and (4) slow growth of the economy until the 1980s.[31] The last point, however, is not relevant to explain the subsequent phenomenon that even with higher economic growth, the youth unemployment rate has worsened, as explained above. Furthermore, unemployment of educated young people has existed side by side with shortage of labour in different segments of the economy, which has raised the issue of mismatch in two senses: one between existing skills and the needs of employers; and two the aspirations of those waiting for jobs and available employment opportunities.[32] These issues have been debated by another body of literature addressing the issue of youth unemployment in relation to education. In general, strong criticism has been raised against a lack of coordination both in theory and praxis in the spheres of employment, education, and development.[33] For example, Padmini Swaminathan asserts that India lacks worthwhile discourse on school-to-work transition or link between vocational education and employment and consequently issues of industrial development, employment, and education are disengaged and compartmentalized.[34] In the nexus of education and employment, others say that a mismatch of type of degrees and jobs has increased; although jobs have been on the increase in the professional stream, degrees in general education, mainly in the arts and humanities have been multiplying. This trend has led to degree devaluation and unemployability among graduates.[35]

POTENTIAL SCOPE OF JOINT COMPARATIVE RESEARCH

Based on a cursory review of the circumstances and literature related to youth unemployment in India and Japan, some scope for possible joint research can be suggested. Without any intention to claim sufficient knowledge of both countries and the issue of youth unemployment, in particular, I present conclusions that are neither exhaustive nor exclusive. Rather, the inferences achieved through this study might suggest action including critical evaluation of these observations of the issues and proposals for joint research, which would engender further exploration of this issue.

India and Japan differ considerably in terms of their economic, social and cultural parameters as well as historical trajectories, especially with respect to the development of economy and modern education. Consequently, without considering those contextual differences, it would be meaningless to compare the two countries at a macroscopic level. Nevertheless, young people in both countries who are struggling to find good employment opportunities present many common points, irrespective of differences in social and cultural contexts, economic status, educational background, and in many other attributes. Therefore, experiences of young people in India and Japan might be a starting point.

First, regarding India, micro-scale and ethnographical studies of unemployment of educated young people or on problems in school-to-job transition are fewer than such studies of Japan. Non-Indian authors have conducted few such studies.[36] A study by Craig Jeffrey, Patricia Jeffery, and Roger Jeffery explored the manner in which education transformed the subjectivities of rural young people and described the struggles faced by marginalized educated men in acquiring work, political leverage, and respect in situations of economic uncertainty. Based on fieldwork in the villages in Western part of Uttar Pradesh, they interviewed young educated people (males 20-34 years and those who had passed Eighth Class) belonging to specific caste/religious communities: Jats, Chamars (a Dalit caste), and Muslims. Whereas Jeffrey and others' work has examined rural young people, Hiroshi Sasaki analysed the problems of urban educated young people (males and females; 17-25 years) based on fieldwork in a city in eastern Uttar Pradesh. Sasaki described the effects of education of different types on their upbringing, perceptions, and life chances including prospects of getting a 'good' job by taking samples of those who had studied in English and those who studied in Hindi, in addition to young people who left school before completing primary education.

Results of these studies provide important insights both in their approaches and findings. Notwithstanding, in our interest in the investigation of the whole process of the transition from school to job, their emphasis was placed mostly on education, especially Sasaki's study. For that reason, analysis about the job including the function of the labour market and nature of jobs was insufficiently covered, although economic problems such as limited employment opportunities in the organized sector were recognized as an extremely important factor to mediate the impact of education. Moreover, the transition process itself can be studied further.

Some topics of joint research are suggested below:

- *School-to-work transition*:
  (1) Longitudinal follow-up of school leavers;
  (2) Institutional analysis of formal and non-formal process of obtaining jobs *(shuukatsu)*. It might include analyses of institutions or media providing job hunting services such as the internet, employment exchanges, school/college/university support, and placement agencies;[37]
  (3) Ethnographical study of *shuukatsu* at individual levels.
- Ethnographical studies of various jobs where educated young people are increasingly absorbed.[38] Compared to work done by

poorer or less educated people such as factory work or various informal work, jobs performed by better educated young people are given less attention, except for work in IT and IT-enabled services.[39]

Regarding the topics described above, some studies are available as for the Japanese case in varied volume and depth, which enables us to draw some useful methodological and theoretical implications in order to investigate Indian cases. We can expect to do the same exercise in the opposite direction, i.e., from studies of India to those of Japan.

NOTES

1. Based on OPAC data compiled in the Institute of Developing Economies (IDE) Library (http://webopac.ide.go.jp/webopac/catsrd.do). In this paper, studies comparing only India and Japan are covered. Additional comparative studies have incorporated other countries in addition to the two countries.
2. Most of these studies were conducted by Indian scholars who stayed at the IDE, Japan for a certain period as Visiting Research Fellows.
3. Andre Béteille, 'Some Observations on the Comparative Method', *Economic and Political Weekly*, vol. 25, no. 40, 1990.
4. Ibid., p. 2262.
5. Ibid., pp. 2256, 2262. A strand of opinion has held that comparison between neighbouring cultures is better.
6. ILO, *Global Employment Trends for Youth.* August 2010, p. 1.
7. Ministry of Youth Affairs and Sports, National Youth Policy 2003, India. Ministry of Health, Labour and Welfare, '*Jakunensha koyou jittai chousa* (Survey of employment conditions of youth)' 2009, Japan.
8. National Sample Survey Office, *Employment and Unemployment Situation in India 2009-10*, p. 160.
9. http://www.guardian.co.uk/business/2011/nov/16/youth-unemployment-hits-1m-uk, (accessed on 16 December 2011). There were 2.62 million unemployed people. Although the total unemployment rate was 8.3 per cent, that of youth was 21.9 per

cent. One caveat about the figure is that it includes 2,86,000 people, more than a quarter of all unemployed young people, who were students, looking for part-time work.

10. *Asahi Shimbun*, 10 August 2011.
11. http://www.ilo.org/global/about-the-ilo/press-and-media-centre/insight/WCMS_154078/lang--en/index.htm (accessed on 16 December 2011). The youth unemployment rates in the region are averaging more than 23 per cent.
12. See ILO, *Global Employment Trends for Youth*. August 2010 Issue and ILO, *Global Employment Trends for Youth 2011 Update*.
13. ILO, *Global Employment Trends for Youth 2011 Update*, p. 1. In the ILO's definition, 'unemployed people' comprise all persons above a specified age who during the reference period were: (a) 'without work', i.e., were not in paid employment or self-employment, (b) 'currently available for work', i.e., were available for paid employment or self-employment during the reference period; and (c) 'seeking work', i.e. had taken specific steps in a specified reference period to seek paid employment or self-employment. The specific steps might include registration at a public or private employment exchange; application to employers; checking at worksites, farms, factory gates, market or other assembly places; placing or answering newspaper advertisements; seeking assistance of friends or relatives; looking for land, building, machinery or equipment to establish their own enterprise; arranging for financial resources; applying for permits and licences, etc.
14. ILO, 2010, p. 23.
15. Ibid., p. 21.
16. Ibid., pp. 11-12.
17. Related to this topic, a substantial volume of literature exists in Japanese, but see OECD, *Jobs for Youth*, 2009 for a concise English review of the condition of youth employment in Japan. The Japanese translation, *Nihon no wakamono to koyou: OECD jakunensha koyou rebyuu: Nippon*, was published by Akashi Shoten in 2010.
18. Yuki Honda, *Kishimu shakai: kyouiku, shigoto, wakamono no genzai* (Squeaking Society: Education, Work, Current Condition of Youth), Tokyo: Kawade Shobou Shinsha, 2011, p. 6.

19. G.K. Chadha, 'Youth Unemployment in India: Past Policy Gaps and Future Strategic Options', *The Indian Journal of Labour Economics*, vol. 43, no. 4, 2000, p. 591.
20. Pravin Visaria, *Unemployment Among Youth in India: Level, Nature and Polity Implications*, Employment and Training Papers 36, ILO. 1998. The objectives of the ILO's programme were (1) to raise awareness amongst constituents concerning the problems associated with the labour market entry of young people; (2) to improve their understanding of the advantages and disadvantages of the principal policy and programme options for tackling the problem of youth unemployment; and thus, (3) to enhance the capacity of member States to design and implement policies and programmes for promoting youth employment.
21. Planning Commission, *Report of the Task Force on Employment Opportunities*, 2001 and Planning Commission, *Special Group on Targeting Ten Million Employment Opportunities per Year*, 2002.
22. Planning Commission 2001, p. 28.
23. Child labour issue was adopted as conference theme 10 years earlier in 1990. http://www.isleijle.org/NormalView.asp?m_id=136 (accessed on 31 December 2011).
24. C.P. Chandrasekhar, Jayati Ghosh and Anamitra Roychowdhury, 'The "Demographic Dividend" and Young India's Economic Future', *Economic and Political Weekly*, vol. 41, no. 49, 2006, p. 50-61.
25. See for instance, Visaria 1998 and the articles included in *The Indian Journal of Labour Economics*, vol. 43, no. 4, 2000; as a similar and more recent study, Arabinda Acharya and S.K. Mohanty, 'Youth Unemployment in India: A Situational Analysis', *Journal of Educational Planning and Administration*, vol. 24, no. 2, 2010.
26. G.K. Chadha, p. 595. More recent study by Acharya and Mohanty corroborated that the pattern was further worsened between 1998 and 2004. Acharya and Mohanty, p. 124.
27. G.K. Chadha, p. 597.
28. Ibid., p. 598.
29. U. Kalpagam states that female youth unemployment is underestimated because of the patriarchal ideologies as well as frames used to for statistical measurement of unemployment. U. Kalpagam, 'Gender Dimensions of Youth Unemployment in India', *The Indian Journal of Labour Economics*, vol. 43, no. 4, 2000.

30. Data presented here are based on the 'usual status' defined in the National Sample Survey. A person is classified as unemployed if he or she is 'not working but seeking and/or available for work' for the majority of time during the 365 days preceding the date of survey.
31. Visaria, pp. 32-3.
32. G.K. Chadha, p. 605.
33. See for example, C.S.K. Singh, 'Skill, Education and Employment: A Dissenting Essay', *Economic and Political Weekly*, vol. 38, no. 31; Padmini Swaminathan, 'The Interface between Employment and Education in India: The Need for a Discourse' in *Education and Social Change in South Asia*, ed. Krishna Kumar and Joachim Oesterheld, Orient Longman, 2007; Avinash Kumar Singh, 'Degree Devaluation in Higher Education: Unemployment and Unemployability among the Graduates in India', *Journal of Education Planning and Administration*, vol. 20, 2006.
34. Swaminathan, 2007. The paper states that compared with the way the colonial Madras Presidency grappled the problem of linking employment and employment, the aforementioned two task forces set up by the post-Independence Indian government were superficial in their engagement and unable to come up with substantive issues. Her critique was also directed against academics saying that the interface between education and economic development in general and employment in particular has merited very little academic attention, p. 349.
35. Avinash Kumar Singh, op. cit.
36. Craig Jeffrey, Patricia Jeffery and Roger Jeffery, *Degrees Without Freedom: Education, Masculinities, and Unemployment in North India*, Stanford University Press, 2008; Hiroshi Sasaki, *Indo ni okeru kyouiku no hubyoudou* (Education and Social Inequality in India), Tokyo: Akashi Shoten, 2011 (in Japanese).
37. Related studies include Sujoy Chakravarty and E. Somanathan, 'Discrimination in an Elite Labour Market? Job Placements at IIM-Ahmedabad', *Economic and Political Weekly*, vol. 43 no. 44.
38. According to the ILO report, information about quality of work for youth is quite limited globally (ILO 2010, p. 22).
39. See for example, *In and Outpost of the Global Economy: Work and Workers in India's Information Technology Industry*, ed. Carol Upadhya and A.R. Vasavi, London: Routledge, 2008.

Contributors

TAKENORI HORIMOTO was Professor of Contemporary South Asian Studies at Shobi University. Currently he is engaging in a study on India's contemporary foreign policy under Grants-in-Aid for Scientific Research (B) of Ministry of Education at Kyoto University. He heads the study project. He has published a book *India-Globalizing Giant Elephant* (2007) along with other 10 books on South Asia. His main fields of study are international relations of South Asia and India's relations with US, China, SEA and Japan.

LALIMA VARMA is Professor of Japanese Studies in the Centre for East Asian Studies, School of International Studies, Jawaharlal Nehru University, New Delhi, India. She has published numerous papers on Japan's foreign policy and domestic issues. A recipient of Japan Foundation fellowship twice over (1987-8 and 2005-6) she was affiliated to the University of Tokyo, Japan. She is the author of *Making of Japan's China Policy*, edited volumes which include 'United Nations in a Changing World'.

SRIKANTH KONDAPALLI is Professor in Chinese Studies at Jawaharlal Nehru University. He was educated in Chinese studies in India and China. He was a Visiting Professor at National Chengchi University, Taipei in 2004, Visiting Fellow at China Institute of Contemporary International Relations, Beijing in May 2007, Honorary Professor at Shandong University, Jinan in 2009 and 2011 and a Fellow at Salzburg Global Seminar in 2010. He has written two books, two monographs and two edited volumes, besides articles, on China.

EMI MIFUNE is Professor at the Faculty of Law, Komazawa University. He is a specialist on Contemporary China's foreign policy and politics.

TORU ITO is Associate Professor at Department of International Relations & Graduate School of Security Studies at National Defense

Academy of Japan. He is a specialist on international relations in South Asia. He has authored about 20 academic papers on India and South Asia.

SWARAN SINGH is Professor and Chairperson, Centre for International Politics, Organisation and Disarmament, School of International Studies, Jawaharlal Nehru University, New Delhi. He is President of the Association of Asian Scholars and General Secretary of Indian Congress of Asian and Pacific Studies.

KAZUTOSHI TAMARI is a doctoral candidate at Graduate School of Law, Chuo University, Tokyo. He finished his M. Phil. programme at the Centre for International Politics, Organization and Disarmament (CIPOD), School of International Studies (SIS), Jawaharlal Nehru University (JNU), New Delhi, India, in 2010.

MARIE YOSHIOKA-IZUYAMA is a Senior Research Fellow at the National Institute for Defense Studies (NIDS).

MAKOTO KOJIMA is Professor of Indian Economy at the Faculty of International Studies, Takushoku University, Tokyo. He served as Chairman of the India Study Group at the Ministry of Finance in 2004-5 and a Member of Japan–India Joint Government Study Group in 2005-6. He has authored many books and articles in the field of current Indian economy and industries.

SRABANI ROY CHOUDHURY is an Associate Professor in Japanese Studies, Centre for East Asian Studies, School of International Studies, Jawaharlal Nehru University. Her Ph.D was on human resource management of Japanese multinationals and its transferability to India. During her Ph.D. she was a recipient of Japan Foundation fellowship and affiliated to Institute of Social Science, University of Tokyo.

P.A. GEORGE presently is the chairperson of the Centre for Japanese, Korean, and North East Asian Studies, School of Languages, Literature and Culture Studies. He is a Professor of Japanese Language. Prof. George was a visiting scholar to Waseda University (Tokyo); Iwate University (Morioka); and International Research Centre for Japanese

Studies (Kyoto). He is a recipient of the coveted Miyazawa Kenji Shoreisho award and has done extensive research in modern Japanese literature and is an authority on Shimazaki Toson, Miyazawa Kenji, and Ishikawa Tokuboku.

MAYUMI MURAYAMA is Deputy Director-General, Inter-disciplinary Studies Centre at the Institute of Developing Economies (IDE-JETRO), Chiba, Japan. Her main research fields are labour and gender issues in India and Bangladesh and sub-regional relationships in South Asia. Her publications include *Gender and Development: The Japanese Experience in Comparative Perspective* (Editor, 2005) and *Globalization, Employment and Mobility: South Asian Experience*, (Co-editor 2008).

Index

Abe Shinzo 43; visit to China 43; and Wen for strategic relations 44
Acquisition and Cross-servicing Agreement 194
all-weather relations, of Pakistan 80, 104-5
anti-China protests 45, 57, 66, 116
anti-Japanese movements 23, 42-3, 45-6, 52, 116, 165
anti-piracy naval operations 145, 193, *see also* Indian Ocean
Anti-Terrorism Special Measures Law 73, 179
Antony, Arackaparambil Kurien 53
Arc of Freedom and Prosperity 110, 118
Armitage, Richard, visit to India 73
ASEAN + 3 217
ASEAN + 6 217
ASEAN Regional Forum 53, 109, 118, 138, 191-2
ASEAN–India summit 191
Ashraf, Jawed 143
Asia Cooperation Dialogue 78
'Asia-literate Australia' 135
Asian: financial crisis 272; Japan into economies of 233; triangles 136-9, 149
Asia–Pacific Economic Cooperation 100, 109
Asia–Pacific Partnership on Clean Development and Climate 79, 138
Asia-Pacific region 33, 99-100, 133, 148, 185, 195; security mechanism in 49
Association of Southeast Asian Nations 28, 30, 34, 55, 95, 100, 134, 191-2, 201, 205, 217-18, 224, 233, 236; economic zones of 30
Australia 23, 29-31, 33, 75-6, 79, 99, 109, 118, 134-5, 145, 154, 156, 185, 188, 194, 202

balance of power 71-5
ballistic missile defence system Patriot PAC-3 74
Bambawale, Gautam 143
Basic Defense Force concept 50
Bengal Initiative for Multi-Sectoral Technical and Economic Cooperation 28
Béteille, Andre 266
bilateral: relations 20-3, 30, 33-6, 48, 59, 63, 67, 70, 72, 76, 137-8, 142, 153, 170, 202, 218-20; strategy 30-2
Blake, Robert 143
Brazil–Russia–India–China–South Africa grouping 78
Buddhism 223, 246-7
Bush, George (Jr) 141
Bush, George W. 121

Campbell, Kurt 143
Centre for Japanese, Korean and North East Asian Studies 258-9
Centre for Strategic and International Studies 139
Chadha, G.K. 275
Chellaney, Brahma 21, 121

China and India 48, 79, 101, 104-5; problem of water resources 106; relations between 54, 100, 103, 107-8
China and Japan 43, 64-6, 69, 71, 75, 78; for cooperation on security issues 58
'China factor' 52-4, 144-6
'China threat' theory 50, 113, 115-21, 123, 125
China: ASEAN policy of 30; bilateral trade with 134; claims over islands 65; its concept of foreign diplomacy 101; droughts in 107 foreign policy of 63, 65, 68, 71, 140; Japan–India–Us relations 99-100; Japan's FDI flows into 78; as Japan's largest trading country 23; labourers of 107; Laws of Territorial Waters and Contiguous Zone of 65; oil-drilling vessel Kantán of 66; relations with Pyongyang and Islamabad 80; riposte of 29-30
'China's rise' 63-4, 72, 80, 93, 97, 133-6, 144, 148
China–ASEAN trade 134
China–India–Pakistan 137
China–Japan–India, differences between 78
China–Japan–Korea 58
China–North Korea axis 134
China–Pakistan nexus 103, 105, 124
China–South Korea bilateral trade 134
Chinese: language education 246; Studies 246
Chunxiao Islands 64
Clinton, Bill 47, 115, 160, 167; visit to India 24
Clinton, Hillary 32, 47, 124
coast guards of Japan, Chinese vessels collided with 58
Cohen, Stephen P. 121
Commandant Ishikawa 26
Comprehensive Economic Partnership Agreement/ Economic Partnership Agreement 23-4, 56, 76-7, 157, 161, 204-5, 235-8, 241
Confederation of Indian Industries 139
cooperative patrols 191
COP13 Bali conference 122
COP15 Copenhagen 122
counter-terrorism 76, 143, 180
Cui Tiankai 77

Dasgupta, Sunil 121
Dedicated Freight Corridor 24, 211, 218, 240
Delhi Mass Rapid Transport System Project 234
Delhi–Mumbai Freight Corridor 76, 218, 234
Delhi–Mumbai Industrial Corridor 24, 56, 211, 220, 234, 240
Democratic Party of Japan 58, 119-20
Deng Xiaoping 68, 101, 103
developing countries 48, 77, 121-2, 228, 235, 270, 275
Diaoyu Islands 26, 66
Diaoyutao Islands 45, 64-5
Dynamic Defense Force 50

East Asia Summit 47, 72, 109, 117, 141, 217-18
East Asian Financial crisis 134, 148
East China Sea 41, 123-4
economic partnership agreement 23-4, 56, 76, 158, 161, 204, 235-6, 251
economic: cooperation 24-5, 158, 236-7, 251; policies 20, 48

Eightfold Initiative 52, 141, 251-2, 256, 259
8th ASEAN–India summit in Vietnam 55
English communications skills 216, *see also* youth unemployment
exclusive economic zones 65

Fernandes, George 52, 121
foreign direct investment 56, 201-2, 206, 212, 219, 224, 228-33, 235
Foreign Minister Okada Katsuya 45
foreign policy of India 30, 34, 147, 250
four-nation alliance 118
Free Trade Agreement 55, 134, 261
Free Trade Area of Asia Pacific 100
Fu Xianquiang 31
Fukuda Takeo 44

Gandhi, Indira 114; visit to Japan 20
Ganga Action Plan Project 234
generic medicines 205, 210; import of 205
Global Peacekeeping Operations Initiative 142
Goldman Sachs 51
Grant Aid Cooperation and Technical Cooperation 234
Great East Japan Earthquake 25, 49, 59, 96, 219
Great Recession 95
Greater Middle East Plan 110
Green Revolution 233
Group Four format 75, 77
Guam Doctrine 176
Gulf War 179-80

HABU NAG exercise 190
Han Min 74
Hatoyama 157; visit to India 76
Hitachi tie-up with BCE Energy Systems 211
Hong Kong 66, 70, 72-3, 109
Howard, John 29, 121
Hsu Li-The 69
Hu Jintao 44, 48, 121; and Medvedev 46; visit to New Delhi 121
human exchange 215-17
Humanitarian Assistance/Disaster Relief, Cooperative Security 185-8, 195, *see also* Tsunami relief

Ikeda Hayato 20, 68
IMF 122, *see also* WTO
India and Eastern Asia 97-9
India–ASEAN trade 203
India–Japan CEPA 237
India–Japan Maritime Security Dialogue 53
India–Japan–United States trilateral dialogue 143
Indian Farmers Fertilizer Cooperative Limited 212
Indian Navy 28, 177-8, 180; INS *Vikramaditya* 28; and Japanese Self-Defense Forces 26, 53, 185, 218
Indian Ocean 26, 28, 53, 73, 80, 101-2, 123-4, 142, 145, 154, 178-9, 189-90, 218
Indian Ocean Navy Symposium 28
Indian Ocean Rim-Association for Regional Cooperation 28
Indian–Americans 215
India–Pakistan war 178
India–US: defence cooperation 178; relations 162
Indo–China: 75, 80, 94, 96, 100-8, 121-2, 203, 266; cooperation on UNFCCC 122; trade

between 201, 203-4; relationship 122
Indo–Japan 21, 36, 50-1, 56, 59, 64, 72, 75-8, 77-80, 141-2, 153, 236-7, 246-8, 251-2, 256-7, 261, 265-9, 280; bilateral Strategic Dialogue 143; economic partnership and security cooperation 29, 50-1, 55-6, 194-5, 218-20, 252; relations 19-24, 63, 141, 161, 217, 250; Strategic and Global Partnership 251-2; trade relations 203, 205, 224, 235
Indo–Japan Cultural Exchange Agreement 249
Indonesia 31, 52, 55, 57, 78, 99, 188, 191, 193-4, 240
Indo–Pacific region 138, 143
Indo–Soviet Treaty of Friendship and Cooperation 114
Indo–US Framework for Maritime Security Cooperation 189
Indo–US: agreement, for civilian nuclear cooperation 141; defence agreement 29; global partnership 141; naval exercises 145-6; relations 141, 161
Information–Technology Promotion Agency 213
infrastructural development 24, 210-12
Integrated Industrial Region, in southern India 211
International Finance Corporation 212
international terrorism, countering 140
International Thermonuclear Experimental Reactor 138
IT companies: of India 213-15; offshore investment of 212-15
Jain, Purnendra 154
Japan and India 25-6, 30-6, 52-5, 63-4, 71-2, 76-8, 80, 100-1, 108-10, 113, 120-5, 153-4, 156-7, 195, 216-17, 237-8; disagreement over China between 120-5; maritime operations 185; Strategic and Global Partnership between 156; ties with 114
Japan Foundation 252-3, 256
Japan–India EPA 206
Japan Institute of International Affairs 139
Japan Maritime Self-Defense Force 176-7, 179-80, 185, 188-9, 191, 193-4; ship *Kunisaki* of 179, 189
Japan Self-Defense Forces 194
Japan Steel Works Ltd 219
Japan: Chinese trawler collided with Coast Guard vessel of 58; foreign policy 47, 141, 154-9, 162-3, 169, 257; imports of 52; import basket 225; imports from Bangladesh 55-6; investment into India 206-12; maritime policy of 26; measures by 68-9; and Peoples Republic of China 30, 41-2, 44, 47, 55, 58, 72, 79, 97, 109, 119, 122, 215; relations with ROK 57; and South Korea 57, 109; trade expansion of 24
Japan–ASEAN summit 192
Japan–Australia Acquisition and Cross-servicing Agreement 194
Japan–China: relation 41-6, 58-9, 97, 116; war 248
Japanese 44-5, 70, 119, 145, 214-15; Area Studies in India 255-6; companies in India 98, 201, 205-6, 209-16, 218-19, 224,

229-30, 233, 238, 240, 252; Emperor's visit for non-isolation of China 42; financial institutions 211; FDI 206, 208-10, 219, 230, 232; foreign policy of 154, 163, 168, 217; IT companies of 215; investments into India 56, 208, 212, 230; language education in India 252-5, 249, 252-3, 257, 259, 261; language teachers 248, 253-4; literature and culture studies in JNU 256, 258-9; Maritime Self-Defense Force of 53, 64; occupation of *wuzhudi* islands 64, 71; policy of India 155, 160, 162-3, 167-70; studies of 245-52, 248-53, 255-6
Japan–India: bilateral relations 30, 32, 75-7, 115, 125, 154, 156, 158-9, 164, 202; CEPA/EPA 205, 218; civil nuclear cooperation 163; economic partnership agreement 158, 251; economic relations 24, 201, 203, 205-6, 217; Global Partnership 22, 52, 117, 156, 158-9; and India–US relations 161; Joint Declaration on Security Cooperation 29, 153, 194; merchandise trade between 202-6; Nuclear Agreement 219-20; Strategic and Global Partnership 156-7, 218, 251; summits of 135; trade between 159, 201, 204; 2 + 2 Dialogue 25
Japan–India-US relations 73, 94, 108
Japan–Republic of Korea 56-7
Japan–Southeast Asia 57-8
Japan–US: Alliance 20, 30, 35, 47-8, 57, 73, 97; and India–US relations 175; Security Treaty 33, 73
Japan–US–India trilateral strategic dialogue 121
Jaswal, Gen. 73
Jeffery, Patricia 280
Jeffery, Roger 280
Jeffrey, Craig 280
JETRO 205
JFE Steel tie-up with JSW Steel 209
Jiang Zemin 105
Jihadist terrorism 180
joint military exercises 53, 57, 76, 176, 218, 261
joint naval exercise 26, 28, 52, 154, 179
Junichiro Koizumi 75, 115, 154

Kajima Construction 211
Kan Naoto 31, 46, 56, 58, 119-20
Katsuya Okada on China 120
Kim Jong Il 47
Kishi Nobusuke, visit to Taiwan 69
Kobe Steel with SAIL 209
Koizumi Junichiro 42, 52-3, 75, 116, 118, 141, 157-8, 251
Koji Tsuruoka 143
Kokario dormitory incident 69
Kondapalli 32
Kono Yohei 71
Kotak Mahindra Bank 212
Krishna, S.M. 93, 143

Lama, Dalai 67
land-power-cum-sea-power 26-7
Larsen & Toubro 211
Lee Teng-hui 70
liberalization of Indian economy 233
Life Insurance Corporation 212; Mutual Asset Management Company 212
Liu Jianchao 77

Liu Weimin 144
logistics companies, operations in India 209
Look East Policy 28, 54-5, 93, 191, 201, 203, 224, 230, 250, 252
Lu Guangsheng 100

Macao 66
Maeda Tadashi 56
Malaysia 31, 34, 52, 55, 57, 78, 99, 191, 193, 210, 240
maritime multilateralism 185-8
maritime power 175-7; of India 177-9; of India and Japan 179-85
Maruti-Suzuki venture 228
Masaki, General 25
Masashi Ishihara, pro-Taipei statements by 70
Masood, Syed Ross 248
Mauritius 28, 206
Medvedev, Dmitry 46, 105
Memorandum on Promotion of Japanese Studies in India 249, 257
Mifune, Emi 32
MILAN 191
military-to-military cooperation 179
Mine Countermeasure Exercise and Diving Exercise 2 188
Minister Hatoyama Yukio 53
Ministry of Economy, Trade and Industry 98
Mitsubishi Heavy Industries 211
Mizuho Corporate Bank 212
Mizuho Securities Co 212
Mori Yoshiro 22, 25, 52, 115, 160, 167, 251
Morihiro Hosokawa 192
Myanmar 78, 105, 123, 145

NAFTA–China trade 96
NAFTA–Japan trade 96
Nakasone, Prime Minister 20, 177
Nanjing massacre 71
Nara Declaration 58
National Defense Program 49-50
1991 'bubble' burst 49
Nippon Steel, alliance with Tata Steel 209
Nomura Asset Management Co. 212
Non-Aligned Movement 20, 114, 191
non-regular employment 273-4
North Atlantic Treaty Organization 49
North Korea 46-8, 80, 115, 123-4, 144; rivalry with South Korea 134

Official Development Assistance 22-3, 42-3, 45, 48-9, 71, 141, 148, 193, 201, 219, 224, 233, 235-6
Okakura Tenshin 248
Okinotorishima 66
'One China' principle 73, 103-4
operation Castor 188
operation Enduring Freedom-Maritime Interdiction Operations 179-80
operation Gambhir 188
operation Madad 188
operation Rainbow 188
operation *Sea Wave*
Organization for Economic Cooperation and Development 49
Overseas development assistance 233-5

Panda, Rajaram 121, 154
Pant, Harsh V. 125, 169
Paracels and Spratly's Islands 65
People's Republic of China. *See* China

people–to–people exchanges 215, 217, 251-2
Philippines 52, 57, 78, 99, 102, 133, 192-3
pirates, in Malacca and Singapore Straits 52
PLAN's expansion 30
Pokharan nuclear tests 22, 51
Pokhran II 158

Quad approach 29

Rao, Narasimha 34, 224
Rao, Nirupama, visit to Tokyo 143
Regional Cooperation Agreement on Combating Piracy and Armed Robbery against ships in Asia 192-3; countries of 194
Reliance Capital Asset Management 212
reparation. *See* Official Development Assistance
Republic of Korea 43, 56-7, 78, 93
'return to Asia', American policy of 99, 110
Rice, Condoleezza 118
rising China 21, 93-4, 100, 135, 138-40, 146-7
Rodrigues, General 179
Rudd, Kevin 135, 144
Russia–China–India strategic triangle 137, 140
Russo–Japan War 248

Sait, Admiral 25
San Francisco Peace Treaty 70, 223
Saran, Shyam 31
Sasaki, Hiroshi 281
Satu Limaye 35
security cooperation 23, 25, 29, 53, 100, 118-19, 125, 157, 175, 194
Seiji Maeharar 57, 120
Seiroku Kajiyama 69
Self Defence Force 27, 50, 146, 177, 188-9
Sen, Ronen 140
Senkaku/Diaoyutao Islands 26, 44, 46, 58, 64, 66, 76, 99, 116, 119, 124
7 September incident, and Japan 45
Shanghai Cooperation Organisation 59, 144
Shi Yunsheng 102
Shih Chun-yu 71
Shinzo Abe 29-30, 76, 118, 121, 144, 153
shipping companies, production in India 209
shuukatsu 267-8, 275
Singapore 33-4, 75, 78, 99, 118, 145, 156, 185, 188, 191, 193-4, 205-6, 231, 237
Singh, Manmohan 22, 25, 27, 29, 31, 34, 55, 70, 73, 75-6, 104, 117, 121, 153, 156-8, 160: Joint for Declaration on Security Cooperation by 118; visit to Japan 119, 217; visit to Malaysia 55; yen credit to 76
Singh–Koizumi meeting 117
Sino–Japanese war 65
skill-development opportunities 273
Sony in India 210
South China Sea 27, 34, 44, 57, 64, 103, 109, 123, 144, 191; Japanese and Indian policies on dispute of Islands in 64
South Korea 57-8, 79-80, 134, 148
Southeast Asia: in Indian maritime strategy 190-1; in Japan's maritime strategy 191-4
Soviet: invasion of Afghanistan 114; withdrawal from Afghanistan 178

strategic and global partnership 51-2, 113, 125-6, 153; security relations 25-6
String of Pearls operation 30, 123, 144-5
Sumitomo Metal Industries with Bushan Steel 209
Susilo Bambang Yudhoyono 55
Suzuki and President Reagan 33, 177, 209
Swaminathan, Padmini 279

Ta Kung Pao 66, 70
Tagore 248, *see also* Japanese, language studies
Taiwan 41, 64-6, 68-70, 75, 102-4; claim over 64 (*see also under* China); into Japanese rule 68; Japanese and Indian policies on 64; Japan 'Peace Treaty' with 69; Japan relations with 41
Taiwan–Guam–Tokyo triangle 191
Takei, Rear Admiral 191
Taro Aso 29, 71, 110, 118, 120, 157
Tata Capital 212
Tellis, Ashley 31
Tenjiku (Buddhism) 223, 246-7
territorial disputes 34, 41, 56, 63-8, 70-1, 110; with China 57, 64, 67; with Japan 64
Tetsuya Nishimoto, visit to China 72
Tiananmen Square 42, 72
Tibet Autonomous Region, and India 54, 70, 103-4, 106
Tokyo Electric Power Company 219
Tokyo Marine & Nichido Fire Insurance 212
Toshiba with Jindal South West 211
Toshiki Kaifu 157
Toshimi Kitazawa and Liang Guanglie 72
trade 224-8, *see also* India–ASEAN trade; between Indian and China 201, 203-4; between India–Korea 203; between India and Japan 202-6, 224
trafficking in narcotics 140
Trans Pacific Partnership 34
Treaty of Good-Neighbourliness and Friendly Cooperation 105
Trilateral meetings 33, 47, 138, 143-4
Tsunami relief 188-9
Tsunami core group 141, 188-9

Ultra Mega Power Projects 211
UN peacekeeping in Cambodia 179
unemployment 269, 271; in Japan 271-5; in India 275-80; Indian Society of Labour Economics on 276; in UK 269; of youth 266-72, 275-80;
United Nations Framework Convention on Climate Change 122
United Nations Security Council 77, 116; and China 116; India becoming a permanent member of 59; reform of 77-8
United Services Institute's Centre for UN Peacekeeping 142
United States: and ASEAN countries 32-5; and India 26, 146, 160, 189; India policy of 155, 160-2, 166-7; Trade between 166; ballistic missile defence system 74; foreign policy 162, 168; re-engagement across Asia-Pacific 135-6
US–China–India triangle 137

US–China–Pakistan relationship 114
US–India: cooperation in disaster relief 189-90; defence cooperation mechanism 180; Disaster Relief Initiative 189; relations 64, 99
US–Japan, alliance 99-100, 175, 177; Defense Cooperation 176; Strategic dialogue 137, 142; treaties between 64, 69-70, 250
US–Japan–Australia trilogue 137
US–Japan–India triangle/trilogue 110, 133, 137-44, 145-9; director-generals meeting of 33; naval cooperation 145; parleys of 136; rapprochement of 139, 144
US–Japan–South Korea strategic triangle 137
USS *Trenton* 190

Vajpayee, Atal Behari 22, 154, 158
value oriented diplomacy, Taro Aso's vision of 110
Vietnam 25, 31, 34, 57-8, 72, 78, 80, 99, 109, 133-5, 144, 194; Indian approach to 123
Visaria, Pravin 275
Vivekananda, Swami 247-8

Wang Guangya 77
Wen Jiabao 30, 44, 54, 68, 74-5, 104, 117; and Manmohan Singh joint declaration of 73; to Pakistan 104; visit to India 104
Western Dedicated Freight Corridor 56
Western Pacific, multilateral exercises in 185-8
WTO 96, 122
Wu Bangguo 44

Yamamoto Ichita 51
YasukuniInoki 79
Yasukuni Shrine 42, 71, 75, 116
Yomiuri Shimbun 27, 50
Yoshida, General 25
Yoshihiko Noda 25, 27, 120, 218, 235; visit to India 25, 110
Yoshiro Mori 115, 158, 251
Yukio Hatoyama 119

Zangmu hydropower station 106
Zhang Jie 99
Zhang Yan 54, 99; on 'Flying Wild Goose Security Model' 99
Zhou Enlai 68-9